1,001 Grammar Practice Questions

FOR DUMMIES®

A Wiley Brand

1,001 Grammar Practice Questions

FOR DUMMIES®
A Wiley Brand

by Geraldine Woods

FOR DUMMIES®
A Wiley Brand

1,001 Grammar Practice Questions For Dummies®

Published by: **John Wiley & Sons, Inc.,** 111 River St., Hoboken, NJ 07030-5774, www.wiley.com

Copyright © 2014 by John Wiley & Sons, Inc., Hoboken, New Jersey

Media and software compilation copyright © 2014 by John Wiley & Sons, Inc. All rights reserved.

Published simultaneously in Canada

No part of this publication may be reproduced, stored in a retrieval system or transmitted in any form or by any means, electronic, mechanical, photocopying, recording, scanning or otherwise, except as permitted under Sections 107 or 108 of the 1976 United States Copyright Act, without the prior written permission of the Publisher. Requests to the Publisher for permission should be addressed to the Permissions Department, John Wiley & Sons, Inc., 111 River Street, Hoboken, NJ 07030, (201) 748-6011, fax (201) 748-6008, or online at http://www.wiley.com/go/permissions.

Trademarks: Wiley, For Dummies, the Dummies Man logo, Dummies.com, Making Everything Easier, and related trade dress are trademarks or registered trademarks of John Wiley & Sons, Inc., and may not be used without written permission. All other trademarks are the property of their respective owners. John Wiley & Sons, Inc., is not associated with any product or vendor mentioned in this book.

LIMIT OF LIABILITY/DISCLAIMER OF WARRANTY: WHILE THE PUBLISHER AND AUTHOR HAVE USED THEIR BEST EFFORTS IN PREPARING THIS BOOK, THEY MAKE NO REPRESENTATIONS OR WARRANTIES WITH RESPECT TO THE ACCURACY OR COMPLETENESS OF THE CONTENTS OF THIS BOOK AND SPECIFICALLY DISCLAIM ANY IMPLIED WARRANTIES OF MERCHANTABILITY OR FITNESS FOR A PARTICULAR PURPOSE. NO WARRANTY MAY BE CREATED OR EXTENDED BY SALES REPRESENTATIVES OR WRITTEN SALES MATERIALS. THE ADVICE AND STRATEGIES CONTAINED HEREIN MAY NOT BE SUITABLE FOR YOUR SITUATION. YOU SHOULD CONSULT WITH A PROFESSIONAL WHERE APPROPRIATE. NEITHER THE PUBLISHER NOR THE AUTHOR SHALL BE LIABLE FOR DAMAGES ARISING HEREFROM.

For general information on our other products and services, please contact our Customer Care Department within the U.S. at 877-762-2974, outside the U.S. at 317-572-3993, or fax 317-572-4002. For technical support, please visit www.wiley.com/techsupport.

Wiley publishes in a variety of print and electronic formats and by print-on-demand. Some material included with standard print versions of this book may not be included in e-books or in print-on-demand. If this book refers to media such as a CD or DVD that is not included in the version you purchased, you may download this material at http://booksupport.wiley.com. For more information about Wiley products, visit www.wiley.com.

Library of Congress Control Number: 2013954227

ISBN 978-1-118-74501-4 (pbk); ISBN 978-1-118-74475-8 (ebk); ISBN 978-1-118-74474-1 (ebk)

Manufactured in the United States of America

10 9 8 7 6 5 4 3 2

Contents at a Glance

Table of Contents

Introduction

A bestselling book once claimed that anyone hoping to reach the highest level in a particular field must put in 10,000 hours of practice. That's a lot of hours! I'm pleased to inform you that you won't need 10,000 hours to work your way through these 1,001 grammar questions. I'm even more pleased to report that practicing the skills these questions address, even for only a few hours, *will* improve your grammar. If you already speak and write English well, this book helps you refine your knowledge of proper usage. If English is a language you're still learning, you can concentrate on questions that address basic concepts and gradually work your way to more advanced points.

In addition to 1,001 questions, this book provides answers and explanations, so you know *why* a particular expression is correct (or incorrect). In the explanations, I stay away from technical terms as much as possible, including only the specialized vocabulary you absolutely need to grasp the underlying logic or traditions of the language. I stay with the simplest terms and define them as they appear, in case you're not familiar with a term or you learned a different one in school. And you may have! Grammarians love jargon. For example, many bloody battles have been fought between those who favor the terms *predicate nominative* and *predicate adjective* and those who prefer the label *subject complement*. (Both apply to a word that follows a form of the verb *to be*.) Okay, I'm exaggerating a little. Maybe blood hasn't been shed, but an ocean of ink has! My view is that as long as you know proper usage, you can call something a *cantaloupe* for all I care.

One warning: According to one study, English has nearly a million words that may be combined in varied — and grammatically correct — ways. For each question I provide the most common response, but at times you may come up with another answer that's also acceptable. In such a situation, measure your version by the standards I provide in each explanation, and count yourself "right" if you've followed the rules.

What You'll Find

This book contains 1,001 questions, neatly divided into 22 chapters. I take you through parts of speech (verbs, pronouns, and so forth), parts of a sentence (subjects, verbs, objects, descriptions, and the like), and what English teachers call mechanics (punctuation and capitalization). I also cover the most common mistakes, such as incomplete sentences, commonly confused words, and nonstandard expressions. Each chapter begins with a list of topics, followed by tips and traps — points to remember when you're answering the questions in that chapter. You don't have to complete every question in a section, and you don't have to work on the chapters in order. You're in charge! Select only the topics that stump you, if you want. When you're checking your answers and reading the attached explanations, you may discover other areas worth exploring. For example, suppose you're asked to select the proper pronoun for a sentence. In the answer section, you see that you need a subject pronoun. The problem is that you're not sure how to locate a subject. No worries: Turn to Chapter 4 for practice in finding subjects.

How This Workbook Is Organized

This workbook includes 1,001 questions in Part I and answers to all of them, plus explanations, in Part II.

Part I: The Questions

Here are the topics covered by the 1,001 questions in this book:

- **Verbs:** Chapter 1 deals with locating the verb and selecting the right tense. Chapter 2 covers irregular verb forms, helping verbs, and verb forms that function as descriptions (*participles,* in grammar terminology). On a more advanced level, Chapter 17 deals with verbs in active and passive voice and subjunctive verbs.

- **Nouns and pronouns:** Chapter 3 checks your knowledge of singular and plural nouns and pronouns. The questions in Chapter 6 concern pronoun case — the difference between *he, him,* and *his,* for example.

- **Agreement:** In grammar, the principle of agreement is that singular pairs with singular and plural with plural. Chapter 4 focuses on subject-verb agreement, and Chapter 5 checks whether pronouns agree with the words they represent, also known as their antecedents.

- **Sentence completeness:** The building block of writing is a complete sentence. The questions in Chapter 7 deal with complete (and therefore correct) sentences, as well as run-ons (sentences improperly joined) and fragments (incomplete sentences).

- **Descriptions and complements:** Adding to the bare bones of the sentence, the subject-verb pair, are complements and descriptions. In Chapters 8 and 9 you distinguish between an adjective and an adverb, select the correct form, and place it in the right spot. In Chapter 10 you work on comparisons, so that yours are clear and logical.

- **Capitalization:** Names, quotations, seasons, titles — Chapter 11 checks whether you understand where to place a capital letter in these situations and many others.

- **Punctuation:** Lots of people shudder when they think about punctuation, but the rules actually make sense. In Chapter 12 you practice inserting and deleting commas. Chapter 13 hits you with questions about apostrophes and quotation marks.

- **Parallel structure:** *Parallel* is the word English teachers use to describe balance. In Chapter 14 you work on questions about parallelism, including lists, paired conjunctions (*either/or, not only/but also,* and so forth), tense, and person.

- **Style:** Do your sentences need to go on a diet? Chapter 15 permits you to trim some repetitive or wordy sentences. Chapter 16 prods you to vary sentence patterns.

- **Electronic media:** Do you know how to make a grammatically correct presentation slide or bulleted list? Chapter 18 questions you on this topic and tests the appropriate form and language for e-mail and texts. In Chapter 19 you examine formal and informal English and decide when each is appropriate.

- **Word traps:** Some word pairs can trick you — *accept/except, affect/effect, rise/raise,* and so on. In Chapters 20, 21, and 22, you practice choosing the appropriate word so that your writing always expresses your intended meaning.

Part II: The Answers

Scheherazade, a legendary Persian queen, told a story each night for 1,001 nights. She had to strike just the right note to keep the king's interest. Mistakes were not an option, because the penalty facing her was execution. Luckily for you, the consequences for mistakes in answering 1,001 grammar questions are not so terrible. In fact, you receive no penalty at all. Instead, you have a chance to read the explanations and learn more about English grammar. Scheherazade, by the way, survived — and so will you!

Beyond the Book

This book gives you plenty of grammar questions to work on. Perhaps you want to track your progress as you tackle the questions, or maybe you're having trouble with certain types of questions and wish they were all presented in one place. You're in luck. Your book purchase comes with a free one-year subscription to all 1,001 practice questions online. You get on-the-go access any way you want it — from your computer, smartphone, or tablet. Track your progress and view personalized reports showing what you need to study the most. You can study what, where, when, and how you want.

What you'll find online

The online practice that comes free with this book offers the same 1,001 questions and answers that are available here. The beauty of the online problems is that you can customize your online practice to focus on the topics that give you the most trouble. So if you need help forming comparisons or placing commas, just select those question types online and start practicing. If you're short on time but want to get a mixed bag, you can specify the number of problems you want to practice. Whether you practice a few hundred problems in one sitting or a dozen, and whether you focus on a few types of problems or practice every type, the online program keeps track of the questions you get right and wrong so you can monitor your progress and spend time studying exactly what you need.

You can access this online tool using an access code, as described in the next section. Keep in mind that you can create only one login with your access code. After the access code is used, it's no longer valid and is nontransferable, so you can't share your access code with other users after you establish your login credentials.

This product also comes with an online Cheat Sheet that helps you increase your odds of improving your grammar skills. Check out the free Cheat Sheet at www.dummies.com/ cheatsheet/1001grammar. (No access code required. You can access this info before you even register.)

How to register

To gain access to the online version of all 1,001 practice questions in this book, all you have to do is register. Just follow these simple steps:

1. **Find your PIN access code.**

   - **Print book users:** If you purchased a hard copy of this book, turn to the back of this book to find your access code.

   - **E-book users:** If you purchased this book as an e-book, you can get your access code by registering your e-book at `www.dummies.com/go/getaccess`. Go to this website, find your book and click it, and answer the security question to verify your purchase. Then you'll receive an e-mail with your access code.

2. **Go to** `http://learn.dummies.com` **and click Already have an Access Code?.**

3. **Enter your access code and click Next.**

4. **Follow the instructions to create an account and establish your personal login information.**

That's all there is to it! You can come back to the online program again and again — simply log in with the username and password you chose during your initial login. No need to use the access code a second time.

If you have trouble with the access code or can't find it, please contact Wiley Product Technical Support at 877-762-2974 or `http://support.wiley.com`.

Your registration is good for one year from the day you activate your PIN. After that time frame has passed, you can renew your registration for a fee. The website gives you all the important details about how to do so.

Where to Go for Additional Help

Each chapter begins with short explanations of the tips and traps associated with each topic, and the answer explanations give you still more information about grammar rules. If you need longer explanations and more examples, you may want to check out *English Grammar For Dummies, English Grammar Workbook For Dummies,* or *Grammar Essentials For Dummies,* all of which I wrote and Wiley published. My royalty statement and I thank you!

Part I
The Questions

In this part...

You may have a love-hate relationship with answering questions; you enjoy challenging yourself, but you don't like to fail. This part — 1,001 grammar questions — is set up so you *won't* fail. When you have trouble, you can check the answer and read the explanation in Part II and then return to the questions, better prepared to answer the next one correctly. Specifically, here's what you'll find in this part:

- Basic parts of speech and essential elements of a proper sentence (Chapters 1–7)

- Descriptive elements and mechanics of capitalization and punctuation (Chapters 8–13)

- Ways to add style to your writing (Chapters 14–17)

- Considerations when writing for electronic media and varying levels of formality (Chapters 18–19)

- Commonly misused words and expressions (Chapters 20–22)

Chapter 1

Time Travel: Identifying the Verb and Choosing the Correct Tense

• •

*I*n science fiction films, a character can zoom into the past or hop into the future, usually with the help of a machine resembling a giant vacuum cleaner. You time travel too, when you choose verbs for your sentences. Verbs express action or state of being in the past, present, and future. In this chapter you practice locating the verb and selecting the appropriate tense. You also tackle singular and plural forms, plugging the right one into every sentence.

The Questions You'll Answer

Here you find sentences that allow you to sharpen your verb skills in these ways:

- ✔ Locating the verb(s) in a sentence
- ✔ Selecting simple past-, present-, or future-tense verbs to fit the meaning of a sentence
- ✔ Choosing progressive verb forms to indicate ongoing action
- ✔ Placing past perfect, present perfect, or future perfect forms where they're needed
- ✔ Finding the right tense to summarize speech and discuss literary or artistic works
- ✔ Expressing unchangeable facts in present tense
- ✔ Determining whether you need a singular or plural form

What to Watch Out For

Verb tense can be tricky, as can *agreement* — the matching of singular verbs to singular subjects and plural verbs to plural subjects. When you work through these questions, watch out for these issues:

- ✔ Zero in on the time period(s) covered in the sentence.
- ✔ Establish a timeline if more than one action or state of being is expressed in the sentence.
- ✔ Stay in the same tense unless the meaning of the sentence justifies a shift.
- ✔ Check whether the subject is singular or plural and match the verb to the subject.
- ✔ Ignore words that resemble verbs but function as descriptions or nouns.

Locating the Verb

1–15 Identify the verb(s) in the sentence.

1. Eric and his band played five songs by the Beatles, to the delight of the audience.

2. Maria slipped out of the room quietly at the end of the lecture on the causes of World War I.

3. The twins will be happy on their birthday when they receive your present!

4. Perhaps because of my brother's illness, my dog Tweet seems sad today.

5. The child searched for a tissue but found only a dirty candy wrapper.

6. The screaming figure at the left of the painting represents a mother's grief.

7. Glenn has always carried the sizzling pizza in a special, heat-proof box.

8. The puppies, along with the kittens, were displayed in the shop window for all to see.

9. The last meeting of the council was bittersweet, as the members were now scattering for distant destinations.

10. To go faster, try not to look at the keyboard as you type.

11. Smiling, Barbara wrestled with the math problem until she calculated the correct answer.

12. Daniel's pen, having run out of ink, sat on the shelf, unused and forgotten.

13. While copying the letter, Mike stuck his finger in the moving paper tray.

14. Norman has been judged "normal" by his doctor, but his friends view him differently.

15. Sliding down the mountain, the ski instructor guided his students.

Choosing Simple and Perfect Tense Verb Forms

16–55 Select the tense and form of the verb in parentheses that fits the meaning of the sentence.

16. I _____ (to start) my blog a year ago, and I do not intend to stop now.

17. Sheryl and her friend always _____ (to shop) on a Tuesday, when the store offers double discounts.

18. Next year, four boys _____ (to compete) for a single spot on the wrestling team.

19. Emma _____ (to snap) a picture of her brother Eric every year on his birthday, including today.

20. Last week I tossed a bit of my dinner under the table because the dog _____ (to beg) for scraps while I ate.

21. Start working on your lab report as soon as you _____ (to arrive) home.

22. Mr. Martin _____ (to trim) the tree after he had watered it.

23. While Harry _____ (to wash) the clothes, Oliver was brushing the dog's matted fur.

24. Jackie _____ (to learn) Arabic when she lived in Tunisia.

25. Carla _____ (to fill) the gas tank before she realized that her credit card was not in her wallet.

26. By the time George gets home, Maria _____ (to gobble) all the cookies, and George hates all the other snacks.

27. When I _____ (to bake) the cookies, I placed them on the dining room table.

28. Although the king commands instant obedience, his followers sometimes _____ (to disobey).

29. Marlene _____ (to lecture) for two hours before she noticed that several audience members were asleep.

30. I _____ (to live) in this neighborhood for about a year, and despite its problems, I still love my home.

31. The yellow and brown leaves began to fall; the autumn soon _____ (to end).

32. No one _____ (to work) harder than Ellen, who spent eight or nine hours a day on this project for the first two weeks and is now allotting ten or twelve hours a day to it!

33. Jared _____ (to jog) four miles every day as soon as he wakes up.

34. From now on, David _____ (to complete) his homework on time, to avoid detention and poor grades.

35. Elliot always _____ (to return) his library books late, so he pays many fines.

36. While Meredith _____ (to paint) the ceiling, a dog jumped on the ladder.

37. Place the dough in a warm spot, and in a few hours it _____ (to double) in size.

38. It _____ (to rain) every day for a month, including today, but tomorrow's forecast calls for sunshine.

39. The soda had soaked into the carpet by the time the janitor _____ (to arrive) with a mop.

40. Right now, Catherine's friends _____ (to gather) for her surprise party.

41. Once George _____ (to chop) down the cherry tree, the fruit was lost.

42. I paid the electric bill on the 17th, so I _____ (to receive) the next bill in about a week.

43. Although Eddie _____ (to dance) happily, Shirley turned off the music.

44. Clancy never _____ (to brush) his teeth by himself, even though he is five years old now.

45. As we speak, our enemies _____ (to attack) with great force, but we will not surrender.

46. The teacher _____ (to staple) the drawings on the bulletin board so that the parents could admire their children's artwork.

47. By the time Eleanor and Henry are satisfied with the renovation, they _____ (to exceed) their budget by a wide margin.

48. Where the tulips _____ (to bloom), weeds eventually covered every inch of the garden.

49. In Maya's fantasy novel, a wizard's curse _____ (to turn) a little boy into a frog.

50. Amanda and her friends _____ (to study) Chinese for four years by the time they travel to that country.

51. Joe _____ (to practice) karate for many years and still takes an advanced class every Saturday.

52. In Shakespeare's *Othello,* the title character wrongly _____ (to trust) Iago, one of the most evil villains in literature.

53. LGA Manufacturing has an old-fashioned policy; the company _____ (to market) its products only in a store, not on the Internet.

54. If my dog buries a bone every three days, how many _____ (to bury) by the end of the month?

55. In Dickens's classic novel *Great Expectations,* Pip _____ (to learn) the identity of his benefactor in a chilling scene.

Consistently Choosing the Right Verb Tense

56–65 Select the tense and form of the verb in parentheses that fits the meaning of the sentence. Take care to avoid unnecessary shifts from one tense to another.

56. In my dream, a giant dinosaur ran into my dining room, and then he _____ (to stroll) around the room.

57. Perhaps because the president _____ (to campaign) for the mayor, the mayor won by a huge margin.

58. Linda _____ (to enter) the cafeteria and sits next to the most hated teacher in the entire school!

59. The orchestra _____ (to insure) the instruments every year, so no one ever worries about storm damage after the hurricane.

60. Last year I traveled to Europe, but next year I _____ (to tour) Asia.

61. In response to the reporter's question, the zookeeper said that the lion _____ (to be) very friendly.

62. Morty declared that eight added to ten _____ (to equal) eighteen.

63. Arthur told me that he _____ (to need) a loan until payday and asked me to give him $10.

64. Shana reported that at the end of every show, the ballet dancers _____ (to bow) and ignored the boos from the audience.

65. The astronomer told the youngsters that the earth _____ (to revolve) around the sun.

Chapter 2

Taking a Look at Irregular, Helping, and Descriptive Verb Forms

• •

*E*very year, my students are upset to discover that English has so many irregular verbs. If I were the Queen of Grammar, I'd outlaw irregular verbs. Unfortunately, without them I wouldn't be able to fashion the first sentence of this chapter, because *are* would be behind bars. So would *has!* Like it or not, and because I'm *not* the Queen of Grammar, you and I are stuck with irregulars. Not to worry: In this chapter you practice selecting irregular verbs, changing meaning with helping verbs (*should, can, may, do, does, did,* and the like), and employing verb forms that can act as descriptions, which grammarians call *participles* and *infinitives* and the rest of us call "pains in the neck."

The Questions You'll Work On

In this chapter, you work on questions that develop these skills:

- ✔ Using irregular past-tense and participle forms correctly
- ✔ Selecting the proper form and tense of the irregular verbs *to be* and *to have*
- ✔ Adding shades of meaning with the helping verbs *should, must, can, could, may, might,* and *would*
- ✔ Creating questions with helping verbs
- ✔ Identifying participles functioning as descriptions
- ✔ Choosing the best form of participles and infinitives used as descriptions

What to Watch Out For

Keep these points in mind when you answer the questions in this chapter:

- ✔ Check whether the past-tense form or participle is regular or irregular.
- ✔ Choose the correct tense of irregular verbs based on the meaning of the sentence.
- ✔ Employ reading comprehension skills to detect the need for a helping verb expressing obligation, possibility, condition, or ability.
- ✔ Rearrange word order and add helping verbs to create questions.
- ✔ Select present participles or infinitives as descriptions for actions in the past, present, or future.

Handling Irregular Verbs

66–90 Choose the proper past, present perfect, past perfect, or future perfect form of the irregular verb in parentheses so that the verb fits the meaning of the sentence.

66. Joe _____ (to catch) the ball as it reached the top of the outfield fence.

67. The car was cruising along the highway smoothly until it _____ (to hit) a huge bump.

68. Dorothy and the baby _____ (to sleep) for two hours when they returned from a visit to Grandma.

69. At the end of the trial the judge _____ (to rise) from her chair and left the courtroom.

70. Last week the Yankees _____ (to beat) their fiercest rivals.

71. From 2010 through 2011, the confused clerk _____ (to put) all the forms in the wrong file cabinet.

72. The helicopter _____ (to fly) straight up into the sky and then headed south.

73. Glenn _____ (to see) the little dog and grabbed her before she could run away again.

74. I didn't know that you _____ (to swim) in the deep water last summer; I thought you were less advanced in your swimming skills.

75. Nelson wouldn't _____ (to get) sick if he had washed his hands more frequently.

76. The bully approached, but because my uncle _____ (to teach) me how to handle difficult people, I wasn't afraid.

77. The doctor _____ (to do) everything in his power; now Allison must wait for the medicine to take effect.

78. Miriam _____ (to let) the dog out for a few minutes, but she will call him inside soon.

79. Although Adam _____ (to find) a good candidate already, the boss continued to interview others for the job.

80. "Who _____ (to begin) the fight, you or your brother?" asked Mother as she separated her battling children.

81. After you _____ (to send) the letter, shred the scrap copies.

82. At first the rain was simply annoying, but when it _____ (to freeze), the streets became very slippery and many pedestrians fell.

83. Albert _____ (to tear) his shirt when he crawled through the obstacle course.

84. "I _____ (to know) it!" exclaimed the detective as the murderer confessed.

85. When she attempted to pay for her coffee, Lee discovered that she _____ (to lose) all her coins because of a small hole in her pocket.

86. By midnight Angie _____ (to sing) that aria enough times to set a world record.

87. In ancient times, murderers were often _____ (to hang) in the public square.

88. The picture _____ (to hang) on the wall for years, but no one noticed it.

89. The janitor _____ (to sweep) the sidewalk before the students arrive, so expect a clean path.

90. The riflemen _____ (to lay) down their weapons but are ready to resume target practice at a moment's notice.

Dealing with To Be and To Have

91–105 *Select the proper form of the verb* to be *or to* have *to fit the meaning of the sentence.*

91. The marble statue _____ (to be) on the shelf right now, but earlier it was in the sculptor's studio.

92. Along with Jack, I _____ (to be) bored and decided to watch a different show.

93. The co-presidents _____ (to have) no trouble persuading club members to go out for pizza when they suggest the excursion at the end of the meeting, because everyone will be hungry then.

94. Louisa rejected the sofa when it was delivered because it _____ (to have) a stain on one cushion.

95. Max _____ (to be) sick for the last two days, but the doctor predicts that his temperature will be normal tomorrow.

96. The lottery winners _____ (to be) difficult; they refuse to share their winnings.

97. If the referee and the coach can't agree, our efforts _____ (to be) fruitless because we will forfeit the game.

98. Shelley _____ (to have) difficulty getting up on time ever since her alarm clock broke, but she plans to buy a new one soon.

99. While the elevators were rising, the mechanic _____ (to have) doubts about the strange noises below.

100. We _____ (to be) here, patiently waiting, for more than four hours before Justin arrived.

101. When Doreen _____ (to be) 13, she struggled to start her business, but one day sales began to rise.

102. By the time it opens on Broadway, the show _____ (to have) four different directors.

103. Gina, who _____ (to be) your friend, begs you to forgive her.

104. Doug, who _____ (to be) very immature in those days, used to stick gum under everyone's desk.

105. Sam thought that his mom _____ (to have) a stroke, but fortunately he was wrong; it was just a headache.

Adding Meaning with Helping Verbs

106–120 Choose the verb form that expresses the tense of the verb and the shade of meaning shown in parentheses.

106. Shelly's song _____ (to win, present tense, ability) her an award for "Best New Artist."

107. Alice _____ (to fly, future, possibility) to Buenos Aires on business next week.

108. Your hands _____ (to be, present, obligation) clean before you perform surgery, Doctor!

109. Because she loves that color, Helen _____ (to choose, present, possibility) only green blocks for her playhouse.

110. On Saturday mornings, the whole family _____ (to attend, past, repeated action) Wendy's softball games and cheer her on.

111. The workers _____ (to pave, past, obligation) the street more smoothly, but they did a sloppy job.

112. Margaret _____ (to jump, past, ability) over the fence easily, but instead she waited patiently for the guard to open the gate.

113. Enter the house quietly because the baby _____ (to be, present, possibility) asleep.

114. The mathematician was told that she _____ (to calculate, present, obligation) the odds of failure before making a recommendation.

115. The sheriff _____ (to arrest, present, obligation) Josephine for murder, as he has collected an overwhelming amount of evidence of her crime.

116. If he graduates from high school with honors, Walter _____ (to enroll, future, ability) in college and continue on the path to success.

117. Seven hours ago, Otis said that he _____ (to prepare, past, possibility) dinner, but we are still waiting, hungrier than ever.

118. "You _____," (to continue, present, permission) remarked the teacher as the student hesitated.

119. If it had not rained, Sam _____ (to go, past, condition) for a walk.

120. With a sharp pencil, Eliza _____ (to poke, past, repeated action) through the flimsy paper and then ask for a new sheet to write on.

Creating Questions with Helping Verbs

121–130: *Change the underlined portion of the sentence, as needed, to turn the statement into a question. **Note:** The period at the end of the sentence has been replaced by a question mark already.*

121. <u>Mary owns</u> a small but valuable art collection?

122. <u>Bert was carrying</u> a large carton of crayons to the daycare center?

123. <u>Jefferson will attend</u> the committee meeting this afternoon, despite his busy schedule?

124. Eugene has too many video games, according to his friend James?

125. After he had chewed his gum for an hour, Steven blew an enormous bubble?

126. The wire between the fenceposts sags so low that cattle cross easily from one field to the next?

127. Deborah is not interested in reading that poem aloud?

128. You will have eaten by the time George arrives at the restaurant?

129. Ellie went to the skating rink when it was closed?

130. The winning essay compared face-to-face communication with social media relationships?

Detecting and Placing Descriptive Verb Forms

131–140 In the sentence, which word or words function as descriptive verb forms (participles) and not as verbs?

131. In the flowing stream, Hank found a little paper boat.

132. Tom, pleased with his high test score, will celebrate with his family this evening.

133. In the last scene of the play, Daniel walks rapidly toward the setting sun.

134. Confused, Eliza is sorting through the instructions for her new computer and printer.

135. The mountains rising majestically in the background are a symbol of nature's power.

136. The printed word, carrying meaning for centuries, will never be obsolete.

137. "I have done my homework!" screamed Andrew, tired of his mother's nagging.

138. The research was done by laboratories around the world, all funded by one generous donor.

139. Amelia is performing in the play, although she hates the conceited director, who, hired under a long-term contract, does whatever he wishes.

140. The snake, sunning itself on the rock, slithered away when hikers came near him.

Selecting Tense for Descriptive Verb Forms

141–150 Which form of the verb in parentheses works best as a description in the sentence?

141. _____ (to prepare) the room for redecoration, Vincent discovered a crack that grew longer with every tug of the wallpaper he was removing.

142. _____ (to speak) with intense emotion, the actor recites his lines every night without a trace of boredom.

143. _____ (to water) the plants during vacations, Caroline installed an automatic sprinkler.

144. The mayor, _____ (to vow, to fight) crime, will increase the number of police officers.

145. The cat raked sharp claws across the new desk _____ (to stand) in the corner of the living room.

146. His funds _____ (to exhaust), Nelson called home and begged for a loan from his parents.

147. Annie walked ten miles _____ (to visit) her Aunt Marie.

148. _____ (to walk) the entire shoreline this morning, Ed can assure the reporters at tonight's news conference that all the beaches are ready to reopen.

149. Barbara and Arnie, _____ (to confer) already, will need no introduction when they attend the next meeting.

150. "It's great _____ (to meet) you!" exclaimed Paul as he shook hands with his new tennis partner, who had never seen Paul before in his life.

Chapter 3

One to Many: Forming Plurals of Nouns and Pronouns

According to one website, as of January, 2013, the English language was made up of 1,019,729.6 words. I don't believe that anyone actually knows — or can know — how many words are in any language. (And what on earth is 0.6 of a word?) So you can forget about numbers when you study proper English, with one huge exception: You have to pay attention to singular and plural forms of nouns and pronouns. In this chapter, you practice with nouns, turning one (the singular form) into many (the plural form). You also sort singular and plural pronouns, so that you can match them appropriately with the words they represent.

The Questions You'll Work On

In this chapter, you work on questions that cover the following concepts:

- ✔ Forming plurals of common and proper nouns, both regular and irregular
- ✔ Creating plural forms of hyphenated and compound words
- ✔ Tackling difficult pronouns such as *everything, one, either, all, some, that, which, who,* and so forth

What to Watch Out For

Keep these points in mind when you're answering the questions in this chapter:

- ✔ Most nouns form the plural by adding the letter *s*. For nouns ending in *ch, sh, x, s,* and *z,* add *es.*
- ✔ Nouns ending in a *y* change the *y* to *i* and add *es* if the letter preceding the *y* is a consonant (any letter except *a, e, i, o,* or *u*).
- ✔ Add *s* or *es* to the most important word in a hyphenated or compound noun.
- ✔ These pronouns are always singular: *one, everyone, everything, everybody, no one, nothing, nobody, someone, something, somebody, either, neither, each, other,* and *another.*
- ✔ These pronouns are always plural: *few, both, several,* and *many.*

- ✔ Relative pronouns *(that, which, who)* are singular if they refer to singular nouns or pronouns and plural if they refer to plural nouns or pronouns.

- ✔ These pronouns can be either singular or plural: *all, any, most, some,* and *none.* If one of these pronouns refers to a plural (for example, *all of the shows,* in which *all* refers to *shows*), the pronoun is plural. If the pronoun refers to a singular (for example, *most of the air,* in which *most* refers to *air*), the pronoun is singular.

Forming Plural Nouns

151–165 What is the correct plural form of these nouns?

151. stitch, telephone, tax

152. dye, splash, sandal

153. tomato, catch, mug

154. monkey, turkey, baby

155. zoo, success, edge

156. child, woman, man

157. deer, elephant, month

158. light, batch, biography

159. microphone, jelly, virus

160. delivery, essay, wife

161. Smith, Jones, O'Toole

162. leaf, pitch, copy

163. son-in-law, kangaroo, tooth

164. alumnus, mass medium, Woods

165. species, statistic, vice president

Sorting Singular and Plural Pronouns

166–195 Identify the singular (S) and/or plural (P) pronouns in the sentence.

166. Isaac asked his aunt to reduce her workload, but she refused.

167. As the children opened their presents, they told Santa how great his selections were.

168. We must apply sunscreen to our arms, according to my mother.

169. "Where is your sneaker?" asked the babysitter as he searched the room I share with my little sister.

170. "Your yoga class will be delayed an hour," I announced when the students had gathered in front of their lockers.

171. A friend of mine wants to go on vacation with them, but they prefer to travel by themselves.

172. The cookies are in his pocket; I saw them myself.

173. The football coach remarked, "Everyone is counting on you," but I was too stressed to play.

174. Something is wrong with the computer, because it blinks constantly and flashes a warning sign every hour.

175. Several of the engineers have examined the platform and declared it safe, but when someone screamed, everyone ran.

176. One of the books has an index, but those on the top shelf do not, so we use them infrequently.

177. Both of us entered the international math competition; however, no one from our country won.

178. Neither of my uncles attended the graduation ceremony, so the principal mailed a diploma to each of them.

179. The talk show host directed the question to her audience, but someone on stage answered it anyway.

180. All of the birds flew to the pond, but most of the water had evaporated, and they soon left.

181. Either of the restaurants is fine with me, if anyone would like to stop for a snack.

182. Arthur located most of the films, but a few were hard to find, so we had to substitute others.

183. The hungry man asked me to give him some of my sandwiches.

184. Someone rang the bell, but no one was there when Judy opened the door, expecting to see her brother.

185. Everyone was required to bring his or her swimsuit to camp, but Anna forgot to pack hers.

186. All of the orange juice spilled, but no one wiped the table until Billy called the manager and asked for her help.

187. Each of Bobby's bicycles is missing one wheel, but Bobby thinks both of the bikes can be repaired.

188. Much of Gene's trouble stems from his reliance on everyone's admiration.

189. Sharla and Alex like one tattoo but hate the other; they have mixed opinions about mine, a blue star.

190. The shoes that Mark bought weren't comfortable, but they were more stylish than anything else he purchased yesterday.

191. Someone who should know better washed my best pair of pants in hot water.

192. The branches that tapped on the window made too much noise, so I cut them off.

193. While she waited to hear the winner's name announced, Lulu, who had bought three lottery tickets, crossed her fingers for luck.

194. The envelope and writing paper, which were stored in the desk, are hers, but the stapler is theirs.

195. The doctor treated eight patients who were stricken by the same disease, which was fatal for nearly all of them.

Chapter 4

Identifying Subjects and Perfecting Subject-Verb Agreement

· ·

What are you talking about, at this exact moment? That's the *subject* of your conversation. While I'm on the subject of subjects, I must mention that every sentence has a subject — the *who* or *what* being discussed. The most important aspect of subjects is agreement: not smiling and saying, "Yes! Yes!" but rather ensuring that a singular subject pairs with a singular verb form and a plural subject pairs with a plural verb form. In this chapter, you find the subject and then play matchmaker between subjects and verbs. (If you have trouble identifying the verb, turn to Chapters 1 and 2 for extra help.)

The Questions You'll Work On

In this chapter, you work on questions that cover the following concepts:

✔ Finding the subject in statements, questions, and commands

✔ Identifying compound subjects and pronouns acting as subjects

✔ Choosing the correct verb for every subject-verb pair

What to Watch Out For

Keep these points in mind when you're answering the questions in this chapter:

✔ To find the subject, first locate the verb(s) in the sentence. Ask *who?* or *what?* is performing the action or is in the state of being expressed by the verb.

✔ Don't be fooled by location. Most subjects appear before the verb, but some follow the verb. Use your reading comprehension skills to answer the *who?* or *what?* questions.

✔ Most subjects and verbs show up with descriptions attached. Ignore distracting words or phrases and concentrate on the real subject-verb pair.

✔ Verb forms used as descriptions or as nouns may resemble verbs without functioning as the verb in the sentence. When you ask *who?* or *what?* to find the subject, be sure you're working from the real verb.

✔ The subject in a command may be an understood, but not stated, *you*.

✔ Pronouns acting as subjects can be tricky. Check out Chapter 3 for help distinguishing singular and plural pronouns.

Locating the Subject

196–215 Identify the subject(s) in the sentence.

196. The plastic tip of the shoelace slowly slipped through the hole as Juan marched down the street.

197. Marina and Tom are in the grocery store on the corner of Appleton Avenue.

198. Eight security cameras constantly swiveled in their holders on the ceiling of the jewelry store.

199. In the garden behind the house, the bride and groom solemnly recited their vows.

200. Only one girl in the crowd of 200 fans actually got an autograph.

201. Jumping on the trampoline is fun for Lily and Jane during the long weeks of summer vacation.

202. Stop talking back to the teacher now!

203. Henry distributed sheets of paper to whoever needed some.

204. Does the new brand of peanut butter taste odd to you?

205. There on the shelf sat four large statues of historical figures.

206. Above the clouds and far from the violent storm, the plane flew safely toward its destination.

207. The bus full of delighted tourists slowly circled the famous monument.

208. Each of the coffee cups has a small crack near the rim.

209. Both of the parakeets happily land on my finger for a bit of birdseed and a bite of lettuce.

210. Allison and her former friend Pete parted angrily, snarling at each other and walking in opposite directions.

211. Grandpa, who loves hockey, was the goalie on his college team.

212. Either the apartment with a terrace or the townhouse will surely please that buyer.

213. The dog that I believe should win the contest is over there.

214. Courtney, along with her mother, spoke politely to the mayor about the need for longer library hours.

215. The fire truck, which is heading to a blaze downtown, speeds through the intersection.

Fine-Tuning Subject-Verb Agreement

216–240 In the context of the sentence, what form of the verb (V) in parentheses is correct, and what is the subject (S) of that verb?

216. Every morning Anna _____ (to open, present tense) the gate and _____ (to allow, present tense) her poodle to play in the yard.

217. On the way to work, Clare and David always _____ (to share, present perfect tense) funny stories about their boss.

218. The large-sized bottle of my favorite shampoo _____ (to be, past tense) on sale last week.

219. Alicia and I _____ (to plan, present progressive tense) a talent show to raise money for needy children.

220. The Cub Scouts _____ (to place, past progressive tense) candy apples in small, sticky piles in preparation for the Halloween party.

221. _____ (to be, past tense) Hank pleased when he _____ (to read, past tense) your letter?

222. The best exhibits in the museum _____ (to seem, present tense) more crowded lately.

223. Matthew and I _____ (to sing, past progressive tense) every single song until our voices _____ (to break, past tense) from overuse.

224. _____ (to have, present tense) you any extra icing for my birthday cake?

225. Through the dark, damp tunnel _____ (to crawl, present tense) the chipmunks, eager to reach the picnic tables.

226. Ham and cheese _____ (to be, present tense) my favorite sandwich, but salad _____ (to be, present tense) a more nutritious choice.

227. "Your problem _____ (to be, present tense) 17 unexcused absences," commented the teacher as she explained why the student was scheduled for detention.

228. Politics _____ (to influence, present tense) much of the debate on that issue, but the senators from that state always _____ (to vote, present tense) according to their consciences.

229. John, not his friends, _____ (to go, present progressive tense) to attend the ceremony.

230. Any of the solutions he _____ (to offer, present tense) to the panel _____ (to be, present tense) acceptable.

231. _____ (to be, present tense) the House of Representatives in session now?

232. Most of the salt in those diets _____ (to come, present tense) from natural sources.

233. Two or three of the plants with red leaves _____ (to droop, present progressive tense) to the ground because of the drought.

234. The study of economics _____ (to seem, present tense) interesting, but I have never taken any courses about this subject.

235. Two hours of homework _____ (to be, present perfect tense) my usual amount, but I _____ (to expect, present tense) to spend more time on my studies next year.

236. Every girl and boy in the kindergarten _____ (to play, present tense) with the plastic blocks, not the wooden ones.

237. That little girl _____ (to be, present tense) the only one of the dancers who _____ (to make, present tense) friends easily.

238. A thousand dollars _____ (to be, present tense) too much to pay for that broken-down car, which _____ (to look, present tense) like a rusty bucket.

239. Neither Ginger nor her aunts _____ (to have, present tense) keys to the house, but the landlord _____ (to be, present tense) able to supply an extra set.

240. Shelby _____ (to sell, present progressive tense) me one of the cars that _____ (to be, present tense) energy efficient.

Chapter 5

Coming to a Clear Agreement: Pairing Pronouns and Antecedents

· ·

*P*ronouns are like socks. They have to fit perfectly, because if they don't, you spend the day walking around with a lump around your toes or pulling up a too-short heel. They also have to match: no green and blue mixing allowed! Pronouns are stand-ins for other nouns or pronouns — their *antecedents.* Don't worry about the terminology. Just be sure to select the correct pronoun. In this chapter you find practice for every situation likely to arise in matching pronouns to antecedents correctly and clearly.

The Questions You'll Work On

In this chapter, you work on questions that develop these skills:

- ✔ Identifying pronouns and their antecedents
- ✔ Pairing singular and plural pronouns with the appropriate antecedents
- ✔ Matching the gender of pronouns and antecedents
- ✔ Ensuring that the antecedent of every pronoun is clear

What to Watch Out For

Keep these points in mind when you're answering the questions in this chapter:

- ✔ To determine whether you're using the proper pronoun, first identify the antecedent.
- ✔ Singular pronouns take the place of singular nouns or other singular pronouns.
- ✔ Plural pronouns take the place of plural nouns or other plural pronouns.
- ✔ Match masculine pronouns to masculine nouns, and feminine pronouns to feminine nouns. Use neuter pronouns for objects and ideas (*it, those,* and the like).
- ✔ Some personal pronouns refer to the speaker (*I, me, we,* and so forth) or to the person addressed (*you, your,* for example). These pronouns have no antecedent in the sentence. Other pronouns that refer to an undetermined person or thing (such as *whatever* or *something*) may also lack an antecedent in the sentence.
- ✔ Pronouns must express only one meaning. If the reader can't grasp the pronoun-antecedent relationship, you have to reword the sentence.

Identifying Pronouns and Their Antecedents

*241–250 Identify each pronoun in the sentence as well as the word(s) the pronoun replaces (the antecedent). **Note:** More than one pronoun may refer to the same antecedent, and sometimes a pronoun has no antecedent in the sentence.*

241. Martin told his players they had to work harder.

242. Mary and her uncle watched their favorite show at his house.

243. In his sonnets, Shakespeare inspires readers to think deeply about the meaning of their lives.

244. My dog wants to chew on his bone, but I can't find it.

245. Whoever broke the window should pay for it!

246. The motorcycle that Jean built from a kit won the race, which was sponsored by a local bank.

247. None of the computer programs work until someone enters a password and username.

248. John, who needs a shave, broke his own razor and then borrowed mine.

249. What you want is impossible, but I will try to do everything anyway!

250. The dentist to whom Mary entrusted her teeth took good care of them.

Pairing Pronouns and Antecedents Correctly

251–260 What are the correct pronouns for each blank in the sentence? The intended meaning of each pronoun appears in parentheses.

251. Sara was delighted to receive the book and read _____ (book) aloud to _____ (Sara's) friends.

252. Gregory prepared three reports for _____ (Gregory's) supervisor, but when _____ (Gregory) handed _____ (reports) in, the supervisor was not happy.

253. Dora and I liked the dresses, but _____ (Dora and I) decided _____ (dresses) were too formal for the occasion.

254. The company where _____ (Arthur's) father works is expanding _____ (the company's) business to Asia.

255. The audience sat in _____ (audience's) seats, patiently waiting for the performance to begin, but _____ (performance) was delayed.

256. Counting _____ (a group including the speaker) votes is a simple task; _____ (inspectors) will ensure that _____ (task) is done properly.

257. James, _____ (James) loves football, plans to play _____ (football) in college.

258. Because neither of the athletes has _____ (athlete's) sneakers tied properly, _____ (the speaker) expect one of _____ (athletes) to fall.

259. Everyone in the restaurant wants _____ (everyone's) meal right away, but Chef Helen will cook at _____ (Chef Helen's) own pace.

260. When a person wins a prize, _____ (a group including the speaker) clap for _____ (someone).

Avoiding Vague Pronoun References

261–270 Which sentence(s) in the group of three use pronouns clearly and correctly?

261.
   I.   Ellen and her sister thought she got a good grade.

   II.   The pitcher and catcher worked on his throwing speed.

   III.   The umpire found his glasses just in time for the playoffs.

262.
   I.   The bowl was on the table with the green tablecloth; I washed it.

   II.   Joe and I hung our posters on the south wall.

   III.   I hope you like the figs; I picked them myself.

263.
   I.   He is tall and strong; those are attractive qualities.

   II.   Summer gives me more free time than winter, so I prefer it.

   III.   When I slammed the vase into the wall, I broke it.

264.
   I.   The boy Mary insulted walked away from her angrily.

   II.   I love that horror film; there are five wonderfully scary monsters in it.

   III.   Patrick wants to study law because his father is one.

265.
   I.   The tacks and nails from that store are very sharp, so I always buy them.

   II.   The tacks covered all the seats, which were dangerous.

   III.   I read many modern novels, and I usually like them.

266.
   I.   The library book has a stain on the cover, but I can't remove it.

   II.   The fish that Catherine bought had red spots on its tail.

   III.   His grandmother introduced Mark to opera, and he loved it.

267.
   I.   The architect likes the new building, which was designed by his competitor.

   II.   Gloria explained that she was late because her train left an hour past its scheduled time.

   III.   Charlie watches football and baseball games all day long and wishes he could be a professional at it.

268.
   I.   Georgina put one more card on top of the four she had fashioned into a little house, but it fell.

   II.   The computer mouse I dropped broke into three pieces, but I glued them back together.

   III.   I did my homework in the middle of the night without a flashlight, which was a problem.

269.
   I.   In the paper it says that war may break out within the next two days.

   II.   In an article in the paper it says that soldiers will report for duty tomorrow.

   III.   The government hopes to avoid war because of its high cost in both money and lives.

270.
   I.   The Yankee was a great hitter, but the other team's star was better at it.

   II.   The shades let in some light; they were translucent.

   III.   Allowing some sunlight reduces the need for strong electric lights, which may not be efficient in energy use.

Chapter 6

Solving the Case (of Pronouns)

· ·

You don't have to be a detective to know that pronouns — the part of speech that takes the place of nouns — are important. The issue with pronouns is that their form sometimes changes depending upon how they're used in the sentence — a quality known as *case*. In this chapter you work on all three cases — subject (also known as *subjective* or *nominative* case), object (also known as *objective* case), and possessive.

The Questions You'll Work On

In this chapter, you work on questions that involve these concepts:

- Identifying pronouns as subject, object, or possessive
- Choosing the correct pronoun case according to the pronoun's role in the sentence

What to Watch Out For

Keep these points in mind when you're answering the questions in this chapter:

- Subject pronouns act as subjects, the who or what performing the action or in the state of being expressed in the sentence.

- Subject pronouns also follow linking verbs (forms of the verb *to be* or verbs that express sensory information, such as *to sound, to feel,* and so forth).

- Object pronouns act as objects: direct objects, indirect objects, and objects of a preposition or verbal (a verb form not functioning as a verb). You don't need to worry about what type of object you have, as long as you know that the pronoun is acting as an object. An object answers the questions *whom?* or *what?* after a verb, preposition, or verb form.

- Possessive pronouns express ownership. When you say *my book* or *our vacation, my* and *our* are possessive pronouns.

- Some possessive pronouns function as subjects, objects, or other roles commonly played by nouns. In *that book is mine, mine* is a possessive pronoun because it expresses ownership, even though in this sentence it's acting as a subject complement.

- You may run across a verb form ending in *-ing* that acts as a noun — a gerund, in English-teacher terminology. The pronoun preceding it is possessive. For example, in this sentence the possessive pronoun *my* precedes the gerund *swimming: The coach doesn't like my swimming, but he can't stop me!*

- Don't confuse possessive pronouns with contractions — shortened forms of other words. *It's* means "it is," and *its* is a possessive pronoun. No possessive pronoun has an apostrophe.

Sorting Subject, Object, and Possessive Pronouns

271–285 Identify the underlined pronouns as subject (S), object (O), or possessive (P) pronouns.

271. As <u>they</u> built the shelter, the guides told <u>us</u> to watch carefully, in case <u>we</u> ever had to erect a hut like <u>it</u>.

272. Doreen and <u>I</u> caught five fish yesterday, but <u>she</u> threw <u>them</u> back into the water because <u>we</u> don't like to eat salmon.

273. Lola is <u>my</u> friend; however, <u>you</u> are <u>her</u> enemy.

274. The flight attendant told <u>him</u> to turn off <u>his</u> computer and confiscated <u>it</u> when <u>he</u> refused.

275. Al has placed Kerina and <u>you</u> at a lively table, but if <u>you</u> want to change seats, the choice is <u>yours</u>.

276. <u>I</u> know <u>it</u> was <u>she</u> on the phone because <u>I</u> always recognize voices.

277. Lulu's parents hate <u>her</u> adding an extra course because <u>they</u> think <u>she</u> is too busy already.

278. After Helen had examined the clothing thoroughly, <u>she</u> tried on a coat and declared, "<u>Mine</u> is more stylish and warmer," as she threw <u>his</u> away.

279. <u>My</u> jumbo slice of cake didn't tempt <u>him</u>, perhaps because <u>yours</u> was dry and tasteless.

280. The director loved <u>your</u> jumping in front of the runaway horse in the final scene, but <u>your</u> mom told <u>herself</u> not to look at the screen while <u>you</u> were in danger.

281. <u>Their</u> pitcher has a better record than <u>I</u>, but <u>my</u> team wins more games than <u>his</u>.

282. Give <u>your</u> food to <u>whoever</u> is hungry, even though <u>our</u> supply is low.

283. Melissa, <u>whom</u> the proctor scolded for lateness, says <u>she</u> actually arrived earlier than <u>I</u>.

284. When <u>our</u> computer crashed, James shook <u>its</u> screen and yelled, "<u>Whose</u> program was running recently?"

285. <u>I</u> won't go to the pool with <u>his</u> family because that cousin splashes <u>whoever</u> is nearby.

Using Subject and Object Pronouns Correctly

*286–320 What pronouns should be inserted in the blanks? **Note:** Check the parentheses for identifying information.*

286. Scott and _____ (Scott's) fellow racewalkers swing _____ (Scott's and the racewalkers') arms as _____ (Scott and the racewalkers) hurry to the finish line.

287. Keith and _____ (Pam) gave _____ (Pam's) nephew five crayons, because Pam always prefers to select the colors_____ (Pam) likes.

288. Woody saluted _____ (Dan) before _____ (Woody and Dan) bowed to the audience and thanked _____ (referring to the speaker) for directing the play.

289. _____ (David) and _____ (referring to the speaker) will order food for 100 people, in case _____ (guests) all come.

290. Everyone but _____ (referring to the speaker) plays the guitar, but _____ (referring to the people being spoken to) understand the instrument and _____ (the instrument's) construction too.

291. _____ (Toni-Anne) and _____ (Toni-Anne's) favorite singer, Bob Cassino, have never met, but _____ (Toni-Anne) thinks of _____ (Bob Cassino) as a friend anyway.

292. Amy Tan's novels provide Ira and _____ (Beth) with many hours of pleasant reading, but _____ (referring to the speaker) prefer the films and watch _____ (films) often.

293. Daniel and _____ (Pamela) weeded the garden together, but _____ (Daniel and Pamela) hired _____ (the speaker) to mow the lawn.

294. _____ (a group including the speaker) and the managers explain the insurance policy to clients whenever _____ (clients) request _____ (referring to the group including the speaker) help.

295. Did _____ (Derek) hit _____ (the ball) and run around _____ (the bases)?

296. Seeing Laura and _____ (James) pulling _____ (Laura and James's) wagon up the hill was impressive, because_____ (the hill) was very steep.

297. To satisfy _____ (the teacher), Mr. Palgrove, Beth and _____ (the speaker) handed in an excellent paper that we wrote by _____ (Beth and the speaker), without extra help.

298. Do _____ (Helen and Maria) know the boy _____ (the boy) designed the winning sailboat for _____ (Henry)?

299. All of _____ (referring to the group of speakers) students worried about the test _____ (the test) was scheduled for _____ (referring to the group of speakers).

300. Everyone _____ (referring to *everyone*) borrowed bowling shoes must return _____ (the shoes) to _____ (referring to the speaker) by 5 o'clock.

301. It was _____ (Eve) at the front desk; Peter and _____ (referring to the speaker) are sure _____ (Peter and the speaker) recognized _____ (Eve).

302. When a stuffed toy loses _____ (toy's) nose, _____ (toy) looks even more adorable.

303. Ken doesn't know _____ (referring to ownership by an unknown person) chewing gum is stuck to the table, but _____ (Ken) wants _____ (gum) removed.

304. Deborah, _____ (referring to Deborah) is sitting in the second row, will watch _____ (Bill) with great attention in case Bill forgets _____ (Bill's) lines.

305. Please don't tell _____ (Allison) and _____ (the speaker) any jokes while _____ (Allison and the speaker) are trying to concentrate.

306. The bus with _____ (the bus's) 20 passengers flew by _____ (referring to the speaker) stop, so _____ (the speaker) was late for _____ (referring to the person listening) barbecue.

307. Watson and Sons pays _____ (Watson and Sons') employees too little compared to _____ (Watson and Sons') competitors.

308. Are Jason and _____ (Frank) the funniest comedians in the show, or is _____ (Valerie)?

309. Jeff told _____ (Jeff) that _____ (Jeff) would understand the question and write _____ (essay) quickly.

310. Mack told the secret to Al and _____ (Wendy) before _____ (Mack) told _____ (the speaker), but _____ (Mack) gave _____ (the speaker) more details.

311. Jeremy is as nervous as _____ (Gloria) when _____ (Jeremy and Gloria) visit _____ (Gloria's) parents.

312. Elizabeth hates _____ (referring to the speaker) calling _____ (Elizabeth) "Liz" and has forbidden _____ (referring to the speaker) to do so.

313. Fran, _____ (Fran) Charlie thinks should take a course in public speaking, is not open to _____ (the course's) subject matter.

314. Between you and _____ (referring to the speaker), no one is happier about _____ (referring to the person being spoken to) getting a new puppy than _____ (referring to the speaker).

315. Don't _____ (referring to the person or people being spoken to) think _____ (anyone in the group) wants to succeed should study harder than _____ (Christopher)?

316. Alex and _____ (referring to the speaker) plan to read the article and respond to _____ (anyone in the group) has complaints about _____ (referring to the speaker) work.

317. The top students, Nick and _____ (James), will receive awards from the school, which always honors _____ (the school's) scholars at the end of the year.

318. The letter tucked into the bottle began, "To _____ (referring to any person) finds this bottle"; _____ (referring to the speaker) read _____ (the letter) eagerly.

319. The dancer and _____ (referring to the speaker) believe that it is _____ (Frances) _____ (Frances) stole the salt shaker.

320. When Jason told you to ask _____ (referring to anyone in a group) you like to work on the project with _____ (Jason), did you choose _____ (Mary and Frances)?

Chapter 7

Forming Complete Sentences

• •

In court, witnesses must swear to tell "the truth, the whole truth, and nothing but the truth." In grammar, you have to write "the sentence, the whole sentence, and nothing but the sentence." In other words, complete sentences rule — not fragments (partial or incomplete sentences) or run-ons (two or more ideas improperly thrown together). In this chapter you practice identifying and creating complete and grammatically correct statements and questions.

The Questions You'll Work On

In this chapter, you work on questions that involve these skills:

✔ Recognizing whether a sentence is complete or incomplete

✔ Joining two or more ideas correctly

✔ Editing fragments and run-ons to create complete sentences

What to Watch Out For

Keep these points in mind when you're answering the questions in this chapter:

✔ Every sentence must express a complete thought.

✔ Be sure the sentence has a matching subject-verb pair.

✔ All sentences need endmarks — periods for statements, question marks for questions, and exclamation points for exclamations.

✔ Don't assume that short sentences are incomplete and long sentences are complete. Meaning, not length, is your guide.

✔ Semicolons (;) and conjunctions such as *and, but, or, nor, for, since, because, where, when,* and others link one clause (a grammatical unit containing a subject-verb pair) to another.

✔ Relative pronouns — *who, whoever, whom, whomever, that,* and *which* — relate one idea to another, usually by replacing a noun. For example, in this sentence the relative pronoun *that* replaces *book: The book that I bought is very heavy.*

✔ Adverbs such as *however, consequently, therefore, then, also, nevertheless,* and others may not link one complete sentence to another. Use these words to add meaning, but be sure that you use a semicolon or a conjunction between the sentences.

Recognizing Complete Sentences

321–331 Identify the complete sentence(s).

321.
  I.   Have eaten?

  II. Have you eaten

  III. Have you eaten?

322.
  I.   Boris, along with Helena and her best friends from school.

  II. Boris, along with Helena and her best friends from school

  III. Boris, along with Helena and her best friends from school!

323.
  I.   At the army museum, many exhibits caught our attention.

  II. At the army museum, many exhibits caught our attention

  III. At the army museum, many exhibits catching our attention.

324.
  I.   Balloons of all colors of the rainbow above us in the sky!

  II. Balloons of all colors of the rainbow floated above us in the sky!

  III. Balloons of all colors of the rainbow floated above us in the sky

325.
  I.   Around the corner on tiptoes came the burglar.

  II. The burglar came around the corner on tiptoes.

  III. On tiptoes, around the corner the burglar came.

326.
  I.   I dance.

  II. I dance on stage.

  III. On Sundays, I dance.

327.
  I.   Standing in the aisle, Charlotte scanned the audience, searching for an empty seat.

  II. Standing in the aisle, Charlotte scanned the audience and searched for an empty seat

  III. Standing in the aisle, Charlotte, scanning the audience, searching for an empty seat.

328.
  I.   The little dog, chewing his food quickly and then running off to play.

  II. The little dog chewed his food quickly and then ran off to play.

  III. The little dog chewed his food quickly and then ran off to play

329.
  I.   Who is solving the puzzle.

  II. Who is solving the puzzle?

  III. Who is solving the puzzle!

330.
  I.   Alan, having changed his clothes, was ready for the dance.

  II. Having changed his clothes, Alan, ready for the dance.

  III. Having changed his clothes, Alan was ready for the dance.

331.
  I.   Nice to meet you.

  II. Nice meeting you!

  III. It was nice to meet you.

Combining Ideas Correctly

332–346 Identify the sentence(s) in which ideas are joined correctly.

332.
  I.   The table fell over, but it didn't break.

  II. The table fell over, it didn't break.

  III. The table fell over but didn't break.

333.
 I. Miami has a warm climate, Greenland is much colder.

 II. Miami has a warm climate, and Greenland is much colder.

 III. Miami has a warm climate, but Greenland is much colder.

334.
 I. Although she had reviewed the material thoroughly, Lisa was still nervous before her test.

 II. Lisa was still nervous before her test, although she had reviewed the material thoroughly.

 III. She had reviewed the material thoroughly, Lisa was still nervous before her test.

335.
 I. Tomorrow Laura will hike two miles, or she will work out for an hour at the gym.

 II. Tomorrow Laura will hike two miles, and she will work out for an hour at the gym.

 III. Tomorrow Laura will hike two miles, she will work out for an hour at the gym.

336.
 I. The baby cried for hours, no one could quiet her.

 II. The baby cried for hours, and no one could quiet her.

 III. The baby cried for hours, because no one could quiet her.

337.
 I. Before she met the ambassadors, the President examined their credentials carefully.

 II. The President examined their credentials carefully before she met the ambassadors.

 III. The President first examined their credentials carefully, and then she met the ambassadors.

338.
 I. The can is full, so please empty it.

 II. The can is full, you should empty it.

 III. The can is full, please empty it.

339.
 I. Although they had arrived late, the manager refused to shorten the team practice.

 II. The manager refused to shorten the team practice, although they had arrived late.

 III. They had arrived late, but the manager refused to shorten the team practice.

340.
 I. Even though George has never studied French, he understands a few simple words.

 II. George has never studied French, however, he understands a few simple words.

 III. George has never studied French, he understands a few simple words anyway.

341.
 I. Stamp collecting is a fascinating hobby, it can be expensive.

 II. Stamp collecting is a fascinating hobby, although it can be expensive.

 III. Stamp collecting is a fascinating hobby, additionally it can be expensive.

342.
 I. Jim dropped the fragile vase, consequently, it shattered into a thousand pieces.

 II. Jim dropped the fragile vase; consequently, it shattered into a thousand pieces.

 III. Jim dropped the fragile vase, and consequently it shattered into a thousand pieces.

343.   I.   Penny turned off her phone, for she didn't want to be interrupted.

II.   Penny turned off her phone, she didn't want to be interrupted.

III.   Penny turned off her phone because she didn't want to be interrupted.

344.   I.   I went to Vermont, where I met many skiers.

II.   I went to Vermont, there I met many skiers.

III.   I went to Vermont, I met many skiers there.

345.   I.   Jack's suit is old, nevertheless, he still looks good in it.

II.   Jack's suit is old, however, he still looks good in it.

III.   Jack's suit is old; he still looks good in it though.

346.   I.   The mechanic checked the steering wheel, which was fine, but he said that the brakes were defective.

II.   The mechanic checked the steering wheel, which was fine, and then he said that the brakes were defective.

III.   The mechanic checked the steering wheel, which was fine, although he said that the brakes were defective.

Correcting Run-Ons and Fragments

347–361 What changes, if any, should be made to the underlined words in order to create a complete sentence?

347.   Teresa <u>holding the tray</u> as I placed the glasses on it.

348.   Generous donors drop coins in the <u>box their contributions fund</u> scholarships.

349.   <u>Who likes ice cream</u>

350.   <u>Place the carton</u> in the corner of the lobby, Margaret.

351.   <u>The dictionary resting</u> on a shelf in the corner.

352.   I find knitting <u>relaxing, my aunt prefers</u> embroidery.

353.   Those mountain peaks <u>covered</u> with snow even in the summer.

354.   Mattie, <u>having read</u> the paper, went for a walk.

355. Park the truck in the <u>lot, be sure</u> to lock it.

356. <u>A pen and pencil on the desk in the corner of the living room.</u>

357. Which <u>performs better in the annual talent show</u>

358. <u>Accepting an internship, Bert, always planning</u> his next career move, which will lead him to success.

359. When the handle turns, the fire hose sprays water with great force <u>in the direction indicated on the dial.</u>

360. Picasso's statue has a gently curved <u>side, which highlighting</u> the grain of the marble.

361. While <u>swimming</u>, Harriet tangled her foot in a fishing line.

Chapter 8

Moving Beyond the Basics: Adding Descriptions

● ●

A complete sentence (see Chapter 7) can be as short as two words: *Marjorie raps,* for example. Life would be very boring, though, if you relied only on subjects and verbs to get your meaning across. Add in some adjectives and adverbs — the descriptive parts of speech — and your listener or reader perks up. These "extras" give us *Marjorie raps often* or *Marjorie raps superfast* or *Little Marjorie raps every single day.* In this chapter you practice with short descriptions — one-word or slightly longer expressions that attach to nouns, pronouns, verbs, and other adjectives and adverbs.

The Questions You'll Work On

In this chapter, you work on questions in these areas:

- ✔ Identifying adjectives and adverbs
- ✔ Selecting the appropriate adjective or adverb for a particular situation
- ✔ Knowing when to use *a* or *an*
- ✔ Inserting hyphens in compound descriptions

What to Watch Out For

Keep these points in mind when you're answering the questions in this chapter:

- ✔ Adjectives describe nouns and pronouns, telling you how many, which one, how much, or what kind of thing or person you're talking about.
- ✔ Adverbs describe verbs, telling you how, when, where, why, or under what conditions an action or state of being occurs.
- ✔ Adverbs also describe adjectives and other adverbs, expressing the intensity or degree of the quality the adverb describes.
- ✔ The article *an* precedes a word beginning with a vowel sound (*a, e, i, o,* or *u*). *A* precedes a word beginning with a consonant sound (any letter except the vowels listed in the preceding sentence).
- ✔ If two or more words function as one description, you generally hyphenate them, as in *second-place finish, green-and-yellow hat, hard-working waiter,* and so forth.

Distinguishing Between Adjectives and Adverbs

362–373 Identify the underlined words (in order) as adjectives (ADJ), adverbs (ADV), or neither (N).

362. The <u>green</u> scarf slipped <u>off</u> her <u>bare</u> head.

363. Put these <u>shiny</u> cups <u>below</u> because I may use them <u>later</u>.

364. <u>Good</u> journalists <u>still</u> cover <u>important</u> stories, not <u>sensational</u> gossip.

365. <u>Five</u> <u>tiny</u> mice curled up and squeaked <u>softly</u> when they sensed <u>danger</u>.

366. The <u>escaped</u> prisoners, <u>tired</u> and <u>hungry</u>, <u>eventually</u> surrendered.

367. Your <u>school</u> shoes are <u>too</u> <u>tight</u>, so we must buy a <u>larger</u> size.

368. When Luke sounded <u>hoarse</u>, his <u>trusted</u> <u>voice</u> coach gave <u>him</u> honey and lemon.

369. <u>Identical</u> twins are <u>playing</u> <u>one</u> role in that <u>Broadway</u> play.

370. A <u>vacant</u> building, <u>unguarded</u>, may attract squatters who live <u>there</u> <u>illegally</u>.

371. Be <u>smart</u>. Drive <u>defensively</u>, and you'll arrive <u>safely</u> and enjoy a <u>lovely</u> vacation.

372. The <u>production</u> crew is <u>responsible</u> for setting the props on stage <u>before</u> the curtain <u>first</u> rises.

373. Chef John is <u>justly</u> <u>famous</u> for his use of <u>extremely</u> <u>fresh</u> ingredients and <u>fast</u> preparation of <u>complicated</u> dishes.

Placing Adjectives and Adverbs in Sentences

374–393 Insert an adjective or an adverb in each blank, choosing from the words in the parentheses.

374. The reporter was _____ (pleased, pleasingly) to see his _____ (local, locally) story attract _____ (national, nationally) attention.

375. Are _____ (common, commonly) electronic devices _____ (bad, badly) for _____ (social, socially) connections?

376. Wading into _____ (deep, deeply) waters, Ron felt _____ (cool, coolly) _____ (immediate, immediately).

377. Ben strummed his _____ (new, newly) guitar _____ (energetic, energetically) but not _____ (good, well).

378. The _____ (large, largely) delivery van runs _____ (smooth, smoothly), so its contents remain in _____ (good, well) condition.

379. Our show's _____ (loyal, loyally) audience protests _____ (loud, loudly) whenever the network _____ (serious, seriously) threatens to cancel it.

380. Jackson's gift was _____ (extreme, extremely) _____ (generous, generously), even though he considered the donation _____ (minimal, minimally).

381. Dave feels _____ (happy, happily) because the voters _____ (sure, surely) agree with his position on the _____ (controversial, controversially) issue.

382. "Play _____ (nice, nicely)," exclaimed the _____ (over, overly) strict babysitter, but the children continued their _____ (rough, roughly) games.

383. It's _____ (real, really) _____ (unusual, unusually) for an amateur to discover such a _____ (rare, rarely) fossil.

384. Mina worked _____ (hard, hardly), but the _____ (low, lowly) grade she _____ (sad, sadly) read on her paper did not reflect her efforts.

385. Children who behave _____ (bad, badly) should be scolded _____ (prompt, promptly) and then given a chance to improve with the _____ (gentle, gently) guidance of their caretakers.

386. _____ (Ripe, Ripely) plums taste _____ (sweet, sweetly), but fruit picked too soon may be _____ (bitter, bitterly).

387. Walk _____ (rapid, rapidly) down the hall and turn _____ (sharp, sharply) when you reach the _____ (first, firstly) door on the left.

388. I feel _____ (bad, badly) that I spoke _____ (insulting, insultingly) to my most _____ (important, importantly) client.

389. Eileen appeared _____ (merry, merrily) at the party, but afterwards she sounded _____ (sad, sadly) and _____ (nervous, nervously).

390. Anything _____ (wicked, wickedly) makes us feel _____ (uncomfortable, uncomfortably), at least for a _____ (short, shortly) time.

391. It's _____ (certain, certainly) true that young children often wait less _____ (patient, patiently) for their turns to play _____ (fun, funnily) games.

392. The _____ (wide, widely) seen broadcast was _____ (sure, surely) helpful to the show's _____ (dismal, dismally) ratings.

393. The senator _____ (sudden, suddenly) interrupted to declare _____ (firm, firmly) that she was _____ (political, politically) neutral.

Dealing with Articles

394–402 Choose a or an to precede each expression.

394. apple, orange, banana

395. card, printer, outdoor trip

396. bicycle, old-fashioned girl, modern woman

397. everyday dish, light, history

398. amusing story, unusual incident, original song

399. initial impression, very happy child, additional payment

400. historic occasion, important dictionary, telephone

401. herb garden, fir tree, balcony

402. orphan, adventure, e-mail message

Hyphenating Descriptions

403–411 Identify the description(s) that correctly include or omit hyphens.

403.
   I.   self-cleaning oven
   II.   best-dressed list
   III.   package of blue-pens

404.
   I.   recently passed law
   II.   brown-eyed boy
   III.   poorly-expressed idea

405.
   I.   third base coach
   II.   very-shallow water
   III.   sixth-grade math

406.
   I.   nine-year-old kid
   II.   constantly-changing world
   III.   nearly-enough candy

407.
   I.   tension-relieving exercise
   II.   a job well done
   III.   newly formed committee

408.
   I.   three-blind mice
   II.   very-happy puppy
   III.   less-valid argument

409.
   I.   elementary school desk
   II.   Yankees baseball team
   III.   book review section

410.
   I.   more interesting story
   II.   red haired ape
   III.   extremely difficult problem

411.
   I.   annual-dental exam
   II.   language-proficiency test
   III.   mostly-boring material

Chapter 9

Taking the Long View: Descriptive Phrases and Clauses

A s you text or tweet, short descriptions seem like a good idea. (Chapter 8 provides practice with almost everything you need to know about these one- or two-word descriptions, also known as adjectives and adverbs.) Longer descriptive elements — phrases and clauses — may not make it into a tweet, but they're valuable nonetheless. In this chapter you have a chance to show that you know where to place descriptions — mostly the long form, plus a couple of tricky short descriptions — so that they express your intended meaning.

The Questions You'll Work On

In this chapter, you work on these concepts:

- ✔ Recognizing the word or words described by phrases and clauses
- ✔ Placing phrases and clauses so that they are clear and describe the appropriate word

What to Watch Out For

Keep these points in mind when you're answering the questions in this chapter:

- ✔ Prepositional phrases may describe nouns or pronouns (adjective phrases) or verbs (adverb phrases).
- ✔ Infinitives and participles may also act as descriptions. Infinitives *(to + verb,* such as *to meet, to greet, to sleep)* may describe nouns, pronouns, or verbs. Participles (the part of a verb you use with *has, have,* or *had,* such as *given, driving,* and the like) may describe nouns or pronouns.
- ✔ Clauses (units of a sentence that contain a subject-verb pair) may describe nouns, pronouns, or verbs.
- ✔ To find any sort of adjective, ask these questions: *How many? Which one? What kind?* To locate an adverb, ask the following: *How? When? Where? Why? Under what conditions?*
- ✔ Every description, no matter how long or short, must be placed as near as possible to the word it describes. *Only, just, almost,* and *nearly* must be placed right before the word or words they apply to, not earlier in the sentence.
- ✔ Steer clear of vague descriptions that may describe one or more words in the sentence. Your meaning must be clear.
- ✔ When a verbal phrase begins a sentence, it must describe the subject of the sentence.

Identifying the Words Being Described

412–431 Identify the word(s) described by the underlined expression.

412. A zookeeper <u>with a long broom</u> stood outside the lions' large, grassy enclosure.

413. Clara sneezed <u>into her handkerchief</u> and then paused before resuming her speech.

414. <u>Above the clouds</u>, the child's green kite soared swiftly.

415. The author <u>of the mystery series</u> says that she will kill her detective in the next installment.

416. The red wool carpet lay <u>over the scratched floor</u> and made the room look much more attractive to the buyer.

417. Monica, <u>sliding her finger around the bowl</u>, did not realize that all the icing was gone.

418. Two puppets, <u>which belonged to my grandmother</u>, played important roles in our show.

419. <u>Before Dennis applied for a scholarship</u>, he researched many possible awards and found several that seemed within his reach.

420. Sheltering <u>beneath their mother's arms</u>, the twins smiled shyly at the doctor, who offered each of them a cherry lollipop.

421. Shirley visited France and took <u>only</u> one photo of the Eiffel Tower.

422. The boy <u>who cried wolf</u> is a famous fairy tale and an accurate depiction of human nature.

423. Nancy's detective stories were always fun to read about, <u>although sometimes she seemed to benefit from too many coincidental clues</u>.

424. No matter how many times he mopped the floor, Doug couldn't keep up with the water <u>flowing through the cracks in the foundation</u>.

425. The team manager discussed the price of new uniforms <u>at his meeting</u> last night.

426. When Tom finally threw down his spoon, he had been stirring the sauce for <u>nearly</u> an hour.

427. <u>While carrying wood</u>, the lumberjack dropped a few logs on the lawn, and the birds quickly scattered in fear.

428. Conscientious assistants take notes of everything <u>their supervisors say</u>, regardless of how unimportant the comments seem.

429. David and his puppy, <u>rolling together in a mock fight</u>, knocked over a lamp and two tables before they were finished.

430. Last month I traveled to Seattle, a beautiful city, <u>to see my family</u>.

431. Receiving a medal <u>for what he accomplished during his time in office</u>, the principal bowed to his audience and praised both students and faculty.

Avoiding Misplaced, Dangling, and Vague Descriptions

432–451 In which of these sentences are the descriptions placed correctly?

432.
 I. The ruby earrings rested on the nightstand next to my bed that I wore to the dance.

 II. The ruby earrings that I wore to the dance rested on the nightstand next to my bed.

 III. The ruby earrings rested on the nightstand that I wore to the dance next to my bed.

433.
 I. The crosstown bus filled with holiday shoppers inched slowly through heavy traffic.

 II. Filled with holiday shoppers, the crosstown bus inched slowly through heavy traffic.

 III. The crosstown bus inched slowly through heavy traffic filled with holiday shoppers.

434.
 I. Elena only has three children, though she had hoped for a larger family.

 II. Elena has only three children, though she had hoped for a larger family.

 III. Elena has three children, though she had only hoped for a larger family.

435.
 I. George's scowling unnecessarily alarmed people.

 II. George's unnecessary scowling alarmed people.

 III. George's scowling alarmed people unnecessarily.

436.
- I. Tracy and the cat licking fur curled up on the couch.
- II. Tracy and the cat curled up on the couch licking fur.
- III. Licking fur, Tracy and the cat curled up on the couch.

437.
- I. The letter said that she had won the lottery in Alice's mailbox.
- II. The letter in Alice's mailbox said that she had won the lottery.
- III. The letter said that in Alice's mailbox she had won the lottery.

438.
- I. He drove the car down the highway that he bought last year.
- II. That he bought last year, he drove the car down the highway.
- III. He drove the car that he bought last year down the highway.

439.
- I. Although the lobby renovation is taking longer than expected, we are sure that everyone will like the new floor tiles from Greece when it reopens in September.
- II. Although the lobby renovation is taking longer than expected, we are sure that when it reopens in September, everyone will like the new floor tiles from Greece.
- III. Although the lobby renovation is taking longer than expected, when it reopens in September we are sure that everyone will like the new floor tiles from Greece.

440.
- I. My hands, breaking into a thousand pieces, were slippery, and the dishes fell.
- II. My hands were slippery, and the dishes fell, breaking into a thousand pieces.
- III. Breaking into a thousand pieces, my hands were slippery, and the dishes fell.

441.
- I. She almost won with 500 votes; the loser received 410.
- II. She won with almost 500 votes; the loser received 410.
- III. With almost 500 votes, she won; the loser received 410.

442.
- I. The highway boundary, painted white, was visible even at night.
- II. Painted white, the highway boundary was visible even at night.
- III. The highway boundary was visible even at night, painted white.

443.
- I. Because Harry is on a diet that emphasizes fruits and vegetables, he just bought ice cream once a month.
- II. Because Harry is on a diet that emphasizes fruit and vegetables, he bought just ice cream once a month.
- III. Because Harry is on a diet that emphasizes fruit and vegetables, he bought ice cream just once a month.

444.
- I. Jack avoided the mugger who was standing still and pointing a gun, running into the woods.
- II. Running into the woods, Jack avoided the mugger who was standing still and pointing a gun.
- III. Jack, running into the woods, avoided the mugger who was standing still and pointing a gun.

445.
- I. Eleanor told me during the class the teacher was boring.
- II. During the class, Eleanor told me the teacher was boring.
- III. Eleanor told me the teacher was boring during the class.

446.
I. When you're dealing with unreasonable people, making decisions quickly causes arguments.

II. When you're dealing with unreasonable people, making decisions causes arguments quickly.

III. When you're dealing with unreasonable people, making quick decisions causes arguments.

447.
I. Lying asleep in her crib, the nanny checked on the child.

II. The nanny, lying asleep in her crib, checked on the child.

III. The nanny checked on the child lying asleep in her crib.

448.
I. The house Agnes once visited sold for a million dollars.

II. The house Agnes visited sold for a million dollars once.

III. The house Agnes visited once sold for a million dollars.

449.
I. Testifying for the defense, the eyewitness account from Mr. Jones was compelling.

II. Testifying for the defense, Mr. Jones's eye-witness account was compelling.

III. Testifying for the defense, Mr. Jones gave a compelling account of what he had witnessed.

450.
I. The commissioner explained the environmental impact of mining with a slide presentation.

II. The commissioner explained with a slide presentation the environmental impact of mining.

III. With a slide presentation, the commissioner explained the environmental impact of mining.

451.
I. The tattoo artist injected ink into the client's upper arm, which was thickly muscled and hard to draw on.

II. Thickly muscled and hard to draw on, the tattoo artist injected ink into the client's upper arm.

III. The tattoo artist injected ink, thickly muscled and hard to draw on, into the client's upper arm.

Chapter 10

For Better or Worse: Forming Correct Comparisons

....

*W*hile everyone else is dabbing away tears or snapping photos, do you find yourself wondering why wedding vows pledge "for *better* or *worse*" instead of "for *more good* or *more bad*"? If so, this chapter is for you. Here, you're challenged to create comparisons of all types — with one word or many. You also identify and correct vague, illogical, or impossible comparisons.

The Questions You'll Work On

In this chapter, you work on questions that involve the following tasks:

- Choosing the correct word(s) to compare two elements (the comparative form, such as *nicer*) or three or more elements (the superlative form, such as *nicest*)
- Inserting *more, most, less,* and *least* properly
- Dealing with irregular comparisons — *good, better, best* and *bad, worse, worst*
- Identifying words that can't be compared
- Avoiding incomplete and illogical comparisons

What to Watch Out For

Keep these points in mind when you're answering the questions in this chapter:

- Short words often form positive comparisons by adding *-er* or *-est* to the base word, and if the base word ends in *y*, you generally change the *y* to *i* before adding *-er* or *-est*.
- Don't double up: If you add *-er* or *-est,* don't use *more* or *most* too.
- Use the comparative (*-er* or *more, less*) when comparing two elements and the superlative (*-est* or *most, least*) when comparing three or more elements.
- Absolutes — *perfect, unique,* and similar concepts — can't be compared.
- *Good, bad, well, many,* and *much* are irregular.
- All comparisons must be complete and clear.
- Use *other* or *else* when comparing someone or something to the group that includes the person or thing being compared.

Creating Comparative and Superlative Forms

452–476 Which comparisons of the base word are correct?

452. Base word: neat

Comparisons: neater, more neater, less neat, neatest, least neat

453. Base word: close

Comparisons: more close, closer, most close, less close, closest

454. Base word: beautiful

Comparisons: beautifuller, more beautiful, beautifullest, most beautiful, less beautiful

455. Base word: scary

Comparisons: scarier, scariest, more scarier, most scariest, least scary

456. Base word: competent

Comparisons: competenter, less competent, less competenter, least competent, least competentest

457. Base word: pretty

Comparisons: prettyer, prettier, prettyest, prettiest, less pretty

458. Base word: softly

Comparisons: softlier, softliest, more softly, most softly, less softly

459. Base word: fast

Comparisons: faster, fastest, less fast, least fast, most fast

460. Base word: tall

Comparisons: taller, tallest, more tall, most tall, less tall

461. Base word: rapidly

Comparisons: more rapidly, most rapidly, less rapidly, least rapidly, rapider

462. Base word: concerned

Comparisons: more concerned, less concerned, most concerned, least concerned, concernest

463. Base word: nimbly

Comparisons: nimblier, nimbliest, more nimbly, more nimblier, most nimbliest

464. Base word: merry

Comparisons: more merry, most merry, more merrier, most merriest, merrier

465. Base word: loudly

Comparisons: loudlier, loudliest, more loudly, most loudly, more loudlier

466. Base word: curved

Comparisons: curveder, curvedest, less curved, least curved, most curved

467. Base word: friendly

Comparisons: friendlier, friendliest, less friendlier, least friendlier, most friendlier

468. Base word: artificially

Comparisons: more artificially, most artificially, less artificially, least artificially, artificialler

469. Base word: dead

Comparisons: deader, deadest, more dead, less dead, most dead

470. Base word: good

Comparisons: better, best, more better, most better, less better

471. Base word: much

Comparisons: mucher, more, muchest, most, less much

472. Base word: bad

Comparisons: worse, worser, worst, worster, more bad

473. Base word: unique

Comparisons: uniquer, uniquest, more unique, most unique, least unique

474. Base word: well

Comparisons: better, best, weller, wellest, more well

475. Base word: perfect

Comparisons: perfecter, perfectest, more perfect, most perfect, more nearly perfect

476. Base word: badly

Comparisons: badlier, more badlier, badliest, less badliest, worse

Avoiding Incomplete, Illogical, or Vague Comparisons

477–501 How should the underlined expression be changed to create a correct comparison? **Note:** Check the parentheses, if present, for clues to the intended meaning of the sentence.

477. Alice is <u>happier</u>. (comparing Alice to her sister)

478. When Peter quit his job, he was <u>poorer</u>.

479. George Washington may be <u>more famous than any</u> President of the United States.

480. This allergy season is <u>equally as</u> bad as last year's season.

481. Compared to his brother, Levi has <u>the most freckles</u>.

482. During the boring lecture, five people fell asleep, and Darian snored <u>the loudest</u>.

483. Dmitri Smith and his wife Alicia Alvarez are both dentists, but Alicia earns <u>the least</u>.

484. My parakeet Robbie has <u>the curviest tail</u>. (comparing Robbie to all birds)

485. Veronica likes Archie <u>less than her friend Bob</u>.

486. The invention of the touch screen was <u>more important than any</u> technological innovation of that year.

487. Ending on page 1,000, that Victorian novel is longer <u>than most modern novelists</u>.

488. The dance teacher claimed that Fred, nervous and self-conscious, tried not to look dumb and "ended up looking <u>dumber</u>."

489. After examining 50 antique statues, the curator said that the one from Mesopotamia was <u>more incomparable</u>.

490. Elizabeth Bennet, the main character in *Pride and Prejudice,* is <u>less self-aware than</u> she thinks she is.

491. "Oranges are juicier <u>than any fruit</u>," exclaimed Ann as she bit into a freshly picked piece.

492. Julia's accent is <u>less comprehensible than Alicia</u>.

493. A circle that is 2 inches in diameter is <u>rounder than</u> one with a 4-inch diameter.

494. Marcy loaned money to her friend, whose house is <u>the messier in the neighborhood</u>.

495. Henry's strategy for achieving a perfect score on the SAT was <u>less efficient as referenced to</u> mine.

496. Of all the minutes in a day, the baby had to pick <u>the worse one</u> to fall asleep!

497. My suitcase is <u>as heavy, perhaps even heavier than</u>, yours.

498. George does <u>a better job repairing shoes than</u> either Mac or Nelson.

499. Sidney's hair, before his recent trip to the salon, was <u>curlier than Anthony</u>.

500. Discussing his role in the negotiations, Mr. Alexander claimed to be <u>the more effective of</u> the two union representatives.

501. This lamp is <u>as bright, if not brighter than</u>, all the others in my house.

Chapter 11

Avoiding Capital Punishment: Placing Capital Letters Properly

• •

Would you like to stay out of Grammar Jail? If so, place your capital letters where they're needed and nowhere else. Sounds easy, right? It is — mostly. Just know the rules and follow them. Then the Grammar Cops won't come after you.

The Questions You'll Work On

In this chapter, you work on these questions:

- ✔ Deciding when to capitalize people's names and titles, relationships, and ethnicity
- ✔ Choosing capitals or lowercase letters for dates, seasons, geographical names, and regions
- ✔ Selecting capitals for the titles of literary and scientific works and historical eras or events
- ✔ Placing capitals in references to school years and courses
- ✔ Following the rules for capital letters in quotations

What to Watch Out For

Keep these points in mind when you're answering the questions in this chapter:

- ✔ Proper names and the personal pronoun *I* are capitalized, as is a title used as a name or preceding the name of the person holding that title.
- ✔ Seasons of the year aren't capitalized, but the names of months and days are.
- ✔ The proper names of countries, regions, and geographical features are capitalized. Generic geographical references are in lowercase.
- ✔ The first letter of a sentence, title, or subtitle is always capitalized. In *headline style*, nouns, verbs, and other important words in titles are capitalized; less important words aren't. Titles of scientific works generally follow *sentence style*, capitalizing only the first word of the title and subtitle, as well as any proper names.

- References to God are customarily capitalized.

- School years are in lowercase. Subject areas, except for languages or references to countries, aren't capitalized. The names of courses are capitalized in headline style.

- The first word of a quotation that is connected to a speaker tag (*he said, I stated,* and so forth) is capitalized. Quotations inserted into a sentence without a speaker tag begin with a lowercase letter, unless the first word is a proper name or the pronoun *I.* The second half of an interrupted quotation begins with a lowercase letter.

Capitalizing Names, Titles, Relationships, and Ethnicity

502–521 Which words should be capitalized?

502. i celebrate thanksgiving with my family at mary's house.

503. the ambassador told president fowler that war was avoidable if both countries signed the treaty.

504. yesterday peter expressed his belief that god is present at all times.

505. recently professor smith, dean of faculty, revised the requirements for promotion to department head.

506. the display of african-american art at the museum drew huge crowds; more than 50 artists were represented.

507. did you know that aunt elizabeth always invites grandma and grandpa to her son's birthday party?

508. louise smith, chief of operations at medico incorporated, introduced vice president ellis to the staff.

509. conchetta, a distant cousin, recently met the president of the united states.

510. a famous grocery, ballocco's italian specialties, has both a website and a physical store.

511. the preacher explained in detail how to worship the lord.

512. the district attorney gave me five pages of testimony from the principal prosecution witness, general rodriguez.

513. his polish girlfriend taught aunt may and me how to dance the polka, playing many songs suitable for that type of dance.

514. one famous secretary-general of the united nations, dag hammarskjold, received the nobel peace prize in 1961.

515. janice jones, treasurer of our religious study group, asked for a moment of silence to praise god and his works.

516. the annual greek-american parade takes place tomorrow, according to archbishop kerakalos, the head of the greek historical society.

517. how many non-european hockey players participate in the international league of ice hockey, the organization that oversees the schedule and salaries?

518. my favorite film star, jeffrey o. phelps, won the oscar for best supporting actor.

519. the mayor fired daniel ellis, a supervisor with the department of parks, after hurricane sandy.

520. her brother worked for consolidated edison, which supplies electricity to the city, until 2012, when he retired with the rank of vice president.

521. does mother know that uncle bill just left for alabama, where he will run for senator?

Capitalizing Geographical Names, Quotations, and School References

522–532 Which words should be capitalized?

522. my french teacher is from tunisia, a country in africa where that language is widely spoken.

523. when alan was a sophomore, he spent every monday in december working on a mural for the school cafeteria.

524. last winter marian said, "every snowy day is a treasure."

525. lucy loves her history class, but she excels in science and math.

526. in the spring you should take introduction to biology instead of nuclear physics.

527. lou thinks that sandals are "light and airy."

528. to reach the rocky mountains, i drove west for three days last summer.

529. ruining the entire month, april 15th is the deadline for filing tax returns for each year.

530. "i invest in fine art," remarked jean, "because i like to support local artists."

531. joe lives in tribeca, a neighborhood in manhattan, but he's originally from the midwest.

532. having gobbled up my french fries, johnny then wiped his greasy fingers on my best egyptian cotton towels.

Capitalizing the Titles of Artistic or Scientific Works

533–541 Which words in each title should be capitalized? **Note:** *Check the parentheses to see whether the work follows headline or sentence style.*

533. the love song of benny and jenny (headline style)

534. penicillin: an examination of the safety and effectiveness of a common antibiotic (sentence style)

535. superbug, snakefeet, and fish teeth: a history of three rock bands (headline style)

536. serafina my love: how two star-crossed lovers met their fate (headline style)

537. traffic circulation patterns: an analysis of driver choice from 2005–2015 (sentence style)

538. hospital sanitary practices: a guide for administrators (sentence style)

539. you get more than you pay for by bargaining! (headline style)

540. basil: an invasive crop or helpful newcomer? (sentence style)

541. are you listening? a musician's memoir of an auditory education (headline style)

Chapter 12

Exercising Comma Sense: Placing Commas Correctly

· ·

A tiny curved line, the comma has more power than most elected officials. It can make your meaning clear or change the meaning of a sentence entirely. Placing commas where they belong isn't rocket science, but it does require you to notice every detail. In this chapter you practice paying attention to commas and exercising "comma sense."

The Questions You'll Work On

In this chapter, you work on questions that exercise the following skills:

- ✔ Punctuating lists with commas and inserting semicolons where needed
- ✔ Differentiating between essential and nonessential information by inserting commas
- ✔ Using commas to set off introductory elements and interruptions in the sentence
- ✔ Creating direct address with commas
- ✔ Separating clauses with commas and conjunctions

What to Watch Out For

Keep these points in mind when you're answering the questions in this chapter:

- ✔ Elements of a list are generally separated by commas. The comma before *and* is optional, though most people include it.
- ✔ If items in a list contain commas, use semicolons to separate the items.
- ✔ Set off nonessential descriptions from the rest of the sentence using commas. Essential information is not set off by commas.
- ✔ Nonessential clauses (subject-verb statements) often begin with *which*. Essential clauses often begin with *that*.
- ✔ Commas set off words in a sentence that interrupt the flow of meaning (direct address, exclamations, and the like).
- ✔ When you join one complete sentence to another with a conjunction (*and, or, but, for, yet, nor*), place a comma before the conjunction.

Commas in Lists

542–556 Punctuate the list by adding commas and semicolons as needed. **Note:** *Some optional commas already appear in the lists.*

542. ham eggs bacon cereal milk, and toast

543. drizzle hurricane hail sleet, and rain

544. vanilla and chocolate

545. vanilla and chocolate and strawberry ice cream

546. slid teetered, and fell flat

547. the dirty ripped faded shoes

548. three blind noisy mice

549. a constantly changing mysterious personality

550. my oldest kindest friend and her extremely strict parents

551. became angry went to the boss, and vented his passionately held beliefs

552. algebra which I hated geometry which I loved, and calculus which I enjoyed

553. your penetrating unusually creative mind

554. Peter Walsh her former sweetheart Richard Dalloway her husband Hugh Whitbread an old friend (**Note:** This list contains the names of three people, each followed by an explanation of his or her identity.)

555. sealed the crucially important envelope and mailed it

556. five sides equal in length width, and height

Using Commas with Identifying and Extra Information

557–576 Identify the word or words (if any) that should be followed by commas.

557. The plant that has drooping leaves needs more water.

558. The football players who are injured want more protective gear, but the quarterback believes that his current equipment is sufficient.

559. The corner of Second Avenue and Fifth Street where the accident took place now has a stoplight.

560. Alice's cousin Charles is the funniest of the five siblings.

561. My bedroom ceiling which has three long cracks will be repaired next week.

562. The house I grew up in was painted yellow and had a green roof.

563. Johnny playing with his toy cars was not old enough to drive a real vehicle.

564. Sodium chloride better known as salt is a flavorful addition to most meals.

565. The toddler playing in the sandbox was reluctant to leave the playground.

566. The chairman of the board Mr. Smith resigned yesterday.

567. The law enacted at midnight represented a compromise between the opposing parties.

568. The office decorated in blue our state color displays paintings with patriotic themes.

569. Six o'clock when my alarm rings is the time I jump onto my exercise bike and pedal for an hour.

570. A cheerleader who doesn't concentrate can easily fall and suffer an injury.

571. I didn't join the club because we're friends; I am interested in its activities.

572. The herb Debby sprinkles on most of her salads dill is easy to grow.

573. Catherine laughed as she told the story.

574. Sarah won't slap you because she avoids violence at all costs.

575. I have seen the funniest film ever made *Caddyshack* about 30 times.

576. Nearly every student of English literature loves Shakespeare's best play *Hamlet*.

Creating a Pause in a Sentence

577–591 Identify the word or words (if any) that should be followed by commas.

577. Yes I hate geraniums and roses.

578. Max however would like to pilot a jet.

579. Oscar I think you could become a superstar.

580. Eloise closed the door and then she locked it.

581. The clerk slapped a price sticker on each tube and placed the merchandise on the shelf.

582. Go to your room Henry before I lose my temper!

583. Oh no one remembered to bring the ketchup or mustard!

584. Really she's so elegant that I can't imagine her in a kitchen laundry, or basement.

585. He walked two miles through the park but he took a bus home.

586. The itsy-bitsy spider went up the water spout you know.

587. Nevertheless you must complete all your chores before you watch the playoffs.

588. Your calculator is broken and your answer therefore is incorrect.

589. By the way Gloria your zipper is open and so is your mouth.

590. Logging more than a thousand hours flying that plane Albert is an expert pilot.

591. Although it's too difficult for beginners the course is great for advanced students.

Chapter 13

Little Things That Mean A Lot: Apostrophes and Quotation Marks

. . . .

Apostrophes and quotation marks cause much confusion, but these tiny bits of ink serve a purpose. Apostrophes indicate ownership and omitted letters or numbers. Quotation marks identify words from someone other than the writer. In this chapter you answer questions about the proper placement of apostrophes and quotation marks.

The Questions You'll Work On

In this chapter, you work on questions in the following areas:

- ✔ Placing apostrophes to show ownership by one or more people
- ✔ Shortening words or numbers with apostrophes
- ✔ Using apostrophes with expressions of time and money
- ✔ Distinguishing between quoted and paraphrased material
- ✔ Situating periods, commas, and other punctuation marks in quoted material, citations, and titles

What to Watch Out For

Keep these points in mind when you're answering the questions in this chapter:

- ✔ Don't use an apostrophe to create a plural. (Exceptions to this rule exist, but they're not in common use.)
- ✔ To create a possessive, singular noun, add *'s*. To create a possessive, regular plural, add an apostrophe after the *s*. To create the possessive form of an irregular plural, add *'s*.
- ✔ In contractions, replace omitted words or numbers with an apostrophe. (A few irregular contractions, such as *won't* for *will not*, don't follow this rule.)
- ✔ Always surround quoted material and titles of short works (poems, short stories, and the like) with quotation marks.

✔ In Standard American English, single quotation marks appear only when one quotation nests inside another quotation. Place periods and commas before the closing quotation mark. Place semicolons and colons after the closing quotation mark.

✔ If you're quoting a question, the question mark precedes the closing quotation mark. If the sentence is a question but the quotation isn't, place the question mark after the closing quotation mark. Follow the same pattern for exclamation points — before the closing quotation mark if the quoted words are an exclamation and after the closing quotation mark if the sentence, but not the quotation, is an exclamation.

Creating the Possessive Form of Nouns

592–600 What is the possessive form of these nouns?

592. Dora, stars, girl

593. lamps, Robin, pencils

594. lawyer, peanuts, parakeet

595. child, children, boys

596. men, rugs, dinosaur

597. workbook, french fries, women

598. son-in-law, deer, Martin

599. buildings, brothers-in-law, who

600. fish, oranges, Ms. Jones

Creating Contractions with Apostrophes

601–609 Where appropriate, create contractions of these word pairs by omitting letters and inserting apostrophes.

601. do not, I will, is not

602. it is, they are, you have

603. he is, she was, we are

604. will not, should not, I would

605. has not, must not, why is

606. cannot, would have, she had

607. might have, it was, does not

608. who would, could have, how is

609. what is, let us, should have

Inserting and Deleting Apostrophes

610–616 Insert apostrophes where they are needed and delete them where they are not appropriate.

610. The class of 55 will celebrate it's reunion in two month's.

611. Jane bought two new camera's but isnt pleased with her purchase.

612. Dont wait until 2018 to start saving; six years earlier, in 12, start to pile up dollar's.

613. They shouldve given us more time to take those exam's.

614. Bagels' were very popular breakfast foods in 1909'.

615. Im tired of doing two hours homework every night; Marys assignments are easier.

616. Whod work two weeks for only a days pay?

Distinguishing Between Quotations and Paraphrases

617–624 Look at this script, in which two friends discuss a baseball game. Read the sentences following the script. What, if anything, should be surrounded by quotation marks?

Script:

JEFF: Hey, did you go to the game last night?

JANE: Yeah, and I'm glad I did. Did you see Marcus hit in the third inning? It was stupendous! It shot over the left-field wall like a rocket. Were you there?

JEFF: No. I stayed home to do the most boring math homework in the universe. You know what? The teacher didn't even collect the homework! She didn't grade it. Isn't that, like, against the law or something?

617. Jane told Jeff that Marcus hit a home run.

618. Jeff explained, I stayed home to do the most boring math homework in the universe.

619. Jane replied, I'm glad I did, when Jeff asked Jane whether she had attended the game.

620. Jane believes that Marcus's home run was stupendous.

621. Jeff asked Jane whether not collecting or grading assigned homework was illegal.

622. According to Jeff, the teacher didn't grade the homework.

623. Did Jeff ask Jane, Were you there?

624. Jeff claims that he did the most boring math homework in the universe.

Placing Quotation Marks and Other Punctuation

625–638 *Place commas, periods, question marks, exclamation points, and quotation marks in the sentence as needed. Also capitalize letters as needed.* **Note:** *Directly quoted words are underlined. You decide whether the quoted words merit quotation marks.*

625. The heat wave will end on Saturday, the forecaster promised.

626. Mark screamed let her go!

627. Wilbur asked did Christine take a taxi to the theater?

628. Pilar was born in Ecuador, where, she says, the weather is often hot and humid.

629. Xavier eventually declared that his unusual name was awesome.

630. <u>I wonder where the birthday candles are</u>, Grandma whispered, <u>and if we have enough</u>.

631. This smartphone app claims to make <u>shopping</u> easier, according to the boy who is selling it.

632. Marisa explained that she was <u>completely exhausted</u>; she and Lola went home immediately.

633. Henry requested many things, including a pocket <u>knife</u> and a <u>pony</u>.

634. <u>When he learned to read, Daryl was five</u>, declared Jordan, <u>not ten years old</u>.

635. Robbie explained <u>the teacher thinks I am supersmart</u>. (**Note:** *Supersmart* is a quotation from the teacher.)

636. <u>It is going to rain</u>, Harry predicted <u>the picnic will be postponed</u>.

637. Will said that the cheese smelled <u>funky</u>: It had been in the refrigerator for more than a year.

638. According to the authorities, police officers were called <u>brave</u> and <u>heroic</u> by all who witnessed the daring rescue.

Punctuating Academic Work

639–646 Place commas, periods, question marks, exclamation points, and quotation marks, as needed, in the sentence. Also insert capital letters where needed. **Note:** *To help you identify titles and directly quoted words, these elements are underlined. (Assume that all titles belong to short works that are normally placed in quotation marks.) Citations appear in parentheses, as they do in academic papers.*

639. In his first paper, <u>A History of the Stuart Family</u>, Professor Milling explores the relationship between the Stuarts and their business partners.

640. Jacobs argues that the colonies <u>were motivated by a desire for freedom</u>, not additional markets for their goods.

641. Rich's poem, <u>Diving into the Wreck</u>, explores gender and other themes.

642. <u>Going to Savannah</u>, a poem by Agnes Little, is on the reading list.

643. The chorus's version of <u>You Are My Sunshine</u> relies on three-part harmony.

644. In homage to Shakespeare, the main character considers whether <u>to be truthful or not to be truthful</u> (line 23).

645. When she wrote <u>Killer Whales and Their Prey</u>, Maxine Davis asserted that these animals are endangered (44).

646. The essay explores the relationship between voter turnout and weather and claims that weather is less important than other factors (Dooley 23).

Chapter 14

Not Just for Railroad Tracks: Parallelism

• •

Picture railroad tracks as a train chugs along. What happens if the tracks aren't perfectly parallel? Derailment and disaster! The damage to your sentence may not be as obvious, but it occurs, nevertheless, if your sentence isn't parallel. Watch out when you write lists, comparisons, and any sentences with two or more matched elements (subjects, verbs, clauses, and so forth); they're only parallel if everything performing the same function has the same grammatical identity — perhaps all infinitives or all gerunds or all clauses. Don't worry about the grammar terms. Just listen to the voice inside your head reading your words. If a sentence or list sounds balanced, it's probably parallel. In this chapter you answer questions on all sorts of parallel situations.

The Questions You'll Work On

In this chapter, you work on these types of questions:

✔ Ensuring that lists are parallel

✔ Keeping elements parallel when they're joined by paired conjunctions (*either/or, neither/nor, both/and, not only/but also*)

✔ Writing parallel comparisons with *rather/than, as much as, more/than,* and other connectors

✔ Avoiding unnecessary shifts in verb tense, person, and active/passive voice

What to Watch Out For

Keep these points in mind when you're answering the questions in this chapter:

✔ When you're dealing with a pair of conjunctions, check that the same grammatical structure follows each half of the conjunction pair. In other words, if a subject-verb pair follows *either*, a subject-verb pair must follow *or*.

✔ Check all comparisons to be sure that the items compared have the same grammatical structure. You can compare a description to a description or a verb to a verb, but not a verb to a description.

✔ Avoid switching from active (*I wrote a speech*) to passive voice (*the speech was read by me*).

✔ Unless the meaning of the sentence requires a change in tense, be consistent.

✔ Don't change from one person (say, third person, as in *they study*) to another (such as the second-person statement *you learn*) unless you have a good reason to do so.

Identifying Parallel Elements in Lists

647–661 Which of these are parallel?

647.
  I.   skiing, skating, complaining
  II.   to plant, to sow, to reap
  III. going to sleep, waking up, ready for work

648.
  I.   smart, creative, has immense energy
  II.   keeps score, notifies the umpire, encourages the team
  III. over the mountain, through the woods, to Grandmother's house

649.
  I.   Jane calculates, Artie summarizes, Peter plans
  II.   riding a bike, walking in the garden, to relax
  III. around the corner, sneaky as a fox, behind the fence

650.
  I.   came, saw, conquered
  II.   coming, seeing, conquering
  III. come, see, conquered

651.
  I.   silk, thread, carefully sewn
  II.   jump, twirl, fall
  III. ignoring, bought, sold

652.
  I.   sung by the Beatles, recording a hit song, performed by the school chorus
  II.   heard everywhere, is popular, has many fans
  III. Ringo plays the drums, Paul strums the guitar, I sing along

653.
  I.   who needs a computer, that costs a fortune, which the store displays in the window
  II.   in the basement, energy-efficient furnace, in need of cleaning
  III. with remote control, flanked by speakers, sharp picture quality

654.
  I.   early opening, excellent service, committed to quality
  II.   Lisa's spying on her neighbors, the detective tapping her phone, the judge hearing the case
  III. because I said so, when the blizzard rages, after the game ends

655.
  I.   a bulldozer piled up sand, the dump truck carted it away, the jackhammer broke the pavement
  II.   gliding, smoothing the ice, stopping by the fence
  III. soil rich in nutrients, in the botanical garden, endangered species of plants

656.
  I.   screamed, threw food, epic tantrum
  II.   buying a cottage, replacing the roof that was damaged in the storm, redecorating
  III. hid under a chair, away from other players, whispered

657.
  I.   as time goes by, if I applied to that college, before midnight at the latest
  II.   why the card is wet, while it is raining lightly, before the monsoon ends
  III. he had been told, he had been warned, he had been suspended

658.
  I. Mary wrote the chapter, she proof-read it, the chapter was revised by her
  II. the editor liked it, he praised the writing, reviewers went wild
  III. on the remainder table, off the best-seller list, the book tanked

659.
  I. the apple he picked, the grapes he harvested, the grass he mowed
  II. stop, look, listen
  III. while you cook, Henry irons the scarf, although the wedding is tomorrow

660.
  I. the puppy to watch, to take to the park, the kitten to cuddle
  II. whoever is hungry, whatever you need, whomever I ask
  III. when winter comes, the snow piles up, the plow scours the streets

661.
  I. twist and shout, dance the night away, went to the movies
  II. the parrot with yellow feathers, the dog running away, a zoo is out of control
  III. tomorrow, yesterday, soon

Working with Paired Conjunctions

662–673 How should the underlined words be changed, if at all, to make the sentence parallel?

662. I would rather work in the library than <u>to go home</u>.

663. Style depends not only <u>how you look</u> but also on attitude.

664. Oliver's supposed masterpiece was both tuneless and <u>it was too long</u>.

665. When you apply for a selective school, <u>either you will be accepted</u> or rejected; you won't know unless you try.

666. Recipes in that cookbook contain meat rather than <u>they have vegetables</u>.

667. Both the soldiers and <u>that the general agreed</u>, so the proposed change to the battle plan was accepted.

668. The doctor was pleased with both the patient's blood pressure and <u>slower heart rate</u>.

669. Mary was not only fair but <u>she also was careful</u> to explain her decision to the contestants.

670. Neither Jean's absence nor <u>that her coworkers were on a coffee break</u> mattered, as no customers called.

671. Ximena neither explained nor <u>cared</u> if someone mispronounced her name.

672. The film director will not only emphasize special effects but also <u>she will design</u> them herself.

673. Participants in the study either have worked in a laboratory or <u>they plan</u> to do so within five years.

Creating Parallel Comparisons

674–682 How should the underlined portion of the sentence be changed, if at all, to create a parallel comparison?

674. <u>To play baseball</u> is as appealing to Suri as baking cookies.

675. I would rather go to the movies than <u>walking</u> around the mall.

676. Lillian is equal in height and <u>in weight</u> to her twin, Lola.

677. George's mother was upset with him more because of his lateness than <u>that he tracked mud</u> on the kitchen floor.

678. That small dinosaur was probably more aggressive than <u>it was passive</u>.

679. Are your scores on the real SAT as high as <u>what you got</u> on the practice test?

680. Rather than eating at the diner, <u>Lou enjoys dining in a fine restaurant</u>.

681. Spelling is easier for me than <u>John</u>.

682. We have <u>as much to prepare today as tomorrow</u>.

Keeping Sentences Parallel

683–696 How should the underlined portion of the sentence be changed, if at all, to make the sentence parallel?

683. Pursued by a bear, Nicholas ran as fast as possible to the car, and then <u>he locks the door.</u>

684. Before you disconnect the water pipe, <u>the valve should be turned off by you.</u>

685. <u>To travel</u> in Sweden was relaxing; coming home was not.

686. Dr. Weber admitted the patient, Ms. Smith, to the hospital, and <u>the patient was later examined by him.</u>

687. They should capture the audience's attention right away, so <u>an actor must speak forcefully</u> when the curtain rises.

688. The stage set has colorful lighting, costumes, curtains, and <u>rugs that are colorful too.</u>

689. Shirley smiled when she saw the backyard, which was bordered by daisies, shaded by oak trees, and <u>a pond cooled it.</u>

690. To study other cultures, <u>learn new languages, and to visit foreign countries</u> are worthwhile pursuits.

691. Bicycle riding helps people become physically fit and <u>you will find bikes convenient</u> too.

692. Many dictionaries <u>do not include</u> slang words nor common texting abbreviations.

693. <u>An apple, pear, and banana</u> are in the fruit bowl.

694. Successful politicians greet each supporter in person, and <u>social media is used too</u>.

695. As a short-term solution for hurricane victims <u>and in prevention of</u> future storm damage, this plan is excellent.

696. A current teacher must recommend a student applying for an honors course, or <u>they can submit</u> an essay explaining why the workload will not be too challenging.

Chapter 15

Slimming Down: Cutting Repetition and Wordiness

● ●

Do your sentences need to go on a diet? Are they chubby around the middle, with repetitive or wordy elements? If so, consider this chapter your path to trimmer, more powerful expression.

The Questions You'll Work On

In this chapter, you work on these concepts:

- ✔ Identifying synonyms or other repetitious expressions
- ✔ Writing concisely by eliminating unnecessary words

What to Watch Out For

Keep these points in mind when you're answering the questions in this chapter:

- ✔ Many words are close in meaning. *Tense,* for example, refers to how you feel when your muscles clench as tightly as possible. *Nervous,* on the other hand, describes the jitters that zing through your nervous system. Chances are you don't need both *tense* and *nervous* to describe one mood. Look for the right word, the one that truly fits the situation in your sentence.

- ✔ Shorter isn't always better, but nobody likes to waste time. Look for extra words: doubled descriptions, unnecessary explanations, and overly complicated sentence structure. When you find these issues, revise the sentence.

Cutting Repetitive Words and Phrases from Sentences

*697–706 What words, if any, are repetitive in the sentence? **Note:** For the purpose of this exercise, assume that words close in meaning, but not identical, are unnecessary.*

697. Mike, who is a fitness fanatic, jogged on streets and roads each and every morning.

698. Tom, pencil in hand and eraser ready in case of mistakes, drew a four-sided square shape on the paper.

699. The big toe on that statue is 6 inches long in length and weighs 10 pounds.

700. Totally and completely confused, the clown pranced in the circular ring in front of her delighted audience.

701. Try Sparkle-It today — the easiest and most carefree way to clean ovens and other kitchen equipment with no effort!

702. In my opinion, I think that what I experienced emotionally and felt in my heart was truly unique.

703. Georgina's diagnosis — an untreatable disease, fatal in most cases — dismayed and frightened her so much that she retreated to her bed and stayed there.

704. Undoubtedly the best in his field, the biographer is thorough, checking original papers as well as secondary sources.

705. Attempting to cross Niagara Falls on a high wire with an audience of 300 million television viewers, the wire walker tried to reach the other shore.

706. The popular hit series is set in a small Southern town that has 500 inhabitants.

Writing Concisely

*707–721 How should the original sentence best be revised, if at all, to avoid wordiness? **Note:** Be sure the revision you choose is grammatically correct and faithful to the meaning of the original sentence.*

707. Original sentence: The title character in *Macbeth* is ambitious, and it is this ambition that leads him to crime.

I. The title character, Macbeth, has ambition and leads him to crime.

II. Leading to crime, the title character in *Macbeth* is ambitious.

III. Ambition leads to crime in Shakespeare's *Macbeth*.

IV. The ambition of the title character of *Macbeth* leads him to crime.

708. Original sentence: Jill was always fair and reasonable, and she saw the advantages and disadvantages of both sides in every argument.

   I.   Fair and reasonable, Jill saw the advantages and disadvantages of both sides in every argument.

   II. Jill was always fair and reasonable, and she saw each side's advantages and disadvantages.

   III. Jill seeing the advantages and disadvantages of both sides in every argument fairly.

   IV. Jill's fairness and reasonableness led her to see both sides.

709. Original sentence: It was this place, Illinois, that saw the birth of Abraham Lincoln, one of the greatest presidents who ever headed the United States.

   I.   Illinois saw the birth of Abraham Lincoln, one of the greatest presidents who ever headed the United States.

   II. Abraham Lincoln, one of the greatest presidents of the United States, was born in Illinois.

   III. Illinois, which was what saw the birth of one of the greatest presidents, was the place where Abraham Lincoln was born.

   IV. Illinois was where one of the greatest presidents of the United States, Abraham Lincoln, was born and he headed the government.

710. Original sentence: Fifi, who is a dog, loves going to the park; the park is where she plays with other dogs.

   I.   Fifi loves going to the park, where she plays with other dogs.

   II. Fifi, who is a dog, loves going to the park and plays with other dogs.

   III. Fifi, who is a dog, loves going to the park with other dogs.

   IV. Fifi, a dog who loves going to the park, plays with other dogs there.

711. Original sentence: When I asked Dr. Spencer about his training, he told me that he had studied at Oxford University in Britain.

   I.   Dr. Spencer told me that he had studied at Oxford University in Britain.

   II. Dr. Spencer studied at Oxford University in Britain.

   III. Dr. Spencer told me that his studies took place at Oxford University in Britain.

   IV. Dr. Spencer trained at Oxford.

712. Original sentence: Handcuffed with their wrists restrained, the burglars then proceeded to demand phone calls, lawyers, and immediate release.

   I.   Handcuffed with their wrists restrained, the burglars proceeded to demand phone calls, lawyers, and immediate release.

   II. Handcuffed with their wrists restrained, the burglars then demanded phone calls, lawyers, and immediate release.

   III. Handcuffed, the burglars then proceeded to demand phone calls, lawyers, and immediate release.

   IV. Handcuffed, the burglars then demanded phone calls, lawyers, and immediate release.

713. Original sentence: After 12 years of experience at his previous jobs, all positions in marketing, Edward was interested in pursuing a different career path that wasn't marketing.

I. After 12 years of experience at his previous jobs, in marketing, Edward was interested in pursuing a different career path, not marketing.

II. After 12 years of experience in marketing, Edward's previous job was due for a change.

III. After 12 years in marketing, Edward was interested in a different career.

IV. After 12 years of experience at his previous jobs, Edward was interested in a different career path outside of marketing.

714. Original sentence: Smith Publishing, which publishes some books that deal with science and math, employs many experts in science and math to check its publications and eliminate any errors.

I. Smith Publishing, which publishes some books about science and math, employs many experts in science and math to check its publications and eliminate any errors.

II. Smith Publishing employs many experts to eliminate errors in its science and math publications.

III. Smith Publishing, publishing some books about science and math, employs many experts in science and math to check its publications.

IV. Smith Publishing, which publishes some books about science and math, employs many experts to check its publications and eliminate any errors.

715. Original sentence: We were already sitting in seats when the orchestra, all musicians, began to play at the direction of the conductor, who raised his baton to start the performance.

I. We were already seated when the conductor raised his baton and the orchestra began to play.

II. We were already sitting when the orchestra, all musicians, began to play as the conductor, he raised his baton to start the performance.

III. The conductor raised his baton and the orchestra began to play and we were sitting in seats then.

IV. We were already sitting in seats when all musicians began playing at the direction of the conductor, who raised his baton to start the performance.

716. Original sentence: *Oliver Twist,* which some consider Charles Dickens's finest novel, focuses on a young boy, not very old, who is forced to steal.

I. *Oliver* Twist, considered Charles Dickens's finest novel, focuses on a boy who is not too old who is forced to steal.

II. *Oliver Twist,* which some consider Charles Dickens's finest novel, focuses on a young boy forced to steal.

III. *Oliver Twist,* which some consider Charles Dickens's finest novel, focuses on a boy who is forced to steal.

IV. *Oliver Twist,* Dickens's finest novel, focuses on a boy who is forced to steal.

717. Original sentence: It was then, at the moment when the cell divided, that the researchers hoped that the new medication would make a difference.

    I.   It was then, when the cell divided, that the researchers hoped that the new medication would make a difference.

    II.   Then, at the moment when the cell divided, the researchers hoped that the new medication would make a difference.

    III.   The researchers hoped the new medication would make a difference during cell division.

    IV.   The researchers, hoping the new medication would make a difference at the moment when the cell divided.

718. Original sentence: For four hours, quasars — high energy objects — were observed in that galaxy.

    I.   Quasars were observed for four hours in that galaxy.

    II.   For four hours in a galaxy, quasars were observed.

    III.   Galaxy quasars were observed for four hours.

    IV.   For four hours of time, quasars — high energy objects — were observed.

719. Original sentence: Unanimous votes do not (or when they do, only rarely) occur in that committee, the reason for this fact being that committee members hold strong but opposing views.

    I.   Unanimous votes do not (or only rarely) occur in that committee, the reason for this fact being that committee members hold strong but opposing views.

    II.   Unanimous votes rarely occur in that committee, because committee members hold strong but opposing views.

    III.   Unanimous votes only rarely occur in that committee, the reason being that committee members hold strong but opposing views.

    IV.   Unanimous votes only rarely occur in that committee, because committee members oppose each other's views.

720. Original sentence: As I said before, Colles' fractures are fractures of the arm bone near the wrist.

    I.   Colles' fractures are fractures of the arm bone near the wrist.

    II.   As I said before, Colles' fractures occur when the arm bone breaks near the wrist.

    III.   Colles' fractures occur when the arm bone breaks near the wrist.

    IV.   Colles' fractures occur when the arm bone near the wrist breaks, as I said before.

721. Original sentence: In this novel, the author discusses various themes and ideas, all very important concepts that the reader should ponder.

I. In this novel, the author discusses various themes, all very important concepts that the reader should ponder.

II. The novel's author discusses various themes and ideas, all very important concepts that the reader should ponder.

III. In this novel, the author discusses various ideas, all important concepts that the reader should ponder.

IV. This novel presents important ideas that the reader should ponder.

Chapter 16

Aiming for Style: Creating Interesting Sentences

. . . .

You can — and should — develop a sense of style when you're writing. Style comes from many factors. In this chapter you work on combining ideas in interesting, fluid ways and experimenting with sentence patterns.

The Questions You'll Work On

In this chapter, you work on questions targeting the following:

- ✔ Inserting information into basic sentences with clauses and phrases
- ✔ Ensuring that sentences express the intended meaning
- ✔ Punctuating complicated sentences correctly
- ✔ Varying the normal subject-verb-complement pattern of a sentence
- ✔ Experimenting with sentence structure

What to Watch Out For

Keep these points in mind when you're answering the questions in this chapter:

- ✔ Clauses (subject-verb statements) beginning with *who, whom, whose, which,* or *that* usually insert descriptions of nouns or pronouns. Other types of clauses describe verbs, giving information about time, place, method, or reasons.

- ✔ Some clauses play crucial roles inside other clauses, acting as subjects or objects. These clauses often begin with *whoever, whomever,* or *that.*

- ✔ Placed properly, verbals — words that resemble verbs but function as nouns, adjectives, or adverbs — make your writing flow more smoothly. Consider using infinitives (*to* + a verb), gerunds (the *-ing* form of a verb acting as a noun), and participles (a verb form that may function as an adjective) to spice up your sentences.

✔ When you work with participles and infinitives, check the tense. The present form places the action or the state of being at the same time as the verb in the sentence. The past tense places the action or state of being prior to what the main verb of the sentence expresses.

✔ When you add clauses or phrases, take care that your sentence is complete (no fragments!) and properly punctuated (no run-ons!).

✔ Essential, identifying information isn't set off from the rest of the sentence by commas. Extra information is surrounded by commas.

✔ When a sentence begins with a verbal, the subject of the sentence must be the one performing the action or in the state of being expressed by the verbal.

✔ Mature writers vary sentence length and pattern.

Weaving Complex Sentences

722–751 Which sentence or sentences combine the listed ideas smoothly and correctly?

722. Ideas: The lamp is on the table. The lamp shines brightly. The table is next to the sofa.

I. The brightly shining lamp is on the table next to the sofa.

II. Next to the sofa, the lamp is shining brightly on the table.

III. On the table next to the sofa is the lamp, which shines brightly.

723. Ideas: The bus has 50 seats. The bus is stuck in traffic.

I. The bus, which has 50 seats, is stuck in traffic.

II. The bus of 50 seats is stuck in traffic.

III. The bus, it has 50 seats and is stuck in traffic.

724. Ideas: The book contains many pictures. The pictures show forests and mountains. The book is for children.

I. The book contains many pictures, and it shows forests and mountains, and it is for children.

II. The children's book contains many pictures of forests and mountains.

III. The book of many pictures shows forests and mountains, intended for children.

725. Ideas: This container is for food scraps. The food scraps form compost. The compost fertilizes the garden.

I. Food scraps form compost in this container fertilizing the garden.

II. In this container there are food scraps, and they form compost, and they fertilize the garden.

III. This container is for food scraps, which form compost to fertilize the garden.

726. Ideas: The suitcase is heavy. The suitcase has wheels. I don't have to carry the suitcase. I am glad.

I. The suitcase is heavy, but fortunately, it has wheels and I don't have to carry it.

II. I'm glad I don't have to carry the heavy suitcase, which has wheels.

III. The heavy suitcase has wheels, and I don't have to carry it, and I am glad about not carrying it.

727. Ideas: The sun came out. The temperature rose. The ice melted.

I. The sun coming out, the temperature rising and ice melting.

II. When the sun came out, the temperature rose and the ice melted.

III. The sun came out, so the temperature rose, so the ice melted.

728. Ideas: I saw the play. The play was suspenseful. I gasped at times.

    I.   The suspenseful play made me gasp at times.

    II.   Seeing the play, which was suspenseful, was something that made me gasp at times.

    III.   The play was so suspenseful that I gasped at times.

729. Ideas: The air is dry. The plant needs water more often.

    I.   Because the air is dry, the plant needs water more often.

    II.   In dry air, the plant needs water more often.

    III.   Needing water more often, the air is dry for the plant.

730. Ideas: Jonathan has many clients. His clients trust him. He handles their taxes.

    I.   Jonathan has many clients who trust him to handle their taxes.

    II.   Jonathan, with many clients, is trusted by them to handle the taxes they have.

    III.   Handling their taxes, Jonathan has many clients, and they trust him.

731. Ideas: My boss works on Saturdays. He likes Saturdays for work. The office is empty on Saturdays. No one interrupts him on Saturdays.

    I.   My boss, working on Saturdays, likes that the office is empty and that no one interrupts him on Saturdays.

    II.   My boss likes to work on Saturdays because the office is empty and free of interruptions.

    III.   My boss likes working on Saturdays in an empty office without interruptions.

732. Ideas: Consumers like fruit and vegetables that have bright colors. Some fruit and vegetable growers add artificial color. They add color when the fruit and vegetables are harvested.

    I.   At harvest time, some growers add artificial color to fruit and vegetables to satisfy consumer demand for such produce.

    II.   Because of consumer demand for brightly colored fruit and vegetables, some growers artificially add bright color to the fruits and vegetables when the fruits and vegetables are harvested.

    III.   Demanding bright colors for fruit and vegetables for consumers, some growers add the color artificially.

733. Ideas: Smartphones run apps. "Apps" is short for "applications." Apps today are more advanced. Apps written some years ago were less advanced.

    I.   The applications, also known as "apps," for smartphones are more advanced now than the apps were some years ago, being less advanced then.

    II.   Being more advanced now, smartphones running better apps.

    III.   Smartphone applications, or "apps," are more advanced now than they used to be.

734. Ideas: Some trains run at high speeds. At high speeds it takes a while for a train to stop. A sudden stop cannot happen at high speed.

    I.   A train running at high speed cannot stop suddenly.

    II.   Running at high speed, a train cannot stop suddenly.

    III.   Sudden stops, they cannot happen for high-speed trains.

735. Ideas: Fluorescent bulbs are efficient. They use less energy than many other bulbs. Energy costs decrease. Consumers pay less when they use fluorescent bulbs.

    I.   Fluorescent bulbs are energy efficient, so they use less energy, and customers' electric bills are lower.

    II.   Energy-efficient fluorescent bulbs decrease customers' electric bills.

    III.   Fluorescent bulbs, being energy efficient, decrease customers' electric bills.

736. Ideas: Some artists study anatomy. Artists usually draw better drawings of human figures after the artists study anatomy.

    I.   Studying anatomy may help artists draw human figures.

    II.   To study anatomy, which some artists do, is that which helps artists when they draw human figures.

    III.   Studying anatomy, some artists when they are drawing human figures work better.

737. Ideas: Mosquitoes don't fly well. It is hard to fly into the wind. A fan generates wind. A fan can keep mosquitoes away.

    I.   Because mosquitoes don't fly well, especially into the wind, a fan can repel mosquitoes.

    II.   A fan can repel mosquitoes because they fly poorly into the wind.

    III.   Generating wind, a fan may repel mosquitoes, which don't fly well.

738. Ideas: A computer produces sound. Programming can change the sound. Computer sound may resemble the sound of musical instruments.

    I.   Programmed properly, computers can mimic musical instruments.

    II.   Programming different sounds on a computer results in musical instrument sounds.

    III.   To create sounds resembling musical instruments, computer programmers can do that.

739. Ideas: Emily has a mirror. The mirror was her favorite possession. The mirror cracked. It wasn't Emily's favorite then.

    I.   Before the mirror cracked, it was Emily's favorite possession.

    II.   A favorite possession, Emily's mirror was cracking and then wasn't favored.

    III.   Until it cracked, Emily's favorite possession was the mirror.

740. Ideas: Cheating is a disgrace. Henry cheats.

    I.   That Henry cheats is a disgrace.

    II.   Henry, cheating, is a disgrace.

    III.   To cheat is a disgrace for Henry.

741. Ideas: People mishear a word. People misunderstand the meaning of the word. Eventually, the mistaken meaning is accepted. The wrong meaning becomes the right meaning.

    I.   After mishearing and misunderstanding a word, people eventually accept the "wrong" meaning as right.

    II.   To mishear and to misunderstand a word, the meaning is accepted as right, even though it used to be wrong.

    III.   Because people mishear and misunderstand a word, they accept mistakes and go from wrong to right.

742. Ideas: Letter carriers are on strike. They want more money.

    I.   Letter carriers that want higher salaries are on strike.

    II.   Letter carriers, that want higher salaries, are on strike.

    III.   Letter carriers, who want higher salaries, are on strike.

743. Ideas: Some ink washes away. Some ink is permanent. Jim's shirt has ink stains. Jim washed the shirt. Some stains remain. Those stains are from the permanent ink.

   I.   Jim washed his shirt, but the stains made with permanent ink remained.

   II.   Jim couldn't remove stains, made with permanent ink, from his shirt.

   III.   Made with permanent ink, Jim couldn't remove stains from his shirt.

744. Ideas: Charlotte visits Indianapolis. Her grandmother lives in Indianapolis. Charlotte saw her grandmother. She went to Indianapolis for that purpose.

   I.   To see her grandmother, Charlotte visited Indianapolis.

   II.   Charlotte visited Indianapolis to see her grandmother.

   III.   For seeing her grandmother, Charlotte visited Indianapolis.

745. Ideas: The football was in the air. It hurtled through the air. The football cleared the goalposts.

   I.   Hurtling through the air, the football cleared the goalposts.

   II.   To hurtle though the air, the football cleared the goalposts.

   III.   Clearing the goalposts, the football hurtled through the air.

746. Ideas: There is an essay. The writing is polished. The essay will win a prize.

   I.   The essay that is a polished piece of writing and that will win a prize.

   II.   Polished, the essay is a piece and writing and it will win a prize.

   III.   A polished piece of writing, that essay will win a prize.

747. Ideas: Ben stayed up all night. He fought to keep his eyes open at work the next day.

   I.   Staying up all night, Ben fought to keep his eyes open at work the next day.

   II.   Stayed up all night, Ben fought to keep his eyes open at work the next day.

   III.   Having stayed up all night, Ben fought to keep his eyes open at work the next day.

748. Ideas: Everyone wore masks and odd clothes to the costume party. No one recognized anyone else.

   I.   Wearing masks and odd clothes, no one at the costume party recognized anyone else.

   II.   Having worn masks and odd clothes to the costume party, no one recognized anyone else.

   III.   Had worn masks and odd clothes, no one at the costume party recognized anyone else.

749. Ideas: She had a goal. Her goal was to see Mount Everest. Her goal was not easy.

   I.   To see Mount Everest, her goal, wasn't easy.

   II.   Being her goal, seeing Mount Everest not being easy.

   III.   Her goal, to see Mount Everest, wasn't easy.

750. Ideas: A book has an index. I want that book.

   I.   I want the book, that has an index.

   II.   I want the book that has an index.

   III.   Having an index, I want that book.

751. Ideas: I did the laundry yesterday. You should do the laundry today.

    I.   Doing the laundry yesterday, you should do it today.

    II.   Having done the laundry yesterday, I think you should do it today.

    III.   The laundry done yesterday, you should do it today.

Varying Sentence Patterns

752–766 Read these sentences, some of which change the common sentence pattern. Which sentence or sentences, if any, are correct?

752.
    I.   On the bus, did he?
    II.   On the bus, was he?
    III.   Was he on the bus?

753.
    I.   In the courtroom stood the new lawyer, awestruck.
    II.   Awestruck, the new lawyer stood in the courtroom.
    III.   Awestruck, in the courtroom stood the new lawyer.

754.
    I.   Around the corner, just in time, came a police officer.
    II.   Just in time, around the corner came a police officer.
    III.   Coming around the corner, just in time, a police officer.

755.
    I.   Loving Chinese food, avoiding Japanese food.
    II.   Loved Chinese food, he avoided Japanese food.
    III.   Chinese food he loved, but Japanese food he avoided.

756.
    I.   Finished everything, have they?
    II.   Everything finished, have they?
    III.   Have they finished everything?

757.
    I.   Creating perfect ice for hockey, through the pipes flowed Freon under the surface.
    II.   Creating perfect ice for hockey, Freon flowed through the pipes under the surface.
    III.   Through the pipes Freon under the surface flowed, creating perfect ice for hockey.

758.
    I.   His winning a gold medal, no goal more important to him.
    II.   Winning a gold medal, his goal, was more important to him.
    III.   No goal was more important to him than winning a gold medal.

759.
    I.   That Jane's motives were pure was all that mattered to Joe.
    II.   To Joe, that Jane's motives were pure was all that mattered.
    III.   All that mattered to Joe was that Jane's motives were pure.

760.
    I.   No matter what Agatha says, don't listen.
    II.   Whatever Agatha says, it does not matter, don't listen.
    III.   Not mattering what Agatha says, don't listen.

761.
    I.   What he does, you don't have to do too.
    II.   Whatever he does, too, you don't have to.
    III.   You not having to do what he does.

762.
    I.   Breaking through the cloudy skies was a rainbow.
    II.   A rainbow, breaking through the cloudy skies was.
    III.   Was a rainbow breaking through the cloudy skies.

763. I. Whatever attracts attention, such as a feather-and-glue dress, she wants.

II. Whatever attracts attention — a feather-and-glue dress, perhaps — she wants.

III. Wanting a feather-and-glue dress, attracting attention.

764. I. Moving to Lithuania, he experienced his ancestors' culture.

II. His ancestors' culture moving to Lithuania he experienced.

III. He, moving to Lithuania, experienced his ancestors' culture.

765. I. On the track, speeding along, the blue racing car stood out.

II. Standing out, on the track the blue racing car, speeding along.

III. Standing out and speeding along, the blue racing car on the track.

766. I. Of love he knew nothing.

II. Nothing he knew of love.

III. Knowing nothing, he of love.

Chapter 17

Spotlighting Verbs: Voice and Mood

How's your voice? I'm not asking whether you sing in the shower. Instead, I'm inquiring about your knowledge of *active* and *passive* verbs (qualities known as *voice* in the grammar world). In this chapter you also get in touch with *mood* — specifically, when and how to use a verb in subjunctive mood. Sounds complicated, right? It isn't. Those important-sounding grammar terms mask some very simple principles: active verb forms are nearly always better than passive, and *if/then* statements require special attention. In this chapter you find practice questions on the voice and mood of verbs.

The Questions You'll Work On

In this chapter, you work on these types of questions:

- Distinguishing between active and passive verb forms
- Changing passive verbs to active where appropriate
- Selecting the proper verb forms for *if/then* statements

What to Watch Out For

Keep these points in mind when you're answering the questions in this chapter:

- When a sentence has a verb in active voice, the subject performs the action or is in the state of being expressed by the verb, as in *Pete applied for a position with the Peace Corps.*

- With a passive-voice verb, the subject receives the action, as in *The job notice was posted on the bulletin board.*

- In general, use passive voice only when an active-voice sentence is awkward or impossible (when you don't know who performed the action, for example).

- If you discuss a situation that isn't true, use subjunctive mood for the *if* statement and the conditional helping verb *would* for the other portion of the sentence. *Were* creates a subjunctive statement for being verbs; *had* does the same thing for action verbs.

- If you're talking about a real possibility, don't use subjunctive in an *if/then* statement.

- The *if* statement never includes the helping verb *would*.

- Sometimes in an *if/then* statement, the *if* is implied. You still need a subjunctive verb in the clause that sets up the hypothetical situation. Here's an example, with the subjunctive verb underlined: *Had Natalia <u>understood</u> Italian, she would have scolded the waiter.* The hypothetical statement may also begin with *as if* or *as though.*

Identifying Active and Passive Verb Forms

767–774 *Identify active verb forms (AV) and passive verb forms (PV).* **Note:** *In addition to words functioning as verbs, label descriptive verb forms (participles) as active (AV) or passive (PV).*

767. The ruins were uncovered early in 1912.

768. France and England were first connected by high-speed trains when the Chunnel, a tunnel under the English Channel, was constructed.

769. Fog blanketed the area, but somehow Raymond found the path home.

770. Carlos's poetry class is working hard; the poems he writes are imaginative.

771. William rejected 30 applicants representing 16 schools because, he says, not one was properly trained.

772. Played at maximum volume, Doug's music stunned and pleased the crowd.

773. Having been summoned to jury duty, Richard was absent from work last week.

774. Smallpox, which terrified and afflicted so many, has been eradicated.

Changing Passive Voice to Active

775–781 *How should the sentence be changed, if at all, so that the verb is in active voice?* **Note:** *A verb may be active and need no change, or a change to active voice may not be possible.*

775. The letter was stamped by the clerk after Louella had paid the postage.

776. Two candles were blown out by the smiling toddler.

777. Did Max's umbrella hit you when the wind whisked it out of his hand?

778. Isaac hopes that taxes will be lowered when Governor Mary Smith takes over.

779. Helmets should be worn at all times during bicycle rides.

780. Large suitcases must be checked before boarding, but some passengers take them into the cabin anyway.

781. Ten minutes had passed before we realized that she was absent.

Using Subjunctive Verbs Properly

782–796 How should the underlined portion of the sentence be changed, if at all, so that it is grammatically correct?

782. If the heat wave continues, Eric will buy another air conditioner.

783. If I was a lottery winner, I would circle the globe on a first-class ticket. Unfortunately, I didn't win.

784. If Marty was promoted, he would have taken us to a fancy restaurant to celebrate. Instead, we treated him to a hot dog from the corner stand.

785. If Alex would be suspended, he will miss at least 50 games; the commissioner will announce his decision tomorrow, and Alex will know his fate.

786. Anna would have bought more snacks if she had known how hungry her guests were.

787. Being Dmitri an accomplished magician, he would pull a rabbit out of a hat. Because he's still learning, he can retrieve only a scarf from a baseball cap.

788. Had Sparky Firedog gotten lost, the firefighters would not have rested before locating their mascot.

789. On the way to the used car lot, Lola made up her mind: If the convertible were in good shape, she would buy it.

790. <u>If the chef added seasoning</u> to that food, it would have tasted better and more diners would have eaten it.

791. <u>If Maddy were to answer</u> the phone, hang up!

792. The clerk asked <u>if Ali would like to have</u> the toy gift-wrapped.

793. If the pitcher had thrown a fast ball, the batter <u>would of hit</u> a home run.

794. The mathematician spoke <u>as if Jordan was</u> his equal, but Jordan has trouble adding two and two.

795. Cary looks <u>as though he were</u> 60, but he's only 30 years old.

796. Dialing the repair shop, Johnny wishes <u>he bought</u> the computer at a store, not at a flea market.

Chapter 18

Dealing with Electronic Media

One of the best educated people I know recently said, "Grammar in e-mail? You're kidding! I've never put a comma in an e-mail. I don't use them in presentations either." Well, I do. I put commas in text messages too, as well as in instant messages. I don't tweet, but if I did, I'd probably throw in a couple of commas there also. Granted, I'm stricter than normal people (in other words, nongrammarians). Plus, I have to admit that communication media change so rapidly that the rules for writing with them have to be fluid also. Most people feel free to drop at least some conventions of grammar when they pull out a smartphone or a tablet or project a presentation slide. But before you toss all the rules, you should know today's commonly accepted standards for writing e-mails, texts, and instant messages. Furthermore, you should know how to write a list with bullet points — the sort you see on PowerPoint, Prezi, or Keynote presentation slides — without inflicting a fatal wound on Standard English. For help with these skills, read on.

The Questions You'll Work On

In this chapter, you work on questions testing these skills:

- ✔ Capitalizing titles and bullet points in presentation slides and subject lines
- ✔ Punctuating bulleted lists, e-mails, texts, and instant messages
- ✔ Creating parallel bulleted lists
- ✔ Communicating clearly and achieving the right degree of formality in electronic media

What to Watch Out For

Keep these points in mind when you're answering the questions in this chapter:

- ✔ The title of a presentation slide, if it has one, follows the headline style of capitalization. Subject lines of e-mails usually do so also, though you have more leeway there.

- ✔ All the items on a bullet-point list should be parallel. In other words, they should have the same grammatical identity.

✔ If the bulleted list begins with an introductory sentence, use a colon if the sentence is complete or if the bullet points aren't part of the introductory statement. Don't place any punctuation after an introductory statement that ends with a linking verb (any form of *to be*) or if the bullet points combine with the introductory statement to form a complete sentence.

✔ Commonly used (and mutually understood) abbreviations are fine in instant messages and texts. Breaking some rules of capitalization and punctuation is generally accepted in these short forms, as long as the meaning is clear. Words may also be omitted or implied, unless they are necessary for clarity.

✔ When writing to someone who outranks you (a supervisor, a teacher, an elderly relative), follow the rules of Standard English.

Presentation Slides

797–814 What changes, if any, should you make to the underlined material to create a grammatically correct presentation slide?

797.

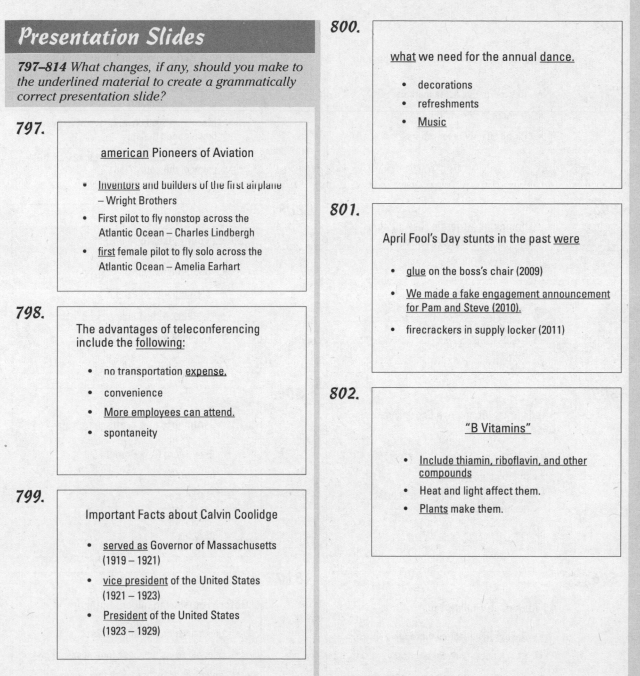

american Pioneers of Aviation

- Inventors and builders of the first airplane – Wright Brothers
- First pilot to fly nonstop across the Atlantic Ocean – Charles Lindbergh
- first female pilot to fly solo across the Atlantic Ocean – Amelia Earhart

798.

The advantages of teleconferencing include the following:

- no transportation expense.
- convenience
- More employees can attend.
- spontaneity

799.

Important Facts about Calvin Coolidge

- served as Governor of Massachusetts (1919 – 1921)
- vice president of the United States (1921 – 1923)
- President of the United States (1923 – 1929)

800.

what we need for the annual dance.

- decorations
- refreshments
- Music

801.

April Fool's Day stunts in the past were

- glue on the boss's chair (2009)
- We made a fake engagement announcement for Pam and Steve (2010).
- firecrackers in supply locker (2011)

802.

"B Vitamins"

- Include thiamin, riboflavin, and other compounds
- Heat and light affect them.
- Plants make them.

803.

Goals for this year include the following.

- to expand our Asian markets
- to increase brand recognition
- hiring 50 new researchers

804.

Themes of Adrienne Rich's Poem
Diving into the Wreck

- gender identity
- self-discovery
- role of perspective
- existential loneliness

805.

Stradivarius Violins Are Expensive
Because Of

- their sound quality
- their limited number
- the inability of modern violin makers to re-create them

806.

All student journalists must

- Research all stories thoroughly
- Check quotations for accuracy
- cite written or electronic sources used
- submit articles before the deadline

807.

Our new Park-It-Now application has

- The app flags unoccupied parking spots within ten blocks.
- More than 3000 drivers have already downloaded the app.
- An approval rating of more than 90% from users of the app.

808.

Check your closet today for

- outdated fashions
- clothing that doesn't fit
- clothing with stains
- possible charity donations

809.

Useful arts and crafts materials

- Glue Sticks (Any Brand)
- Scissors
- Markers
- Felt and Fabric Scraps
- Crayons

810.

Before registering, all students are:

- given a list of available courses
- allowed to visit classes (one session only)
- encouraged to meet with their advisors
- informed about school policies on schedule changes

811.

Infection-Prevention Measures:

- Wash your hands with hot water and soap before examining each patient.
- Use the hand-sanitizer <u>that is available</u> in every room.
- <u>Only disposable equipment should be used.</u>

812.

Films starring Julia Roberts include <u>the following</u>

- <u>(First major role)</u> *Mystic Pizza*
- *Notting Hill*
- *Sleeping with the Enemy*
- *My Best Friend's Wedding*
- <u>many others</u>

813.

<u>Sam Smith</u>, the famous writer, <u>said,</u>

- "Writing is like baking a cake."
- "Aim for quality, not fame."
- <u>"Be true to your message."</u>

814.

<u>Revenue sources</u>

- dues
- donations
- <u>contributions of materials</u>
- <u>should increase by 20%</u>

Composing E-Mails, Instant Messages, and Texts

815–826 Which of these, if any, are acceptable electronic communications? **Note:** *Because some informality is accepted in electronic media, the "situation" information explains the context and medium.*

815. Situation: Instant message, Jean asks her friend whether he wants to go for a walk with her.

   I.   walk today

   II.   walk?

   III.   Want to walk

816. Situation: Text, a parent asks a teacher whether his child's grades are good.

   I.   grades good

   II.   Grades?

   III.   grades good?

817. Situation: E-mail from business to customer, announcing a sale.

I.

> From: Bonanza Hut
> Subject:
> To: Joseph J. Jones
>
> Dear Customer,
> Bonanza Hut is proud to announce our newest branch at 221 Tarpon Way in Elsville. Bring this e-mail for a special discount.
> Sincerely,
> The Bonanza Hut Team

II.

> From: Bonanza Hut
> Subject: Visit Our New Branch
> To: Joseph J. Jones
>
> Dear Customer,
> Bonanza Hut is proud to announce our newest branch at 221 Tarpon Way in Elsville. Bring this e-mail for a special discount.
> Sincerely,
> The Bonanza Hut Team

III.

> From: Bonanza Hut
> Subject: Visit Our New Branch
> To: Joseph J. Jones
>
> Dear Customer, Bonanza Hut is proud to announce our newest branch at 221 Tarpon Way in Elsville. Bring this e-mail for a special discount. Sincerely, The Bonanza Hut Team

818. Situation: Excerpt from a blog post from a food writer hoping for a book contract.

I. This recipe for tomato stew needs a hint of dates.

II. This recipe 4 tomato stew needs a hint of d8s.

III. Add a hint of dates to this tomato stew and wow!

819. Situation: Instant message, history teacher to guidance counselor, in response to a question about the possibility that a student will plagiarize a paper.

I. no   writing paper by herself

II. no, writing paper by herself

III. No. Writing paper by herself

820. Situation: Text from Bill to his grandfather.

I. G2G Gramps ttyl

II. Gotta go Gramps ttyl

III. I have to go, Gramps. I'll talk to you later.

821. Situation: E-mail from client to architect, giving an opinion on preliminary plans

I.

> From: Kit Carton
> Subject: I hate the kitchen layout redo it
> To: Helene Dodgson

II.

> From: Kit Carton
> Subject: Kitchen layout
> To: Helene Dodgson
> Dear Ms. Dodgson
> I hate the kitchen layout. Please redo it. Thanks.
> KC

III.

> From: Kit Carton
> Subject: Kitchen layout
> To: Helene Dodgson
>
> HELENE, I HATE THE KITCHEN LAYOUT. PLEASE REDO IT.
> BEST,
> KIT

822. Situation: Excerpt from a film review on a website for general readers.

I. gr8 CGI in the crashing planet sequence

II. great CGI in the crashing planet sequence

III. great special effects in the crashing planet sequence

823. Situation: E-mail to a potential employer from a job applicant.

I.

> From: Maria Anderson
> Subject: Design Coordinator Position
> To: Jane Allan
> Dear Ms. Allan,
> I'm applying for the position of Design Coordinator advertised in *The Times* on June 25, 2016. Attached is my resume. You can reach me via e-mail or by calling 212-555-5958. I hope to hear from you.
> Sincerely,
> Maria Anderson

II.

> From: Maria Anderson
> Subject: Applying for Position of Design Coordinator
> To: Jane Allan
> Dear Ms. Allan,
> Per your advertisement for employment in *The Times* dated June 25, 2016: I am writing in hopes of securing an interview. I have longed for a position such as you describe, and my qualifications, which I describe in the resume that I have attached to this electronic message, cannot possibly explain all the reasons that you might hire me to your benefit. I hope that you will respond at your earliest convenience. I can be reached at this e-mail address or on the phone (212-555-5958.)
> Very truly yours,
> Maria Anderson

III.

> From: Maria Anderson
> Subject: Job
> To: Jane Allan
> Dear Ms. Allan,
> I'm applying for the position of Design Coordinator advertised in *The Times* on June 25, 2016. Attached is my resume. You can reach me via e-mail or by calling 212-555-5958. I hope to hear from you.
> Sincerely,
> Maria Anderson

824. Situation: Instant message from Jack to Jill, best friends and constant companions, about Henry's claim that he's dating a supermodel.

  I. omg i cant believe it

  II. idnbi

  III. lol your joking

825. Situation: Excerpt from a reader comment on an article in an online newspaper.

  I. Mr. Smith's position, that the waste disposal factory should be relocated, is impractical, as no other sites have been identified.

  II. You're an idiot, Smith! Nobody else will take that factory.

  III. Smith – I hate you and everything you say.

826. Situation: Text from boss to employee about a change in policy.

  I. FYI: Breaks can be 10 minutes tops.

  II. breaks now 10 mins long and no more

  III. 10 min breaks only

Chapter 19

Choosing Language to Suit Your Audience

● ●

When people find out that I write grammar books, some go into "gotcha" mode. They scrutinize everything I say, hoping to catch a mistake. And they do! In fact, they should. Why? Because formal, totally proper English isn't appropriate for all situations. When you're at a party, you probably employ what I call "conversational English" — a less formal version of the language that features shortened or dropped words, incomplete sentences, and similar elements. Conversational English makes you more approachable. One level down is even less formal, what I call "friendspeak." On this level you make some mistakes on purpose, using slang and throwing in *me* instead of *I* or *who* instead of *whom*. Of course, in school or on the job, proper English is generally the goal. In this chapter you practice moving from level to level of correctness, depending upon the situation you're in. These questions check your ability to adapt your oral or written expression as needed.

The Questions You'll Work On

In this chapter, you work on questions that test these skills:

- ✔ Identifying levels of formality
- ✔ Suiting your words to a particular situation

What to Watch Out For

Keep these points in mind when you're answering the questions in this chapter:

- ✔ If you're speaking or writing to someone with more power than you, formal English is best. However, no one likes to hear stiff, old-fashioned, or flowery expressions. Even in formal English, strive for direct and clear expression.

- ✔ When communicating with peers, let the relationship and situation guide you. A friend in the office may be comfortable with conversational English while you're gossiping at the coffee machine but *not* when you're writing a business memo. On Friday night away from the office, friends may "kick off their grammar shoes" and break every rule in the book.

✔ Slang works only when everyone who's supposed to be part of the conversation understands what you're saying. By its nature, slang excludes some people, usually on purpose. Teenagers invent terms all the time specifically to mystify adults — and succeed beautifully!

✔ Jargon — specialized terms, abbreviations, and acronyms — is fine only if the intended audience comprehends. Acronyms are formed from the first letter of each word in a name (*NATO* for *North Atlantic Treaty Organization,* for example).

✔ Electronic communication (text or instant messages, blogs, e-mails) sometimes relax the usual grammar rules, but even there, take care if you're writing to someone of higher status in a given situation.

Identifying Levels of Formality

*827–836 Place these expressions in order of formality, moving from the most formal to the least. **Note:** Two expressions may "tie." For example, your answer may be **1 and 2, 3.** In that answer, the first and second statements have the same level of formality, and the third statement is less formal than the first two.*

827. 1. You just don't get it.
   2. You do not comprehend the situation.
   3. You don't understand what happened.

828. 1. I provide herein
   2. I enclose
   3. Here's

829. 1. Don't worry about that issue.
   2. Hey, don't flip out!
   3. Forget it, please.

830. 1. does not exercise
   2. total couch potato
   3. never exercises

831. 1. C U L8R
   2. See you later.
   3. I will meet you later today.

832. 1. My bad.
   2. Oops! Sorry.
   3. I apologize.

833. 1. Does this interest you?
   2. r u in?
   3. Are you in?

834. 1. about your request
   2. in reference to your request
   3. pursuant to your request

835. 1. You had to ask!
   2. In response to your question
   3. To answer your question

836. 1. the child under discussion
   2. the kid we're talking about
   3. the child we are discussing

The Right Words for the Right Time

*837–851 Which of these statements, if any, are suitable in the specified situation? **Note:** The statement may be excerpted from a longer conversation or piece of writing.*

837. Situation: Student's e-mail to a teacher asking for a letter of recommendation.
   I. Would you please write a letter of recommendation?
   II. You get me. Wanna write for me?
   III. r u ok to write 4 me?

838. Situation: Letter of complaint from a customer to a company about a recent purchase.

    I.   Your vacuum stinks. I want my money back now!

    II.   The vacuum doesn't work, so I want a refund.

    III. Vacuum = busted. Refund = mine.

839. Situation: Text message from Lily, who has known Anthony since preschool, commenting on a mutual friend's unexpected offer to help with a school project.

    I.   2G2BT

    II.   rly? r u sure?

    III. 4 real?

840. Situation: Co-worker speaking to a peer at a committee meeting chaired by their supervisor.

    I.   The marketing stuff's epic, but the neighborhood's sketchy.

    II.   Whassup with the neighborhood? The marketing's okay.

    III. The marketing is fine, but the neighborhood is questionable.

841. Situation: Phone call from a parent to another parent about a play date for their children.

    I.   Saturday okay with you? Maybe the beach? Or the playground? Could be fun.

    II.   How about I take the kids to the beach or the playground on Saturday for a fun afternoon?

    III. Would it be permissible for me to take our children on an excursion this Saturday, perhaps to the beach or to the playground, so that they can amuse each other for a while?

842. Situation: Alice speaks with a traffic patrol officer who has pulled her over to the side of the road.

    I.   You gotta problem?

    II.   What's the problem, Officer?

    III. Is there a problem?

843. Situation: Instant message from a boss to an assistant, requesting a file they've been working on.

    I.   get me file asap

    II.   need file now

    III. file - now

844. Situation: Comment to a citizen from a clerk in a government agency.

    I.   What's your DOB and SSN?

    II.   Tell me your date of birth and social security number.

    III. When were you born, and what's your social?

845. Situation: Text from daughter to mother about a cash-flow problem.

    I.   ATM card no good. What to do?

    II.   ATM no good. ??

    III. ATM?

846. Situation: Class notes for future study.

    I.   war b/c border wasn't where it s/b

    II.   They went to war because the border was drawn where it should not have been.

    III. border wrong, so war

847. Situation: Letter to client from an insurance agent.

    I.   Don't expect us to file Form 112. You didn't supply a copy of the EOB from your PCP.

    II.   We will file Form 112 after you send the "Explanation of Benefits" statement you received from your Primary Care Physician (your doctor).

    III.   No 112 until we get the EOB from PCP.

848. Situation: Comment from a tourist to the tour guide, whose English is minimal and who is speaking in a low voice.

    I.   Speak louder, please.

    II.   Sound off!

    III.   Kick it up a notch.

849. Situation: Text from son to parents after he proposed to his girlfriend.

    I.   she said yes

    II.   she said yes wedding in july

    III.   Wedding in July

850. Situation: E-mail from broker to customer, who asked for information quickly.

    I.   Spoke with Jacobs. Deal's OK with him.

    II.   I had a chance to speak with Mr. Jacobs, as you asked. I called him immediately, as you were in a rush. He indicated that the deal is fine with him.

    III.   Re Jacobs: deal's okay with him.

851. Situation: E-mail to co-workers from their union representative about a possible job action. It's illegal for the union members to strike.

    I.   Tomorrow we should all call in "sick," if that's how the vote turns out at the meeting tonight.

    II.   Important vote at tonight's meeting. Please attend.

    III.   We're getting the flu tomorrow, depending on tonight's vote.

Chapter 20

Tricky Word Traps

. . . .

The road to proper English is full of potholes, including words with vastly different meanings that resemble each other in spelling or sound and words that many people use interchangeably — and incorrectly. In this chapter you perfect your ability to tell these "twins" apart and smooth the highway to better speech and writing.

The Questions You'll Work On

In this chapter, you work on these types of questions:

- ✔ Distinguishing between words such as *passed* and *past* that sound nearly the same

- ✔ Using almost-look-alikes such as *farther* and *further* correctly

- ✔ Selecting possessives and contractions *(their* and *they're, its* and *it's)* as needed

- ✔ Placing commonly misused words *(if* and *whether, like* and *as)* in their proper context

What to Watch Out For

Keep these points in mind when you're answering the questions in this chapter:

- ✔ *Accept* means "to agree or to take"; *except* means "other than." Related forms are *acceptance* and *exception.*

- ✔ In common usage, *affect* is a verb meaning "to influence," and *effect* is a noun meaning "a result." *Effect* is sometimes used as a verb meaning "to bring about," as in *to effect change.*

- ✔ *Farther* measures distance; *further* means "additional."

- ✔ As a noun, *principal* is the head of a school or one of the most important people in a given situation; as an adjective it also means "most important." A *principle* is a "rule or standard."

- ✔ *Stationary* refers to something that's fixed in one place; *stationery* is school or office supplies, especially paper and envelopes.

- ✔ *To compliment* is "to praise," and *to complement* is "to complete, to bring to a better level." Related forms are *complimentary* (which may mean either "praising" or "free") and *complementary.*

✔ A *historic* event is an important moment in *history,* the record or study of the past. *Historical* refers to anything related to the past. The noun *past* refers to everything up until the present moment; *past* as an adverb means "in front of" or "by." *Passed* is a verb meaning "moved by or along" in time or space.

✔ A *capitol* is a building where government meets; the *capital* is the city where the government is located. *Capital* also refers to money for investing and may, as an adjective, mean "chief, most important."

✔ *There* refers to a place, *their* shows possession, and *they're* means "they are."

✔ *To* is a preposition, *two* is a number, and *too* means "also" or "excessive."

✔ *Since* refers to time, and *because* to a reason. *If* begins a statement about a condition or possibility, and *whether* presents two alternatives *(whether or not).*

✔ *Unique* means "one of a kind" and is an absolute term. *Unusual* or *rare* are better words when something is odd, but not unique.

✔ *Disinterested* means "fair and impartial," and *uninterested* means "not interested."

✔ *Like* may be a verb (meaning "to appreciate or enjoy") or a preposition. It may not introduce a subject-verb statement; to introduce subject-verb pairs, use *as* or *as though.*

✔ *Try and* works only when you're discussing two actions; otherwise, use *try to.*

✔ You *emigrate* when you leave a country and *immigrate* when you enter a country. Related words are *emigrant, emigration, immigrant,* and *immigration.*

✔ *A number of* means "some," but *the number* usually refers to a specific quantity.

✔ When you hint at something, you *imply;* when you figure out what the hint means, you *infer.*

✔ *Kind of* or *sort of* means "type of." Don't use these expressions as substitutes for *rather, somewhat,* or *a bit.*

Distinguishing between Words Resembling Each Other

852–881 Which of the underlined words, if any, are used correctly in these expressions?

852. I.   moving <u>to</u> a new house
      II. putting on <u>there</u> shoes
      III. <u>it's</u> a shame

853. I.   taking <u>you're</u> time
      II. thinks <u>two</u> much
      III. <u>accept</u> the offer

854. I.   <u>you're</u> right, not wrong
      II. a dog and <u>it's</u> bone
      III. everyone <u>except</u> Tom

855. I.   <u>too</u> books, one on the shelf and one on the desk
      II. <u>you're</u> right foot
      III. <u>it's</u> raining

856. I.   no one <u>except</u> for Henry
      II. <u>there</u> meeting us later
      III. <u>too</u> the mall

857. I.   me <u>too</u>
      II. <u>it's</u> my turn
      III. every activity <u>accept</u> swimming

858. I.   <u>you're</u> wallet
      II. bicycle losing <u>its</u> wheel
      III. <u>to</u> people who form a lovely couple

859. I.   styling <u>your</u> hair
      II. in <u>their</u> neighborhood
      III. <u>to</u> young for that toy

860. I.   sitting over <u>their</u>
      II. <u>your</u> first job
      III. whether <u>its</u> true or not

861. I.   <u>exception</u> to the rule
      II. college <u>acceptance</u>
      III. the car over <u>they're</u>

862. I.   cause and <u>affect</u>
      II. walking <u>passed</u> the bank
      III. our school <u>principal</u>

863. I.   historians studying the <u>past</u>
      II. <u>principals</u> of fair play
      III. special <u>effects</u>

864. I.   time <u>passed</u> slowly
      II. illness that <u>effected</u> her
      III. when <u>principles</u> scold students

865. I.   <u>past</u> over when promotions were announced
      II. <u>principal</u> reason to sign the treaty
      III. the <u>affect</u> of the drought on crops

866. I.   the parade moved <u>passed</u>
      II. the <u>effect</u> of Barbara's actions
      III. the dome of the <u>capital</u> building

867. I.   heat <u>affects</u> the players
      II. <u>capitol</u> to invest
      III. <u>principles</u> of sportsmanship

868. I.   <u>principal</u> talking to the first graders
      II. spending interest income, not <u>capitol</u>
      III. has an <u>affect</u> on Max's mood

869.
   I.   meeting of the <u>principle</u> signers of the treaty

   II.   visiting the freshly painted and renovated <u>capitol</u>

   III.   factors that <u>affect</u> you

870.
   I.   Paris, the <u>capitol</u> of France

   II.   the <u>principles</u> of investing

   III.   side <u>effects</u> of this medicine

871.
   I.   <u>principles'</u> educational conference

   II.   <u>capital</u> letters

   III.   <u>passed</u> tense verb

872.
   I.   to <u>effect</u> change

   II.   upon <u>further</u> consideration

   III.   not the <u>principle</u> reason

873.
   I.   ran <u>farther</u> than a marathoner

   II.   <u>complements</u> to the chef on a great meal

   III.   <u>historic</u> novels, including those with little readership or influence

874.
   I.   <u>stationary</u> for class, including an extra package of paper

   II.   <u>historical</u> documents

   III.   <u>complimentary</u> tickets

875.
   I.   <u>stationary</u> bicycle at the health club

   II.   no <u>further</u> trouble

   III.   all in the <u>passed</u>

876.
   I.   curtains in <u>complimentary</u> colors

   II.   <u>stationery</u> store having a back-to-school sale

   III.   the <u>principals</u> of good writing

877.
   I.   shoes that <u>complement</u> your outfit

   II.   <u>historic</u> treaty that ended the war

   III.   <u>principal</u> dancers, who enact the lead roles

878.
   I.   buying <u>historical</u> textbooks for class

   II.   vacationing <u>further</u> from home

   III.   monogrammed <u>stationary</u>

879.
   I.   shopping for wedding invitations at a <u>stationary</u> store

   II.   <u>complementary</u> gift when you spend more than $500 on merchandise

   III.   needing <u>further</u> study

880.
   I.   <u>compliments</u> for the hero

   II.   <u>further</u> south along this road

   III.   <u>historical</u> first human step on the moon

881.
   I.   <u>farther</u> reading

   II.   <u>complements</u> on her fine performance

   III.   what the <u>historical</u> records show

Words Incorrectly Seen as Synonyms

882–906 How should the underlined words be changed, if at all, to create a correct sentence?

882. <u>Like</u> I said, I agreed to direct this play <u>since</u> it's very <u>unique</u>.

883. Elena wonders <u>if</u> George <u>likes</u> the subject, <u>because</u> he seldom mentions it.

884. Since birds can fly, they see the world from an <u>extremely unique</u> point of view, one that humans achieve only <u>if</u> they're in an airplane.

885. <u>Since</u> yesterday, Alex has phoned me five times, asking me if I'll sell him the unusual vase — quite rare — I found during my trip to Mexico.

886. <u>Since</u> the concert is sold out, Kira asked <u>whether</u> it would be broadcast, <u>as</u> she'd love to see the event.

887. Joe is <u>like,</u> trustworthy, so <u>if</u> he says he's been ill <u>since</u> Monday, he's telling the truth.

888. <u>Whether</u> you <u>like</u> the role or not, I expect you to do <u>like</u> we agreed and go on stage.

889. Zina will <u>try to</u> wrap <u>a number of</u> presents, <u>because</u> she's always willing to help.

890. Because <u>the number of</u> lions in the zoo is <u>kind of</u> hard to estimate, Jana will have to guess.

891. This <u>kind of</u> plant and <u>the number of</u> others need little water, <u>since</u> they are native to the desert.

892. <u>Since</u> Miranda <u>emigrated</u> from South Africa last year, she's been <u>sort of</u> busy establishing her business.

893. If he plays <u>like</u> I know he can, that pianist will be welcomed as an <u>immigrant</u> in dozens of countries.

894. <u>Since</u> he <u>emigrated</u> from France, Louis has resided in a <u>unique</u> house in Tunisia, one that architectural students often examine.

895. Jacqueline will <u>try and</u> calm down, but she's <u>sort of</u> upset <u>because</u> she has to pay overdue fees for her library books.

896. After <u>immigrating</u> to New York City, Ellen <u>tried and</u> immediately liked hot dogs, the <u>sort of</u> food you can eat while you walk.

897. <u>Try and</u> look <u>like</u> you were born here; don't let the tourists know you're a recent <u>immigrant</u> to this country

898. <u>Like</u> my mom, I <u>try and</u> sometimes fail, but at least I make <u>a number of</u> attempts!

899. <u>If</u> Judge James Smith is <u>disinterested</u>, the trial will be fair and he'll <u>try to</u> reach a proper verdict.

900. Robbie <u>implied</u> that the phone bill was <u>two</u> high <u>as</u> he remarked, "I could fly there and talk in person for less!"

901. Yawning to show that she was <u>disinterested</u>, Jasmine made <u>a number of</u> attempts to be excused from the meeting, which was <u>sort of</u> boring.

902. Deciding <u>whether</u> to <u>immigrate</u> from the country where he was born, Andreas considered <u>the number of</u> visas issued each year and calculated his chances of receiving one.

903. In this <u>sort of</u> mystery novel, the detective often <u>implies</u> the identity of the murderer after gathering <u>the number of</u> clues.

904. <u>Uninterested</u> in human activity, the bear took <u>a number of</u> steps toward the picnic basket to <u>try to</u> locate some food.

905. Mark was <u>kind of</u> happy when the <u>disinterested</u> professor left the university <u>too</u> weeks before Mark was scheduled to be her student, because he liked to be entertained as much as enlightened by his teachers.

906. The program will <u>try and</u> assist new <u>immigrants</u> in <u>their</u> adjustment to a new country.

Chapter 21

Seeing Double: Confusing Word Pairs

You can't always trust your eyes and ears to help you select the right word or phrase. Sometimes a single space or letter changes the meaning *altogether*. That word, which means "completely," proves my point because it resembles *all together,* which refers to a group acting "in unison." To make your life even more difficult, some expressions that you see everywhere, such as *alot* and *could of,* don't exist in Standard English. In this chapter you sharpen your English skills by concentrating on spacing and spelling, so that your word choices will always be correct.

The Questions You'll Work On

In this chapter, you work on these skills:

✔ Selecting the proper word or phrase for a particular context

✔ Eliminating words that aren't correct in Standard English

What to Watch Out For

Keep these points in mind when you're answering the questions in this chapter:

✔ *Altogether* means "completely"; *all together* means "in unison" or "gathered in the same place."

✔ *Some time* refers to a period of time; *sometime* means "at some point in the future"; *sometimes* means "occasionally." *Someday* and *anytime* are adverbs referring to an unspecified time in the future. *Some day* is a noun *(day)* with a description *(some)*. It means "an unnamed day"; *any time* (also a noun + a description) means "any amount of time." *Someplace* is an adverb meaning "somewhere"; *some place* is a noun-description combo that refers to an unspecified location.

✔ *Every day* means "each day"; *everyday* means "ordinary or common."

✔ *Already* means "so soon" or "by this time"; *all ready* means "completely prepared."

✔ These words, though common, aren't Standard English expressions: *alright, alot, might of, could of, would of, should of, might could, eachother, hisself, theyselves, theirselves, anywheres, nowheres, and etc., had of, had ought, this here, that there.*

Selecting the Correct One- or Two-Word Expression

907–923 Which of the underlined expressions, if any, are correct?

907. I.   already finished, and it's only 9 o'clock

II.   thinking about you every day

III.   the choir, altogether in the rehearsal hall, waiting to perform

908. I.   to meet again someday

II.   every body in the morgue

III.   seven snacks, already for the children's lunchboxes

909. I.   visits his uncle some times

II.   not hungry because she's eaten already

III.   the entire jury, altogether in the courtroom

910. I.   altogether corrupt, not a shred of honesty left

II.   everyday dishes, not the ones for special guests

III.   spending sometime on exam prep

911. I.   some times sings professionally

II.   to be a star some day

III.   everybody on the staff, with no exceptions

912. I.   the family, altogether on holidays and birthdays

II.   everyday chores, but nothing extra

III.   buying some place on 16th Street

913. I.   a fitness plan for every body with a few extra pounds on it

II.   to meet someday next week, but not Monday

III.   books Maxine read all ready but would like to read again

914. I.   someplace to relax, such as a spa

II.   a document that is altogether meaningless, as if it were written by a two-year-old

III.   calling any time

915. I.   all ready for the trip — bags packed and passport renewed

II.   every day negotiations, nothing historic

III.   if the boss has anytime this week

916. I.   lifting weights every day

II.   hoping to run for office sometime

III.   planning to meet Helen someday

917. I.   dressed-up seniors, already for the prom

II.   permission to log on to the computer sometimes

III.   going home in one car, altogether

918. I.   getting revenge someday

II.   a plan that is all together ambitious and inspiring

III.   devoting anytime to volunteer work

919. I.   finding some place in the orchestra, perhaps in the string section

II.   everyday challenges for elderly residents

III.   going out because I all ready did my homework

920.
 I. sheltering from the storm, <u>altogether</u> under the awning

 II. asking for <u>sometime</u> off from work

 III. call <u>anytime</u>, day or night

921.
 I. my <u>sometime</u> friend, now my enemy

 II. <u>Everyday</u> of the week

 III. <u>all together</u> majestic and inspiring

922.
 I. vampires, not <u>altogether</u> dead

 II. film making its debut <u>someday</u> next month

 III. nine months old and walking <u>already</u>

923.
 I. may burst out laughing at <u>any time</u>

 II. has <u>sometimes</u> acted on Broadway

 III. danced, <u>altogether</u>, in the chorus line

Eliminating Words that Don't Exist

924–951 How should the underlined expressions be changed, if at all, to correct the sentence?

924. Greg has <u>alot</u> of friends who <u>would of</u> taken care of him if they <u>had of</u> known he was ill.

925. If it's <u>all right</u> with Mike, Tracy and he <u>might could</u> help <u>eachother</u> with their physics homework.

926. "I <u>might of</u> known!" shouted the detective, who added that she had never believed the murder weapon could be <u>anywheres</u> near <u>that there</u> crime scene.

927. <u>This here</u> notebook he bought <u>hisself</u>, but Isabel purchased <u>that</u> one for him.

928. The rowers reassured <u>theyselves</u> that if they <u>had of</u> won, they <u>would've</u> treated the losing team more politely.

929. Betsy <u>should of</u> watered the plants yesterday; now <u>this here</u> garden has <u>a lot</u> of dead plants.

930. Sam is <u>nowheres</u> to be found; he <u>could of</u> told me his location when we spoke with <u>each other</u>.

931. After falling, the skater checked <u>hisself</u> for a minute and then said he was <u>all right</u>, though he <u>could've</u> been lying.

932. <u>A lot</u> of work went into <u>that there</u> art exhibit, the best examples of Picasso's work <u>anywheres</u>.

933. <u>This here</u> janitor was assigned <u>alot</u> of mopping, painting, <u>and etc.</u>

934. The shoppers <u>theirselves</u> packed their purchases (groceries, clothing, dishes, <u>etc.</u>), but the clerk <u>should of</u> taken care of that chore.

935. James and Matt comforted <u>eachother</u>, reminding <u>theirselves</u> that they <u>would've</u> won the spelling bee had it not been canceled.

936. Shelly was frantic because she couldn't find her pet bird <u>anywheres</u>, but the parrot was <u>all right</u>, hiding in <u>that there</u> closet.

937. With <u>nowheres</u> to go, Aaron and Betsy <u>should of</u> stayed home, but instead they drove around nearby suburbs, including Babylon, Massapequa, Bayshore, <u>and etc.</u>

938. Winnie <u>might of</u> chosen <u>this here</u> blue sweater if she <u>had</u> known it was available.

939. The boys upset <u>themselves</u> when they spoke with <u>each other</u> about the math test, which <u>should've</u> been easier than it was, in their opinion.

940. Max and his friends, who <u>could not of been</u> more bored, entertained <u>theirselves</u> by naming the Presidents — Washington, Lincoln, Kennedy, <u>etc., etc., etc.</u>

941. If I <u>had of</u> written <u>that there</u> anonymous letter, the grammar <u>would of</u> been correct!

942. They sold similar cars <u>everywheres</u>, but in <u>this</u> dealership the owner <u>might of</u> given you a better price.

943. Yang <u>had ought</u> to apply for <u>that there</u> scholarship, because then he can achieve admission <u>anywheres</u>.

944. If Mr. Mellon <u>hadn't of</u> tried to satisfy his curiosity by looking <u>everywheres</u> for clues, his neighbors <u>might of</u> avoided calling the police.

945. Ms. Johnson, who <u>ought</u> to know where the photos <u>could've been</u> stored, asked Annie and Sascha to help <u>each other</u> figure out where their work was.

946. Wendy <u>would of</u> given Jim a ride, if she <u>had of</u> seen him waiting for the train all by <u>himself</u>.

947. Johnny <u>had ought</u> to be more careful with <u>hisself</u>, because he <u>could have</u> pulled a muscle by exercising too much.

948. Eloise <u>her self</u> told me that she <u>would of</u> spoken more candidly if she <u>could of</u>.

949. Darius <u>hadn't ought</u> to complain about his score on the test because he <u>could not of</u> done better on algebra, geometry, <u>and etc</u>.

950. "<u>Alright</u>, sit down <u>anywhere</u>," declared Miss Echeva, "and help <u>eachother</u> with your grammar homework."

951. Finding <u>himself</u> in a difficult situation, the spy <u>had ought</u> to give up on his mission, and everything will turn out <u>all right</u>.

Chapter 22

Steering Clear of Incorrect Expressions

I'm the first to admit that some grammar rules make no sense. When my students ask *why* they have to place a comma in a certain spot or change a word, sometimes my only answer is *because you do.* End of story! Occasionally, though, grammar rests on a logical framework. In this chapter you tackle a few rules in that category, as well as a couple that represent nothing more than tradition.

The Questions You'll Work On

In this chapter, you work on questions that focus on the following skills:

- Selecting expressions that are correct in Standard English
- Avoiding double negatives
- Distinguishing between the verbs *rise* and *raise, sit* and *set,* and *lie* and *lay*

What to Watch Out For

Keep these points in mind when you're answering the questions in this chapter:

- *Different than* isn't generally accepted in formal usage. Use *different from,* followed by a noun.

- *The reason is because* is incorrect in Standard English. Use *the reason is that* or simply state the reason, introduced by *because.*

- *Irregardless* and *being that* aren't Standard English expressions. Try *regardless, despite,* or *because.*

- In some languages, the more negatives you include, the more emphatically you're denying the point. In English, though, double negatives are a no-no because the two negatives equal a positive statement. Avoid *can't hardly, can't scarcely, can't help but,* and *can't but.* Go for *can hardly, can scarcely, can't help* (plus the *-ing* form of a verb, as in *can't help snooping*), and *can only.*

- The English language distinguishes between what you measure (*sugar,* for example, or *loyalty*) and what you count (*shoes* or *years,* perhaps). Measuring words include *amount, less, little,* and *much.* To count, select *number of, fewer, few,* and *many.* A few words (*more, all, any, no,* and *some*) work for both measuring and counting. *Between* and *among* are prepositions; use *between* when you have two people or things (*between home and school*) and *among* when you have more than two (*among 50 musicians*).

- ✔ *Rise* means "to get up, to lift oneself." Use *raise* when you're lifting something (or someone!) else. *Rise* is an irregular verb: *rise, rose, rising, risen*. *Raise* is regular: *raise, raising, raised*.

- ✔ *Sit* is what you do when you place yourself in a chair or another surface. *Set* means "to place," and it refers to an action you perform on something else. *Sit* is irregular: *sit, sitting, sat*. *Set* is also irregular: *set, setting, set*.

- ✔ *Lie* means "to rest or recline." *Lay* is "to place, to put down." These verbs are devilish because the past tense of *lie* is *lay*. The past participle is *lain*. The past tense of *lay* is *laid*, which is also the past participle.

Avoiding Double Negatives and Other Errors

952–971 How should the underlined words be changed, if at all, to create a correct sentence?

952. <u>Don't</u> not mix business with pleasure, <u>being that</u> you're <u>not on</u> duty now.

953. May didn't know <u>nothing</u> about spelling, and her handwriting was different <u>from</u> ours because she never attended <u>no school</u>.

954. <u>Being that</u> it's summer, you <u>can't</u> expect no freezing rain or <u>different</u> weather.

955. Greta <u>didn't know</u> nothing, wouldn't do <u>nothing</u>, and <u>refused any</u> help.

956. Mick <u>can't get</u> no satisfaction when he complains to Customer Service that he hasn't received <u>any new guitars</u>, although he <u>has paid</u> for three.

957. Zach won't tell <u>no lies</u>, <u>irregardless</u> of who's asking for information, so do not explain <u>nothing</u> to him.

958. The dog <u>should give</u> you no trouble, <u>being</u> a gentle animal, unless you <u>do not</u> feed him.

959. <u>No</u>, Ellie <u>did not tell</u> her aunt that Karl <u>had completed</u> nothing.

960. Jacques <u>can't help but think</u> that, <u>regardless</u> of salary, his work is no <u>different than</u> his boss's.

961. <u>Irregardless</u> of what he says, the reason I changed jobs is <u>because</u> I <u>didn't</u> feel respected.

962. <u>Being that</u> Katie is dieting, she <u>shouldn't have</u> no candy, <u>never</u>.

963. Steve claimed that he had not done <u>nothing</u>; <u>irregardless</u>, the district attorney <u>couldn't help but charge</u> him with burglary.

964. Walter's approach to the problem was <u>different from</u> Hannah's, <u>but</u> he <u>hadn't</u> expected no criticism from her.

965. Don't you know <u>no</u> better, <u>regardless</u> of the fact that you <u>haven't</u> been taught manners in a formal way?

966. The reason Nick moved is <u>because</u> he <u>couldn't</u> hardly stand his supervisor's denial of <u>any</u> guilt.

967. <u>No engineer but</u> Martin has <u>ever</u> stepped in that room, and you <u>can hardly</u> blame him for bragging about his courage.

968. Charlotte <u>couldn't help but weave</u> a beautiful web; the reason was <u>because</u> she <u>was not</u> an ordinary spider.

969. Judy <u>could scarcely</u> believe her eyes; the reason is <u>that</u> a flying saucer <u>hadn't ever</u> landed on her lawn before!

970. Do you know <u>neither</u> Latin <u>nor</u> Greek, or haven't you <u>never</u> studied an ancient language?

971. King Leo <u>hadn't but</u> five knights, and winning the war was something he <u>couldn't hardly</u> imagine, except under <u>different</u> and unlikely circumstances.

Counting and Measuring Words

972–986 How should the underlined words be changed, if at all, to create a correct sentence?

972. Imelda has <u>much</u> shoes, <u>far more than</u> Jessie, but <u>less</u> time to shop.

973. <u>Much</u> time has passed since Ellery noticed that <u>many</u> trees had <u>some</u> buds on their branches.

974. Put <u>less</u> books on that shelf, which appears <u>less</u> sturdy than the one over there, which holds <u>much</u> thick volumes.

975. The soup needs <u>a little</u> pepper to spice it up; be sure to prepare <u>less</u> than you did last time, as we expect <u>less</u> guests.

976. Let's keep the secret <u>between</u> the three of us, because if <u>more</u> people know, our error will attract <u>many</u> attention.

977. Considering the <u>amount</u> of hours I spent adding <u>much</u> vocabulary words to my flash cards, I should have scored <u>much</u> higher on the test.

978. When Jack is <u>among</u> friends, he is <u>less</u> nervous than when the conversation is <u>among</u> him and only one other person.

979. This dial shows the <u>amount</u> of electricity consumed, which is <u>lesser</u> than last year but <u>much more</u> than the goal we set.

980. <u>Between</u> your options are law, banking, and education. The first two guarantee <u>many</u> salary increases, but the last may give you <u>more</u> success.

981. Dr. Henry pays <u>much</u> attention to his students, though he gives <u>many more</u> homework assignments and <u>fewer</u> extra credit work than other teachers.

982. Charlie and Rose have <u>many fewer</u> money <u>between</u> them than they'd like, but it is as <u>much</u> as they need.

983. <u>Many</u> have complained that the rugs have <u>less</u> natural fibers and soil <u>more</u> easily than they used to.

984. The card read, "<u>Much</u> love to my <u>many</u> fans who give me so <u>many</u> applause."

985. <u>Much more</u> quilts are <u>much better</u> than <u>fewer</u> on a cold night like this!

986. Sayed had <u>much</u> to be thankful for, such as <u>much</u> friends, <u>few</u> enemies, and a loving family.

Strange Verb Pairs

987–1,001 Which of these expressions, if any, is grammatically correct?

987.
  I.   raise the flag
  II. lay down for a nap now
  III. setting on the chair

988.
  I.   sit the fragile antique desk in the corner
  II. the sun, which rose at 5 a.m.
  III. has laid in bed for ten hours

989.
  I.   the audience, raising for a standing ovation
  II. who had sat in the shade on a blanket
  III. laid railroad tracks near the station

990.
  I.   because yesterday he sat the birdcage near a window
  II. has lain the picnic basket on the ground
  III. raised the shelf two inches higher

991.
  I.   setting a spell, to relax
  II. rise for the singing of the national anthem
  III. lay down for a nap about an hour ago

992.
I.   peasants rose in rebellion

II. laid flowers in front of the shrine

III. has set still for the photographer

993.
I.   lay the suitcase on the bench and left it there

II. raises an important point at the meeting

III. the diamond, set in a gold ring

994.
I.   lying carpet on the floor

II. sitting in the principal's office, waiting for an appointment

III. Raise and shine! It's time to get out of bed!

995.
I.   robbers lying in wait for a victim

II. has laid on the sofa, pretending to sleep

III. sitted on the window ledge

996.
I.   will sit the decorations in the carton, ready for storage

II. was lain to rest in the town cemetery

III. his rising hope, as he listened to those encouraging words

997.
I.   set aside funds for college tuition

II. stirring yeast into the mixture and waiting for the bread to raise

III. laying eggs

998.
I.   laying still, not moving a muscle

II. sat on a jury

III. rising your expectations and doing better work as a result

999.
I.   raise money for the homeless

II. had set goals for himself

III. plants laying dormant for the winter

1,000.
I.   a position on the issue that laid her open to defeat in the next election

II. raising a fuss

III. sat down on paper a record of all that had happened

1,001.
I.   set the story in the Victorian era

II. will rise the stakes

III. yesterday lay claim to

Part II
The Answers

In this part...

Here you get answers and explanations for all 1,001 questions. As you read the solutions, you may realize that you need a little more instruction. Fortunately, the *For Dummies* series offers several excellent resources. I highly recommend the following titles (all published by Wiley and written by yours truly):

- ✔ *English Grammar For Dummies*
- ✔ *English Grammar Workbook For Dummies*
- ✔ *Grammar Essentials For Dummies*

Visit www.dummies.com for more information.

Answers

1. **played**

The only word expressing action in this sentence is *played,* which is therefore the only verb.

2. **slipped**

The action word in this sentence is *slipped,* which is the verb.

3. **will be, receive**

The first verb, *will be,* links a state of being — *happy* — to the *twins.* The second is an action verb, *receive.*

4. **seems**

The verb *seems* links a state of being — *sad* — to the subject, *my dog Tweet.*

5. **searched, found**

Two words give you the action in this sentence: *searched* and *found.*

6. **represents**

Although *screaming* and *painting* refer to actions, *screaming* functions as a description and *painting* as an object (a thing) in this sentence. The only verb in this sentence is *represents.*

7. **has carried**

The action in this sentence is expressed by two words, *has carried,* which together make one verb. The word *sizzling* resembles a verb but serves as a description, not the action in the sentence. Are you surprised that *always* isn't included in the verb? It's an adverb, telling when the action happens.

8. **were displayed**

What happened to the puppies? They *were displayed,* the action verb in this sentence. Did *to see* trip you up? That's an infinitive, the "head" of the verb family that never functions as the verb in a sentence.

9. **was, were scattering**

The sentence has two parts, one about the last meeting of the council and one about the actions of the members. The verb in the first part, *was,* expresses a state of being and links a description *(bittersweet)* to the subject *(meeting).* The verb in the second part, *were scattering,* tells you about the actions of the members.

10. **try, type**

Remember that infinitives, the "*to* + verb" form, simply name the verb family. They never function as verbs in a sentence. The action verbs here are *try* and *type*.

11. **wrestled, calculated**

The first word in the sentence, *smiling,* looks like an action verb. However, it functions as a description of Barbara. The true action verbs are *wrestled* and *calculated*.

12. **sat**

Several words in this sentence *(having run, unused, forgotten)* resemble verbs, but because they function as descriptions, they aren't actually verbs. *Sat* is the only action verb.

13. **copying, stuck**

The subject of this sentence, *Mike,* did two actions; he was *copying* and he *stuck* his finger in the tray. The first portion of the sentence begins with a conjunction *(While),* which should be followed by a subject-verb statement. Two words are missing, but *Mike was copying* is implied, so *copying* counts as an official verb.

14. **has been judged, view**

Three words make up the first verb in this sentence, *has been judged,* but the second idea needs only one verb, *view,* to express his friends' actions.

15. **guided**

The first verb form is an introductory participle. In other words, *sliding* is a description of *ski instructor*. You know it doesn't function as a verb because it doesn't follow a conjunction such as *while, after, before,* or a similar word. The action verb that pairs with *ski instructor* is *guided,* the only verb in this sentence.

16. **started (I started my blog a year ago, and I do not intend to stop now.)**

A year ago is a time clue, telling you that the blog began in the past. The sentence includes another time clue also; *now* refers to a specific time, the present. The beginning of the blog, therefore, was in the past, as the past-tense verb *started* indicates.

17. **shop (Sheryl and her friend always shop on a Tuesday, when the store offers double discounts.)**

The first clue in this sentence is *always,* which tells you that the action of shopping happens repeatedly. The next clue appears in the second portion of the sentence, where you find out that the store *offers* special discounts on Tuesdays. Because the second portion of the sentence is in present tense, the present-tense verb *shop* makes a good match for the third-person, plural subject *Sheryl and her friend*.

18. **will compete (Next year, four boys will compete for a single spot on the wrestling team.)**

Because the action takes place in the future, or, more specifically, *next year,* you need the future-tense verb *will compete*.

19. **has snapped (Emma has snapped a picture of her brother Eric every year on his birthday, including today.)**

The first time Emma snapped a picture was in the past, and she's still active *today*. The tense that connects present and past is present perfect. Because only one person is doing this action, you need the singular form, *has snapped*.

20. **was begging (Last week I tossed a bit of my dinner under the table because the dog was begging for scraps while I ate.)**

The verb in the first portion of the sentence, *tossed*, indicates an action that took place while another action occurred. The singular, past progressive tense gives a sense of an action, *begging*, that occurred over some time. The simple past-tense form, *begged*, would also work here, but the immediacy of past progressive tense is better.

21. **arrive (Start working on your lab report as soon as you arrive home.)**

The sentence discusses two actions, arriving home and starting work on the lab report. Both occur (or should occur, according to the sentence) at more or less the same time. You have a command *(start)*, and logic tells you that you can't give a past-tense command such as *arrived*. Therefore, the best tense for the second action is present, or *arrive*.

22. **trimmed (Mr. Martin trimmed the tree after he had watered it.)**

In this sentence the busy Mr. Martin is doing two things, trimming and watering, but these actions occur at different times. Standard English requires that the earlier action, the watering, be in past perfect tense *(had watered)*. The action that occurs second is expressed in simple past tense, *trimmed*.

23. **was washing (While Harry was washing the clothes, Oliver was brushing the dog's matted fur.)**

The second portion of the sentence indicates that the action took place in the past *(was brushing)*. The singular, past progressive form, *was washing*, works nicely here, because the actions happen at the same time and only one person was involved in the washing. (The simple past tense, *washed*, could also work in this sentence.)

24. **learned (Jackie learned Arabic when she lived in Tunisia.)**

The two actions in the sentence, *learned* and *lived*, take place at the same time, so they should be in the same tense (past).

25. **had filled (Carla had filled the gas tank before she realized that her credit card was not in her wallet.)**

Two actions occur in this sentence. Both are in the past, but one takes place before the other. Standard English requires that the earlier action be in past perfect tense *(had filled)*. The action that occurs second is expressed in simple past tense, *realized*.

26. **will have gobbled (By the time George gets home, Maria will have gobbled all the cookies, and George hates all the other snacks.)**

The sentence includes a deadline — *the time George gets home* — and something that happens before the deadline — Maria's snack attack. The future perfect tense, *will have gobbled,* is made for just such a situation.

27. **had baked (When I had baked the cookies, I placed them on the dining room table.)**

Two actions in the past show up in this sentence, the baking of the cookies and their placement on the table. Logic tells you that the baking happened before *I placed* the cookies somewhere other than in the oven. To move one action further in the past than another, use the past perfect tense, *had baked.*

28. **disobey (Although the king commands instant obedience, his followers sometimes disobey.)**

This sentence expresses actions that are happening now, as you learn from the first part of the sentence, which contains the present-tense verb *commands.* The second part of the sentence refers to an action that takes place at the same time, so simple present tense is what you want here. Because *followers* is plural, you need the plural form, *disobey.*

29. **had lectured (Marlene had lectured for two hours before she noticed that several audience members were asleep.)**

Two actions occur in this sentence. Both are in the past, but one takes place before the other. Standard English requires that the earlier action be in past perfect tense *(had lectured).* The action that occurs second is expressed in simple past tense, *noticed.*

30. **have lived (I have lived in this neighborhood for about a year, and despite its problems, I still love my home.)**

The present and past are connected in this sentence, as the speaker *(I)* lived in the neighborhood for the past year and continues to live there in the present. The present perfect tense connects the past and present, so *have lived* works perfectly in this sentence.

31. **ended (The yellow and brown leaves began to fall; the autumn soon ended.)**

Simple past tense does the job here; the leaves *began to fall,* so you know that you're talking about the past, and *ended* is a past-tense verb.

32. **has worked (No one has worked harder than Ellen, who spent eight or nine hours a day on this project for the first two weeks and is now allotting ten or twelve hours a day to it!)**

The project began in the past and continues in the present, so present perfect tense is good here. *Ellen* is singular, so *has worked,* the singular form, is the form you want.

33. **jogs (Jared jogs four miles every day as soon as he wakes up.)**

Jared's fitness routine is an ongoing, customary action, so present tense is best. Because *Jared* is one person, opt for the singular form, *jogs.*

34. will complete (From now on, David will complete his homework on time, to avoid detention and poor grades.)

> The expression *from now on* moves the sentence into the future, so *will complete* is the future-tense form you want.

35. returns (Elliot always returns his library books late, so he pays many fines.)

> Your clue here is *always,* which indicates an ongoing action and calls for present tense. *Elliot* is singular, so you need the singular, present-tense form, *returns.*

36. was painting (While Meredith was painting the ceiling, a dog jumped on the ladder.)

> Because the dog *jumped,* you can assume that the painting took place in the past. Also, only one person *(Meredith)* performs the action of painting. Therefore, the singular, past progressive form *was painting* works well. Did you choose the simple past-tense form, *painted?* That form isn't wrong, but the immediacy of the progressive is better because the word *while* places you in the midst of an ongoing action.

37. will double (Place the dough in a warm spot, and in a few hours it will double in size.)

> The first action in the sentence, *place,* is a command, so you know you are in the present. A few hours after you *place* the dough, you are in the future, so *will double* is a good fit.

38. has rained (It has rained every day for a month, including today, but tomorrow's forecast calls for sunshine.)

> The sentence connects the past *(every day for a month)* to the present *(including today)*. Present perfect tense links the present and past, and the subject, *it,* is singular, so the singular form *has rained* is a good choice. The progressive form, *has been raining,* would also work in this sentence.

39. arrived (The soda had soaked into the carpet by the time the janitor arrived with a mop.)

> The sentence mentions two actions — soaking and arriving. The earlier action is in past perfect tense *(had soaked),* and the more recent action is in past tense *(arrived).*

40. are gathering (Right now, Catherine's friends are gathering for her surprise party.)

> The clue here is *right now,* an expression that tells you an action is happening. The present progressive form, *are gathering,* is what you need.

41. had chopped (Once George had chopped down the cherry tree, the fruit was lost.)

> Two events occur in this sentence: George's unfortunate use of the ax and the loss of the fruit. Both happened in the past, so the earlier must be expressed by the past perfect tense, *had chopped.*

42. will receive (I paid the electric bill on the 17th, so I will receive the next bill in about a week.)

> The first portion of the sentence talks about the past, but the second anticipates an action in the future. The future-tense form, *will receive,* fits well here.

43. **was dancing (Although Eddie was dancing happily, Shirley turned off the music.)**

The second portion of the sentence refers to an action in the past *(turned)*. The first portion is also in the past. Because the action was ongoing and only one person was performing it *(Eddie)*, the singular past progressive tense form, *was dancing,* works best in this sentence.

44. **brushes (Clancy never brushes his teeth by himself, even though he is five years old now.)**

The sentence refers to an ongoing action, so present tense is best here. *Clancy* is just one person, so the singular form, *brushes,* fits the sentence.

45. **are attacking (As we speak, our enemies are attacking with great force, but we will not surrender.)**

The key expression in this sentence is *as we speak,* which tells you that you are in the midst of an action. More than one person *(enemies)* performs this action, so the plural form is appropriate. Therefore, *are attacking,* the present progressive plural form, is just what you need.

46. **stapled (The teacher stapled the drawings on the bulletin board so that the parents could admire their children's artwork.)**

The key phrase here is *could admire,* because the helping verb *could* indicates that the action in this sentence is in the past. *(Could* is the past tense of *can.)* Go for the past-tense verb *stapled.*

47. **will have exceeded (By the time Eleanor and Henry are satisfied with the renovation, they will have exceeded their budget by a wide margin.)**

The sentence includes a deadline in the future *(by the time Eleanor and Henry are satisfied),* and the action of exceeding takes place before that deadline. Future perfect tense is made for this situation: an action before a deadline. Therefore, *will have exceeded* is the verb form you need.

48. **had bloomed (Where the tulips had bloomed, weeds eventually covered every inch of the garden.)**

The tulips' blooming is the earlier of two actions in the past, because the sentence tells you that weeds replaced them. Use past perfect tense, *had bloomed,* for the earlier of two past-tense actions.

49. **turns (In Maya's fantasy novel, a wizard's curse turns a little boy into a frog.)**

To write about literature, use present tense, because the action you describe begins anew every time someone reads the book.

50. **will have studied (Amanda and her friends will have studied Chinese for four years by the time they travel to that country.)**

The deadline in the sentence, *by the time,* indicates that future perfect tense is appropriate. *Amanda and her friends* is a plural subject, but luckily, in the future perfect both the singular and plural forms are the same, *will have studied.*

51. **has practiced (Joe has practiced karate for many years and still takes an advanced class every Saturday.)**

The present perfect tense connects the past and the present. In this case Joe's lessons began in the past and continue *still*. *Joe* is a singular form. Therefore, the singular, present perfect form, *has practiced*, is what you want here.

52. **trusts (In Shakespeare's *Othello*, the title character wrongly trusts Iago, one of the most evil villains in literature.)**

To discuss a literary work, use present tense (*trusts*, in this sentence), because the action begins anew every time the play is read or performed.

53. **markets (LGA Manufacturing has an old-fashioned policy; the company markets its products only in a store, not on the Internet.)**

The first verb in the sentence, *has,* is in present tense, and the second portion of the sentence gives you no reason to change time periods. A company, though composed of many workers, is singular, so the singular, present-tense *markets* is best here.

54. **will have been buried (If my dog buries a bone every three days, how many will have been buried by the end of the month?)**

The deadline in the sentence *(by the end of the month)* signals the need for future perfect tense, *will have been buried.*

55. **learns (In Dickens's classic novel *Great Expectations,* Pip learns the identity of his benefactor in a chilling scene.)**

In the world of literature, present tense rules, so *learns* is the form you seek. Why present? Every time a reader opens the book, the action takes place again.

56. **strolled (In my dream, a giant dinosaur ran into my dining room, and then he strolled around the room.)**

The meaning of this sentence doesn't call for a shift in time. Because the first verb *(ran)* is in past tense, the second *(strolled)* should also be in past tense.

57. **campaigned (Perhaps because the president campaigned for the mayor, the mayor won by a huge margin.)**

You know the election is in the past, because the *mayor won.* Therefore, the first verb is also in the past, so *campaigned* is the form you want.

58. **enters (Linda enters the cafeteria and sits next to the most hated teacher in the entire school!)**

The clue here is *sits,* a present-tense verb. The sentence gives you no reason to change time periods, so you know you need a present-tense verb in the blank. *Linda* is just one person; therefore, go for the singular form, *enters.*

59. insures (The orchestra insures the instruments every year, so no one ever worries about storm damage after the hurricane.)

The second part of the sentence contains a present-tense verb form, *worries,* indicating that the present tense, *insures,* is best for the first part also.

60. will tour (Last year I traveled to Europe, but next year I will tour Asia.)

The sentence moves from the past *(last year)* to the future *(next year).* Therefore, the future tense is best.

61. was (In response to the reporter's question, the zookeeper said that the lion was very friendly.)

The sentence summarizes speech, so past tense is best. The answer is *was.*

62. equals (Morty declared that eight added to ten equals eighteen.)

Math doesn't change, so eight added to ten will not suddenly equal nineteen. To express a fact that is always true, use present tense.

63. needed (Arthur told me that he needed a loan until payday and asked me to give him $10.)

When you summarize speech, use a past-tense verb, unless the speech reports a fact that can never change.

64. bowed (Shana reported that at the end of every show, the ballet dancers bowed and ignored the boos from the audience.)

Two clues in this sentence point to the simple past tense. First, *Shana reported,* so you know that the sentence summarizes speech — a situation generally requiring past tense. Second, *bowed* matches *ignored.* Don't shift tenses unless the meaning of the sentence requires two different time periods.

65. revolves (The astronomer told the youngsters that the earth revolves around the sun.)

The earth's movement is constant; it's not suddenly going to revolve around Mars! To express an unchangeable truth, use present tense — in this case, *revolves.*

66. caught (Joe caught the ball as it reached the top of the outfield fence.)

The action takes place in the past, because the ball *reached* (past tense) the fence when Joe *caught* it. The irregular past-tense form of *to catch* is *caught.*

67. hit (The car was cruising along the highway smoothly until it hit a huge bump.)

The action is in the past, as the first verb, *was cruising,* tells you. The second verb should be in the past also, but because hitting a bump isn't an event stretching over a time period, as *cruising* is, the simple past tense is best. *Hit* is the irregular past-tense form of *to hit.*

68. **slept (Dorothy and the baby slept for two hours when they returned from a visit to Grandma.)**

You need the simple past tense for the first part of this sentence, in order to match the past-tense verb *(returned)* in the second part of the sentence. The irregular past-tense form of *to sleep* is *slept*.

69. **rose (At the end of the trial the judge rose from her chair and left the courtroom.)**

The sentence talks about the past *(left)*, so you need a past-tense verb for the blank. The irregular past-tense form of *to rise* is *rose*.

70. **beat (Last week the Yankees beat their fiercest rivals.)**

The irregular past-tense form of *to beat* is *beat*. You know you need past tense because the sentence refers to *last week*.

71. **put (From 2010 through 2011, the confused clerk put all the forms in the wrong file cabinet.)**

The time range *(2010 through 2011)* tells you that you're in the past. The irregular past-tense form of *to put* is *put*.

72. **flew (The helicopter flew straight up into the sky and then headed south.)**

The copter *headed* south, so you know that past tense is what you need. The irregular past-tense form of *to fly* is *flew*.

73. **saw (Glenn saw the little dog and grabbed her before she could run away again.)**

The sentence includes a past-tense verb, *grabbed*, which should be matched with the irregular past-tense form of *to see*, which is *saw*.

74. **swam (I didn't know that you swam in the deep water last summer; I thought you were less advanced in your swimming skills.)**

The irregular past-tense form of *to swim* is *swam*. The words *last summer* indicate that you need past tense in this sentence.

75. **have gotten (Nelson wouldn't have gotten sick if he had washed his hands more frequently.)**

The irregular past participle of *to get* is *gotten*, not *got*, in American usage. Therefore, *have gotten* is correct here.

76. **had taught (The bully approached, but because my uncle had taught me how to handle difficult people, I wasn't afraid.)**

The sentence covers two time periods in the past — when the uncle *taught* and when the bully *approached*. The teaching takes place before the approaching, so the earlier action should be expressed in past perfect tense. The irregular past perfect form of *to teach* is *had taught*.

77. **has done (The doctor has done everything in his power; now Allison must wait for the medicine to take effect.)**

> The doctor acted and now Allison is waiting, so past and present are connected in this sentence. The present perfect tense does the job here. The irregular present perfect form of *to do* is *has done*. The simple past tense, *did,* is also acceptable.

78. **let (Miriam let the dog out for a few minutes, but she will call him inside soon.)**

> Miriam's action occurred already, so past tense is appropriate for this sentence. The irregular past-tense form of *to let* is *let*.

79. **had found (Although Adam had found a good candidate already, the boss continued to interview others for the job.)**

> The sentence discusses two actions, one earlier than the other. Adam's action is earlier, so the past perfect tense *(had found)* works.

80. **began ("Who began the fight, you or your brother?" asked Mother as she separated her battling children.)**

> The irregular past-tense form of *to begin* is *began*. The mother *asked,* so past tense makes sense. (Also, you can't ask about the beginning of a fight until it has begun!)

81. **have sent (After you have sent the letter, shred the scrap copies.)**

> The sentence deals with two time periods: the present (indicated by the command, *shred*) and the past, which is when the letter is mailed. The present and past are linked by the present perfect form, *have sent.*

82. **froze (At first the rain was simply annoying, but when it froze, the streets became very slippery and many pedestrians fell.)**

> Three events take place more or less at the same time — the change from water to ice, the formation of slippery sidewalks, and the crash landing of many pedestrians. Because these events are simultaneous, the irregular past-tense form, *froze,* is what you want here.

83. **tore (Albert tore his shirt when he crawled through the obstacle course.)**

> The simple past tense works fine here, because Albert *tore* his clothing when he *crawled*.

84. **knew ("I knew it!" exclaimed the detective as the murderer confessed.)**

> The detective's exclamation refers to one action in the past, not to a series of actions that must be put in order, a situation that requires the use of the past perfect tense. The simple past-tense form, *knew,* does the job here.

85. **had lost (When she attempted to pay for her coffee, Lee discovered that she had lost all her coins because of a small hole in her pocket.)**

The sentence mentions several events in the past. Attempting to pay for the coffee and discovering the hole happen more or less at the same time, but losing the coins occurs earlier. The earlier action is expressed with the past perfect tense, *had lost*. The other actions *(attempted, discovered)* are in simple past tense.

86. **will have sung (By midnight Angie will have sung that aria enough times to set a world record.)**

The sentence contains a deadline *(by midnight)* and an action that will take place before the deadline (the singing). The future perfect tense, *will have sung,* is exactly what you need for this situation.

87. **hanged (In ancient times, murderers were often hanged in the public square.)**

The verb *to hang* has two important meanings — one, as in this sentence, refers to the execution of a criminal. The other is the verb that refers to hanging an object on a wall. For this sentence, you want the first meaning. The past-tense form for that meaning is *hanged.*

88. **hung (The picture hung on the wall for years, but no one noticed it.)**

The verb *to hang* has two important meanings — one referring to the execution of a criminal and the other to a painting or other object hanging on a wall. For the second meaning, which is the one you want for this sentence, the irregular past-tense form is *hung.*

89. **will have swept (The janitor will have swept the sidewalk before the students arrive, so expect a clean path.)**

The sentence states a deadline — *before the students arrive.* Future perfect tense works well with deadlines, so *will have swept* is the form you want. The simple future form, *will sweep,* or the present tense, *sweeps,* also fit this sentence.

90. **have laid (The riflemen have laid down their weapons but are ready to resume target practice at a moment's notice.)**

Two verbs, *to lie* and *to lay,* can be confusing. The first means *to lie down,* what you do when you take a nap. The second means *to put* or *to place,* which you do when you place a rifle on the ground. The present perfect form of *to lay* is *has* or *have laid.* Here you pair it with *have* because the subject, *riflemen,* is plural. Why present perfect tense? The action in the past *(have laid down their weapons)* is connected to the present, when they *are ready to resume* their practice.

91. **is (The marble statue is on the shelf right now, but earlier it was in the sculptor's studio.)**

You know that the situation in the sentence takes place in the present tense because of the phrase *right now.* The third-person, singular form *is* works well because you are talking about the statue; therefore, you need a third-person form.

92. **was (Along with Jack, I was bored and decided to watch a different show.)**

The sentence talks about something in the past, when *I decided* to watch anything other than the yawn-producing show on the television. The first-person form (when the speaker is the subject) is what you want. Therefore, the answer is *was*.

93. **will have (The co-presidents will have no trouble persuading club members to go out for pizza when they suggest the excursion at the end of the meeting, because everyone will be hungry then.)**

The clues here are *when they suggest* and *everyone will be,* which indicate that you are in the future tense. Singular and plural forms are the same in the future tense. Go for *will have.*

94. **had (Louisa rejected the sofa when it was delivered because it had a stain on one cushion.)**

The sofa is already in the house *(it was delivered),* so you know you need past tense. The third-person form (the one used to talk about something) is what you want. The verb *had* is the answer.

95. **has been (Max has been sick for the last two days, but the doctor predicts that his temperature will be normal tomorrow.)**

The sentence ranges over the past *(the last two days)* and the present *(predicts).* Present perfect tense connects these two time periods. Go for the singular, third-person form, *has been,* because you're talking about *Max.* When you talk about someone or something, you need a third-person form.

96. **are being (The lottery winners are being difficult; they refuse to share their winnings.)**

The second portion of the sentence talks about something happening right now, so you're in the present tense. The action is ongoing, so the present progressive form is appropriate. Because you have *winners,* a plural, you want a plural form, *are being.*

97. **will be (If the referee and the coach can't agree, our efforts will be fruitless because we will forfeit the game.)**

The sentence talks about a possible event in the future, when *we will forfeit.* The future-tense *will be* matches nicely.

98. **has had (Shelley has had difficulty getting up on time ever since her alarm clock broke, but she plans to buy a new one soon.)**

The first portion of the sentence talks about two time periods — when the *alarm clock broke* (past) and her present *difficulty.* Present perfect tense is, well, perfect for this sentence because it connects past and present. The present progressive form, *is having,* also works here, because Shelley's difficulty is ongoing.

99. **was having (While the elevators were rising, the mechanic was having doubts about the strange noises below.)**

The first part of the sentence tells you about an ongoing action in the past, so past progressive tense makes sense for the second part of the sentence also. The *mechanic* is singular, and you're talking about him, so opt for the third-person, singular, past progressive form, *was having.* **Note:** The simple past tense, *had,* also works here.

100. **had been (We had been here, patiently waiting, for more than four hours before Justin arrived.)**

> Two actions occur in the past, but one, the *waiting*, happened first. Go for *we had been*, the first-person, plural form of the past perfect tense. Past perfect tense places one event in the past prior to another.

101. **was (When Doreen was 13, she struggled to start her business, but one day sales began to rise.)**

> You're in the past when you talk about a business owner at age 13! (Another clue is *struggled*, which also indicates the past.) Go for the singular, past-tense form — *was*.

102. **will have had (By the time it opens on Broadway, the show will have had four different directors.)**

> See the deadline in this sentence? It's *by the time it opens*. A deadline tells you that you need future perfect tense, or *will have had*.

103. **is (Gina, who is your friend, begs you to forgive her.)**

> Because *who* stands in for Gina (in grammar terminology, *Gina* acts as the antecedent of *who*), you need a form that matches *Gina*. The verb *is* works well here, because you're in present tense.

104. **was (Doug, who was very immature in those days, used to stick gum under everyone's desk.)**

> Two things were happening at the same time in this sentence: Doug's immaturity and his pranks with gum. Because the statement about gum is in past tense, the statement about immaturity should be also. *Doug* is singular, so opt for *was*, a singular, past-tense form.

105. **had had (Sam thought that his mom had had a stroke, but fortunately he was wrong; it was just a headache.)**

> This verb form sounds like a typo, but it's actually the past perfect tense. Two actions took place in the past — Sam's thinking and whatever happened to his mom. The thinking occurred after the illness started, so it's expressed in simple past tense *(thought)*. To place the illness earlier in the timeline, go for past perfect, *had had*. Another possible answer is *was having*, in which case the thinking and the illness are simultaneous.

106. **can win (Shelly's song can win her an award for "Best New Artist.")**

> The helping verb *can* expresses ability in the present tense.

107. **may fly (Alice may fly to Buenos Aires on business next week.)**

> The helping verb *may* introduces a possibility in the present time. Did you consider *might fly* or *could fly*? These helping verbs also serve to express a possible action, but the strictest, most formal English generally reserves *might* and *could* for past-tense situations, as in *yesterday Alice could go to Buenos Aires, but next week she cannot.*

108. should be (Your hands should be clean before you perform surgery, Doctor!)

The helping verb *should* introduces a sense of obligation. Another possible helping verb for this situation is *must*.

109. may choose (Because she loves that color, Helen may choose only green blocks for her playhouse.)

The helping verb *may* introduces a possibility in the present time. Did you consider *might choose* or *could choose?* These helping verbs also serve to express a possible action, but the strictest, most formal English generally reserves *might* and *could* for past-tense situations, as in *Helen told me that she might choose only green blocks*.

110. would attend (On Saturday mornings, the whole family would attend Wendy's softball games and cheer her on.)

The helping verb *would* expresses a repeated or customary action in the past tense.

111. should have paved (The workers should have paved the street more smoothly, but they did a sloppy job.)

The helping verbs *should* and *have,* added to *paved,* create a statement about obligation in the past.

112. could have jumped (Margaret could have jumped over the fence easily, but instead she waited patiently for the guard to open the gate.)

The helping verb *could* expresses ability, and *have* moves the action of jumping into the past.

113. may be (Enter the house quietly because the baby may be asleep.)

The helping verb *may* expresses possibility. Other verbs that work are *might* and *could,* but the strictest, most formal English reserves those helping verbs for past-tense sentences.

114. must calculate (The mathematician was told that she must calculate the odds of failure before making a recommendation.)

The helping verb *must* expresses obligation. Another possible answer is *should calculate*.

115. should arrest (The sheriff should arrest Josephine for murder, as he has collected an overwhelming amount of evidence of her crime.)

The helping verb *should* expresses obligation. Another possible answer is *must arrest*.

116. can enroll (If he graduates from high school with honors, Walter can enroll in college and continue on the path to success.)

The helping verb *can* expresses ability in the present or future. Did you opt for *could enroll?* The strictest, most formal English reserves *could* for past tense.

117. **might prepare (Seven hours ago, Otis said that he might prepare dinner, but we are still waiting, hungrier than ever.)**

The helping verb *might* adds possibility to the verb *prepare*. Because you're in the past tense, *might* works better in this sentence than *may*, another helping verb of possibility.

118. **may continue ("You may continue," remarked the teacher as the student hesitated.)**

The helping verb *may* expresses permission in the present tense.

119. **would have gone (If it had not rained, Sam would have gone for a walk.)**

The helping verb *would* expresses a condition — the circumstances needed for Sam's willingness to go for a walk, and *have gone* places the action in the past. Did you answer *might have gone?* That shades the meaning slightly, expressing the possibility of Sam's walking. Because the question specifies condition, *would have gone* is the better choice.

120. **would poke (With a sharp pencil, Eliza would poke through the flimsy paper and then ask for a new sheet to write on.)**

The helping verb *would* expresses a repeated action in the past.

121. **Does Mary own (Does Mary own a small but valuable art collection?)**

The helping verb *does*, together with the main verb *own*, creates a question. The subject, *Mary*, should be placed between the singular helping verb *(does)* and the main verb *(own)*.

122. **Was Bert carrying (Was Bert carrying a large carton of crayons to the daycare center?)**

The singular past progressive verb, *was carrying*, must be split by the singular subject, *Bert*, to create a question.

123. **Will Jefferson attend (Will Jefferson attend the committee meeting this afternoon, despite his busy schedule?)**

The future-tense verb, *will attend*, is interrupted by the subject, *Jefferson*, in a question.

124. **Does Eugene have (Does Eugene have too many video games, according to his friend James?)**

The statement (Eugene has too many video games, according to his friend, James) gets by with one present-tense verb, *has*. Another, less common possibility is *Has Eugene too many video games, according to his friend James?* However, the usual way to begin this question is *Does Eugene have*.

125. **did Steven blow (After he had chewed his gum for an hour, did Steven blow an enormous bubble?)**

The first part of the sentence tells you that an hour passed, so you know that you're in the past tense here. Past-tense questions may be created with the helping verb *did*. The subject, *Steven*, belongs between the helping verb and the main verb.

126. **Does the wire between the fenceposts sag (Does the wire between the fenceposts sag so low that cattle cross easily from one field to the next?)**

The helping verb *does* pairs with the main verb *sag* to create a question. *Wire* is singular, so *does* is the helping verb you need, not *do.*

127. **Is Deborah not (Is Deborah not interested in reading that poem aloud?)**

No helping verbs are needed to turn this statement, which contains the verb *is,* into a question. In fact, if the main verb of a sentence is a form of *to be,* you can usually forget about helping verbs when you're creating a question. However, you should rearrange the word order to ask a question in formal English. Another possible answer is *Isn't Deborah. Isn't* is a contraction, a shortened form that substitutes an apostrophe for the omitted letter *o.*

128. **Will you have eaten (Will you have eaten by the time George arrives at the restaurant?)**

The subject, *you,* slips between two helping verbs, *will* and *have,* to create this question in the future perfect tense.

129. **Did Ellie go (Did Ellie go to the skating rink when it was closed?)**

The past-tense form of the verb *to go* is *went,* but you can't pair a helping verb with *went* to create a question — or for any other reason. Instead, you need to return to the infinitive, pull out the *go,* and add the past-tense helping verb, *did,* to ask a question in Standard English.

130. **Did the winning essay compare (Did the winning essay compare face-to-face communication with social media relationships?)**

The past-tense form, *compared,* drops out of this sentence when you change it into a question. The helping verb *did* (which is a past-tense form) is separated from the main verb, *compare,* by the subject, *the winning essay.*

131. **flowing**

Flowing is a form of the verb *to flow,* but in this sentence it describes *stream.* The main action in the sentence is *found,* which is what Hank did.

132. **pleased**

The action in the sentence — the real verb — is *will celebrate.* The word *pleased* comes from the verb *to please,* but in this sentence it functions as a description of Tom.

133. **setting**

The action in the sentence — the real verb — is *walks.* The word *setting* comes from the verb *to set,* but here it functions as a description of the sun.

134. **confused**

The main action in the sentence is expressed by the verb, *is sorting.* The verb form *confused,* a form of the verb *to confuse,* adds information about Eliza, but it functions as a description.

135. rising

The state of being in the sentence is expressed by the verb *are*. *Rising,* a form of the verb *to rise,* describes the subject of the sentence, *mountains,* but it doesn't function as a verb.

136. printed, carrying

The main verb in the sentence is *will be,* which expresses a state of being. Two verb forms function as descriptions — *printed* and *carrying.* Both describe *word.*

137. tired

The sentence has two parts: one in quotation marks and one that "tags" the quotation by identifying the speaker. Inside the quotation, the verb is *have done.* No word there functions as a description. In the other part of the sentence, *screamed* is a verb that tells you what *Andrew* is doing. The word *tired* gives you more information about *Andrew,* but it doesn't function as a verb. Did you select *nagging* also? In this sentence, *nagging* is a noun — the "thing" *Andrew* can't stand! It's not a description.

138. funded

The main verb in the sentence is *was done.* The verb form *funded* describes *laboratories.*

139. hired

Several words function as verbs in this sentence: *is performing, hates, does,* and *wishes.* Only one verb form is a description: *hired.* Did you choose *conceited?* True, that word resembles a verb because it ends in *-ed.* However, *to conceit* isn't a verb; in fact, it isn't even a word! *Conceited* is simply an adjective.

140. sunning

The sentence contains two verbs, *slithered* and *came.* The word *hikers* may look like the verb *to hike,* but it's just a noun. The descriptive verb form in this sentence is *sunning.*

141. **Preparing (Preparing the room for redecoration, Vincent discovered a crack that grew longer with every tug of the wallpaper he was removing.)**

Your reading comprehension skills tell you that Vincent's tug on the old paper happens at the same time as the preparation of the room for redecoration. Therefore, the present participle, *preparing,* is correct.

142. **Speaking (Speaking with intense emotion, the actor recites his lines every night without a trace of boredom.)**

Two clues tell you that this sentence describes an ongoing situation: the main, present-tense verb *(recites)* and *every night.* For an ongoing situation, the present participle, *speaking,* works nicely.

143. **To water (To water the plants during vacations, Caroline installed an automatic sprinkler.)**

In this sentence, the installation happened in the past *(Caroline installed)*, but the reason for the installation is ongoing. The infinitive, *to water*, states the reason.

144. **vowing to fight (The mayor, vowing to fight crime, will increase the number of police officers.)**

The main verb in the sentence, *will increase*, refers to the future. The present participle *(vowing)* is a good fit for a sentence with a future-tense verb, as is the present-tense infinitive, *to fight*, and the present perfect form, *having vowed to fight*.

145. **standing (The cat raked sharp claws across the new desk standing in the corner of the living room.)**

The present participle, *standing*, indicates that the desk is there at the same time that the cat *raked* his claws on it. Present participles express simultaneous events.

146. **exhausted (His funds exhausted, Nelson called home and begged for a loan from his parents.)**

The past participle, *exhausted*, is a good match for the simple past-tense verb forms, *called* and *begged*.

147. **to visit (Annie walked ten miles to visit her Aunt Marie.)**

The infinitive, *to visit*, gives the reason for Annie's long walk.

148. **Having walked (Having walked the entire shoreline this morning, Ed can assure the reporters at tonight's news conference that all the beaches are ready to reopen.)**

To crack this sentence, make a timeline. First comes the walk, then the news conference, and then the reopening of the beaches. To place the walk before the news conference, use the perfect form, *having walked*.

149. **having conferred (Barbara and Arnie, having conferred already, will need no introduction when they attend the next meeting.)**

The first encounter between Barbara and Arnie took place already. To express an action that occurs before another action in the sentence, use the perfect form, *having conferred*.

150. **to meet ("It's great to meet you!" exclaimed Paul as he shook hands with his new tennis partner, who had never seen Paul before in his life.)**

Your reading comprehension skills tell you that Paul's comment about meeting his partner refers to the same moment he extends his hand for a shake. The simple infinitive, *to meet*, expresses simultaneous events. You don't need the perfect form, which places one event before another.

151. **stitches, telephones, taxes**

To form a plural of a word ending in *ch* or *x*, add *es*. That rule accounts for *stitches* and *taxes*. The word *telephone* needs only an *s* to form its plural.

152. **dyes, splashes, sandals**

The words *dye* and *sandal* need only an *s* to form the plural. *Splash,* however, ends in *sh,* so you need to add *es* to form the plural.

153. **tomatoes, catches, mugs**

The addition of *s* creates the plural of *mug.* The word *catch,* which ends with *ch,* needs *es* to form the plural. So does *tomato.* In general, a noun ending in *o* forms the plural with *es* if the letter preceding the *o* is a consonant. (A consonant is any letter except *a, e, i, o or u.*)

154. **monkeys, turkeys, babies**

To form the plural of a word ending in *y,* you add *s* if the *y* is preceded by a vowel *(a, e, i, o,* or *u).* You change the *y* to *i* and add *es* if the *y* is preceded by a consonant (any letter that isn't a vowel). Therefore, *monkey* and *turkey* need only an *s,* because the second-to-last letter in each word is a vowel, *e. Baby,* on the other hand, changes to *babies,* because the second-to-last letter is a consonant, *b.*

155. **zoos, successes, edges**

To form the plural of a noun ending in *o,* you generally add only an *s* if the letter preceding the final *o* is a vowel *(a, e, i, o,* or *u).* Therefore, *zoos* is the correct plural form. Words ending in the letter *s* form the plural with *es,* so go for *successes.* The word *edge* needs an *s,* and nothing more, to form the plural.

156. **children, women, men**

These three words are irregular. None form the plural with *s* or *es.* Instead, the whole word changes! For help with irregular plurals, check your dictionary. Near the singular form you should see the abbreviation *pl.,* which stands for *plural,* followed by the plural form.

157. **deer, elephants, months**

Animal plurals can be tricky, so you should check your dictionary if you aren't sure of the proper form. The plural of *deer* is *deer!* No change at all. On the other hand, you may see one *elephant* or two *elephants* while you're on a safari. The plural of *month* is *months.*

158. **lights, batches, biographies**

A simple *s* is enough for the plural of *light.* Add *es* to *batch,* because it ends with *ch.* A consonant precedes the *y* in *biography,* so you change the *y* to *i* and add *es.* (A consonant is any letter except *a, e, i, o,* or *u.*)

159. **microphones, jellies, viruses**

Add the letter *s* to form the plural of *microphone.* Because *jelly* ends in a *y* preceded by a consonant (any letter except *a, e, i, o,* or *u*), form the plural by changing the *y* to *i* and adding *es.* Add *es* to *virus* to form the plural, *viruses,* because the singular form ends in *s.*

160. **deliveries, essays, wives**

Remember the rule about words ending in *y:* Add *s* if the letter preceding the *y* is a vowel *(a, e, i, o,* or *u).* Change the *y* to *i* and add *es* if a consonant (any letter that isn't a vowel) precedes the *y.* Using this rule, you get *deliveries* (because a consonant precedes the *y* in *delivery)* and *essays* (because a vowel precedes the *y* in *essay).* The word *wife* has an irregular plural form, *wives.*

161. **Smiths, Joneses, O'Tooles**

To form the plural of names, add *es* to names ending in *ch, sh, x, s,* and *z,* and a simple *s* to everything else. Don't form a plural of a name with an apostrophe!

162. **leaves, pitches, copies**

The irregular plural of *leaf* is *leaves.* (Always check your dictionary if you're unsure whether a plural is regular or irregular.) *Pitch* ends in *ch,* so you add *es* to form the plural. *Copy* ends with *y* preceded by a consonant (any letter that isn't *a, e, i, o,* or *u),* so change the *y* to *i* and add *es* to form the plural.

163. **sons-in-law, kangaroos, teeth**

For a hyphenated word, zero in on the most important word and make that word plural — and nothing else! Therefore, the proper plural form is *sons-in-law,* because the family relationship *(son)* is highlighted. For words ending in *o,* you usually add an *s* if the letter preceding the *o* is a vowel *(a, e, i, o,* or *u).* Therefore, the plural of *kangaroo* is *kangaroos. Teeth* is an irregular plural. (Always check your dictionary if you're unsure whether a plural is regular or irregular.)

164. **alumni, mass media, Woodses**

The irregular plural of *alumnus,* a word that comes down to us via Latin, is *alumni* (or, for a group composed solely of females, *alumnae).* Similarly, the plural of *medium,* another word of Latin origin, is *media,* unless you're using the word to mean a size (three *mediums* sold this morning but no *smalls)* or a psychic *(Jim consulted three mediums in order to communicate with his dead pet).* To form the plural of my last name, *Woods,* add *es* because the name ends with an *s.*

165. **species, statistics, vice presidents**

Trick question here: You can have *one species* or *two species* — same spelling. *Statistic* takes an *s* to form the plural. For the compound word, *vice president,* add an *s* to the most important part, which in this case is *president.*

166. **his (S), her (S), she (S)**

His, her, and *she* are all singular pronouns. Each refers to one person. Did you make a mistake and choose *but? But* is not a pronoun; it's a conjunction — a joining word.

167. **their (P), they (P), his (S)**

They and *their* are plural pronouns, referring to a plural noun *(children). His* is a singular pronoun, referring to a singular noun, *Santa.* Did you mistakenly choose *As? As* isn't a pronoun. It's a conjunction — a joining word.

168. **We (P), our (P), my (S)**

We and *our* are plural pronouns. Each refers to a group. *My* is a singular pronoun; it refers to one person.

169. **your (S), he (S), I (S), my (S)**

Your, he, I, and *my* are singular pronouns. Each refers to one person.

170. **Your (P), I (S), their (P)**

The yoga class contains more than one student, so *your* is plural. So is *their,* because it refers to the group. The personal pronoun *I* is always singular. Did you opt for *had? Had* is a verb, not a pronoun. Don't be fooled into thinking that all short words are pronouns.

171. **mine (S), them (P), they (P), themselves (P)**

The pronoun *mine* refers to one person, so it's singular. The pronouns *them, they,* and *themselves* are all plural because they refer to a group.

172. **his (S), I (S), them (P), myself (S)**

Three pronouns here are singular: *his, I,* and *myself.* All refer to just one person. *Them* is a plural pronoun because it refers to a group.

173. **Everyone (S), you (S), I (S)**

Three singular pronouns appear in this sentence: *everyone, you,* and *I.* Are you surprised to see that *everyone* is singular? All the pronouns that end in *-one* (including *someone, anyone,* and *no one,* as well as *one* all by itself) are singular.

174. **Something (S), it (S)**

All the pronouns that end with *-thing (something, everything, nothing)* are singular. *It* is also singular; in this sentence *it* refers to the singular noun, *computer.* Did *every* give you pause? *Everything* is a pronoun, but *every* is a description (an adjective).

175. **Several (P), it (S), someone (S), everyone (S)**

This sentence contains one plural pronoun, *several. It, someone,* and *everyone* are singular pronouns. All the pronouns that end in *-one* (including *someone, anyone,* and *no one,* as well as *one* all by itself) are singular.

176. **One (S), those (P), we (P), them (P)**

Any pronoun containing *-one,* including the word *one,* is singular. *We* and *them* are plural because they refer to groups. So is *those,* which refers to *books,* a plural noun.

177. **Both (P), us (P), no one (S), our (P)**

The pronouns *both, us,* and *our* are always plural. Any pronoun containing *-one,* including the two-word pronoun *no one,* is singular.

178. **Neither (S), my (S), each (S), them (P)**

Because you're talking about *uncles*, you may be tempted to think that any pronoun nearby is plural. Resist that temptation! The pronoun *neither* is always singular, because it refers to one uncle at a time — *neither* this uncle *nor* the other uncle. The pronouns *my* and *each* are also singular. The only plural here is *them*, which refers to a group.

179. **her (S), someone (S), it (S)**

Three pronouns here are singular: *her*, *someone*, and *it*. Did you think *someone* was plural? Any pronoun containing -*one*, including the word *someone*, is singular. Also, in case you erred in choosing *anyway*, be aware that *anyway* is an adverb, not a pronoun.

180. **All (P), most (S), they (P)**

The pronouns *all* and *most* take their identity as singular or plural pronouns from the words they refer to. If the word referred to is singular, the pronoun is singular. If the word referred to is plural, the pronoun is plural. In this sentence, *all* refers to *birds*, a plural noun. Therefore, *all* is plural here. *Most* refers to *water*, a singular noun, so *most* is singular here.

181. **Either (S), me (S), anyone (S)**

All three pronouns here are singular — always! *Either* is always singular, because it refers to one *restaurant* at a time: *either* this restaurant *or* that one. All pronouns ending with -*one*, including *anyone*, are singular.

182. **most (P), few (P), we (P), others (P)**

All four of these pronouns are plural. Three — *few, we,* and *others* — are always plural. *Most* takes its identity as a singular or plural pronoun from the word it refers to. If the word referred to is singular, the pronoun is singular. If the word referred to is plural, the pronoun is plural. In this sentence, *most* refers to *films*, a plural noun, so *most* qualifies as a plural pronoun.

183. **me (S), him (S), some (P), my (S)**

The pronouns *me, him,* and *my* in this sentence are all singular. *Some* is plural because it refers to more than one sandwich.

184. **Someone (S), no one (S), her (S)**

Pronouns ending in -*one*, including the two-word pronoun, *no one*, are always singular. *Her* refers to one female (in this sentence, *Judy*), so it's singular also.

185. **Everyone (S), his (S), her (S), hers (S)**

Pronouns ending with -*one* are always singular, as are *his* and *her*, each of which refers to one person. The pronoun *hers* may look plural because it ends in *s*, but it is singular because it refers to one female.

Answers
101–200

186. **All (S), no one (S), her (S)**

In this sentence *all* refers to *orange juice,* a singular noun, so *all* is also singular. All the pronouns ending in *-one* are singular, including the compound pronoun *no one. Her* is also a singular pronoun.

187. **Each (S), both (P)**

The pronoun *each* is always singular, and *both* is always plural. Did you add *one* to your list? True, *one* may be a pronoun, but not when it's attached directly to a noun (*one wheel,* in this sentence). In such a situation, *one* is an adjective.

188. **Much (S), his (S), everyone's (S)**

The pronoun *much* is singular, as are the possessive pronouns *his* and *everyone's.*

189. **other (S), they (P), mine (S)**

The pronoun *other* refers to one of the two tattoos that Sharla and Alex agree on, so *other* is singular. *They* is plural because it refers to *Sharla and Alex* (two people). *Mine* is singular in this sentence because it refers to one tattoo, *a blue star.* If you selected *one,* you fell into a trap. *One* is an adjective, not a pronoun, when it's attached to a noun. In this sentence, *one* is attached to *tattoo.*

190. **that (P), they (P), anything (S), he (S)**

The relative pronoun *that* takes its identity from its antecedent — the word it refers to. In this sentence, *that* is a stand-in for *shoes,* a plural, so *that* is plural also. *They* is always plural, and *he* is always singular. *Anything* is a singular pronoun also, just like the other pronouns that end with *-thing: everything* and *something.*

191. **Someone (S), who (S), my (S)**

All the pronouns ending in *-one* are singular. Because *someone* is singular and *who* refers to *someone, who* is singular in this sentence, as is the pronoun *my.*

192. **that (P), I (S), them (P)**

The relative pronoun *that* takes its identity from its antecedent — the word it refers to. In this sentence *that* is a stand-in for *branches,* a plural, so *that* is plural also. The pronoun *I* is always singular, and *them* is always plural.

193. **she (S), who (S), her (S)**

The relative pronoun *who* can be either singular or plural, depending upon the word or words it refers to. In this sentence, *who* stands in for *Lulu,* a singular noun, so *who* is singular too. *She* and *her* are also singular pronouns.

194. **which (P), hers (S), theirs (P)**

The relative pronoun *which* can be either singular or plural, depending on the word or words it refers to. In this sentence, *which* refers to two nouns, *envelope* and *writing paper*. Therefore, *which* is plural. Although the pronoun *hers* ends in *s*, it's singular because it refers to one person. *Theirs,* on the other hand, is plural because it refers to a group.

195. **who (P), which (S), all (P), them (P)**

The relative pronouns *who* and *which* can be either singular or plural, depending upon the word or words they refer to. In this sentence, *who* stands in for *patients,* a plural noun, so *who* is plural too. *Which* refers to *disease,* a singular noun, and thus is singular. The pronoun *all* can also be either singular or plural, depending upon what it refers to. In this sentence, *all* refers to *them. Them* is plural, so *all* is plural as well.

196. **tip, Juan**

The first verb in the sentence is *slipped*. When you ask *who slipped?* you have no answer. When you ask *what slipped?* the answer is *tip*. Next verb up is *marched*. Okay, *who marched?* The answer is *Juan*. Your subjects are *tip* and *Juan*. Did you select *shoelace?* That word appears in a description — the prepositional phrase *of the shoelace.* The subject is never part of a prepositional phrase.

197. **Marina, Tom**

The verb in this sentence is *are*. When you ask *who are?* the answer is *Marina and Tom are*. The word *and* is a conjunction — a word that joins. Ignore it and you see the subjects of this sentence: *Marina, Tom.*

198. **cameras**

The verb in the sentence is *swiveled*. When you ask *who swiveled?* you have no answer. What you ask *what swiveled?* the answer is *cameras swiveled*. The subject is *cameras.* (*Eight* and *security* are descriptions attached to *cameras,* not the subjects.)

199. **bride, groom**

The verb in the sentence is *recited*. When you ask *who recited?* the answer is *bride and groom recited.* Ignore *and,* a conjunction (joining word). The subjects are *bride, groom.*

200. **girl**

The verb in the sentence is *got*. When you ask *who got?* the answer is *girl got*. Your subject is *girl*. Did you stumble over the *crowd of 200 fans?* All those words are extra information.

201. **Jumping**

The verb in this sentence is *is*. When you ask *who is?* you have no answer. When you ask *what is?* the answer is *jumping*. Yes, the subject looks like a verb! In fact, it could be part of a verb in a different sentence. In this sentence, though, *jumping* is a noun and the subject of the sentence. If you answered *jumping on the trampoline,* don't worry. You just added on the description attached to *jumping*. The subject is still there, so your answer is acceptable.

202. **you (understood)**

The verb here is *stop,* a command. If you ask *who stop?* the answer is the person you're commanding. In other words, the subject of a command is always *you,* but the subject in a command is understood, not stated.

203. **Henry, whoever**

This sentence contains two verbs, *distributed* and *needed.* Ask the questions for each verb. *Who distributed?* The answer is *Henry distributed,* so *Henry* is the subject of *distributed.* Now ask *who needed?* The answer is *whoever needed.* Therefore, *whoever* is the subject of *needed.*

204. **brand**

The verb in this question is *does taste.* Ask the usual questions — *who does taste? what does taste?* The answer is *new brand of peanut butter.* In that expression, one word *(brand)* is key and the rest *(new, of peanut butter)* are descriptions. The subject is *brand.* If you answered *the new brand of peanut butter,* you added the descriptions to the subject, but count your answer as correct because it includes the subject.

205. **statues**

Follow the usual procedure to find the real subject in this sentence. Locate the verb, in this case *sat,* and ask *who sat?* and *what sat?* The second question tells you that *four large statues of historical figures sat.* Okay, time to dig the subject out of that long list of words. Ignore the descriptions *(four, large, of historical figures)* and you're left with *statues,* the true subject. If you answered *four large statues of historical figures,* count your answer as correct because it includes the subject.

206. **plane**

The verb in the sentence is *flew.* Ask the questions: *Who flew?* You have no answer. *What flew?* The answer is *plane,* and that's your subject. Notice that this subject is located in the middle of the sentence. Don't choose a subject by location; use the questions, and you'll find the correct answer.

207. **bus**

The verb in this sentence is *circled.* When you ask *who circled?* you may think the answer is *tourists.* Look more closely at the sentence. True, the *tourists* moved, but they moved because they were on the bus. Go back to the verb and ask *what circled?* Now the answer is clear: the *bus circled.* The subject is *bus.* By the way, *full of delighted tourists* is a prepositional phrase, which never contains the subject of a sentence.

208. **Each**

The pronoun *each* is the subject here, and *of the coffee cups* is a description clarifying the meaning of *each.* (In grammar terminology, *cups* is the object of a preposition and not eligible to be a subject.) The verb is *has,* and when you ask *what has?* the answer is *each has.* If you answered *each of the coffee cups,* your answer is acceptable because the real subject, *each,* is included with its descriptions.

209. Both

The verb in this sentence is *land*. Ask your question: *Who land?* The answer, in long form, is *both of the parakeets*. Now take away the description (*of the parakeets*, a prepositional phrase) and you're left with the subject, the pronoun *both*. *Parakeets*, by the way, can't be a subject because in this sentence it functions as the object of the preposition *of*. If you answered *both of the parakeets*, your answer is acceptable because the real subject, *both*, is included with its descriptions.

210. Allison, friend

The main verb in this sentence is *parted*. You may have detected two other verb forms, *snarling* and *walking*. In this sentence those verb forms function as descriptions. Okay, ask the question: *Who parted?* The answer is *Allison and her former friend Pete*. Now you have to excavate the real subjects. Cross out the descriptions (*her, former*) and the conjunction (the joining word *and*). You can also cross off *Pete* because in this sentence, *Pete* and *friend* are the same person. The first one in the sentence, *friend*, is the subject. The second, *Pete*, is an appositive — the grammar term for an equivalent. An appositive isn't a subject.

211. Grandpa, who

This sentence makes two statements, each with its own verb and subject. The first statement is *Grandpa was the goalie on his college team*. The second statement is *who loves hockey*. Take them one at a time. The verb in the first statement is *was*. Ask the question *who was?* The answer is *Grandpa*. There's your first subject. Now check out the second statement. The verb is *loves*. *Who loves?* The answer, oddly enough, is *who loves*. The pronoun *who* is the subject of the verb *was*. (*Who*, of course, is a stand-in for *Grandpa*.)

212. apartment, townhouse

The word *either* is tricky. In some situations it's a pronoun, but when it's paired in a sentence with *or*, both the *either* and the *or* are conjunctions (joining words). In an *either/or* sentence — and also in a *neither/nor* sentence — the subjects are linked by these conjunctions. In this sentence, the subjects are *apartment* and *townhouse*. The verb is *will please*. When you ask *who will please?* and *what will please?*, you discover the answers *apartment* and *townhouse*.

213. dog, that, I

Before you can locate the subjects, you have to untangle the statements in this sentence. You have three: (1) *The dog is over there*; (2) *that should win the contest*; (3) *I believe*. Now zero in on each statement separately. In the first, the verb is *is*. When you ask *who is?* the answer is *the dog is*. *Dog* is your first subject. Now go to the second statement. The verb is *should win*. *Who should win?* Your answer is the pronoun *that*. Did you answer *dog* again? The logic is understandable, but the grammar is clear. The pronoun *that* replaces *dog* in the second statement. The subject of *should win* is *that*. The third statement is easy. *Who believes? I believe*. The subject is *I*. As always, the key to untangling all the statements is to identify the verbs and ask the usual subject questions.

214. **Courtney**

This sentence is easier to figure out if you cross out the prepositional phrase, *along with her mother.* (It's a description.) Now the verb, *spoke,* pops out. *Who spoke? Courtney spoke.* True, your reading comprehension skills may have told you that both *Courtney* and *her mother spoke,* but the word *and* isn't in the sentence. Because *mother* is the object of the preposition *along with,* it can't function as a subject.

215. **truck, which**

To find the subjects of this sentence more easily, untangle the two statements the sentence contains: (1) *The fire truck speeds through the intersection* and (2) *which is heading to a blaze downtown.* Now analyze each statement separately. In the first statement, the verb is *speeds. What speeds?* The *truck.* In the second statement, the noun *truck* has been replaced by a pronoun, *which.* The verb is *is heading.* Ask your question: *What is heading?* The answer is *which.* Did you choose *truck* for both verbs? That's a common mistake, because *which* represents *truck.* However, when one subject works for two verbs, the verbs are joined by a conjunction such as *and* or *but.*

216. **V: opens, allows; S: Anna. (Every morning Anna opens the gate and allows her poodle to play in the yard.)**

The sentence has two action verbs *(to open* and *to allow).* You must stay in the present tense, so you have two possible answers for each verb — *open* or *opens* and *allow* or *allows.* First, ask your subject questions without worrying about which form you need. When you ask *who open or opens?* and *who allow or allows?* the answer is *Anna.* Now you know you have a singular subject *(Anna),* which matches with the singular verbs, *opens* and *allows.*

217. **V: have shared; S: Clare, David. (On the way to work, Clare and David always have shared funny stories about their boss.)**

The sentence contains one verb, which must be in present perfect tense. Your options are *has shared* and *have shared.* First, ask your subject questions without worrying about which form you need. When you ask *who has shared or have shared?* the answer is *Clare and David. And* is a word that adds one subject to another, creating a plural. Now you know you have a plural subject *(Clare, David),* which matches with the plural verb, *have shared.*

218. **V: was; S: bottle. (The large-sized bottle of my favorite shampoo was on sale last week.)**

The sentence contains one verb, which must be in past tense. Therefore your options are *was* and *were.* Ask your subject questions without worrying about which form you need. When you ask *who was or were?* you get no answer. Now ask *what was or were?* The answer is *bottle.* (The other words attached to *bottle* are all descriptions. You can ignore them. In case you're curious about grammar terms, *large-sized* is an adjective and *of my favorite shampoo* is a prepositional phrase.) You have a singular subject *(bottle),* which matches with the singular verb, *was.* If you included the descriptions, *large-sized* and *of my favorite shampoo,* your answer is still acceptable, so long as you included *bottle,* the real subject.

219. **V: are planning; S: Alicia, I. (Alicia and I are planning a talent show to raise money for needy children.)**

The verb *to plan* must be in present progressive tense, so your choices are *is planning* and *are planning*. Ask your subject question: *Who is or are planning?* The answer is *Alicia and I.* In English, as well as in math, one plus one equals two. So add *Alicia* and *I* and you end up with two people, a plural subject, which must match the plural verb form *are planning*.

220. **V: were placing; S: Scouts. (The Cub Scouts were placing candy apples in small, sticky piles in preparation for the Halloween party.)**

The verb *to place* must be in past progressive tense, so you must choose between *was placing* and *were placing*. Ask your subject question: *Who was or were placing?* The answer is *Scouts were placing.* The plural subject *Scouts* matches the plural verb *were placing.* If you chose *Cub Scouts,* consider your answer correct also. *Cub* is a descriptor, telling you what kind of *Scouts* you're discussing.

221. **V: Was, read; S: Hank, he. (Was Hank pleased when he read your letter?)**

Divide this sentence into its two component parts and work on each one separately. The first part is *Was* or *Were Hank pleased. Hank* is singular, so you need *was,* a singular verb form. Now for the second part: *when he read your letter.* The verb is *read,* a handy past-tense form that is the same for both singular and plural subjects. Ask the question *who read?* The answer to that part of the sentence is *he.*

222. **V: seem; S: exhibits. (The best exhibits in the museum seem more crowded lately.)**

The two present-tense choices available to you are *seems* and *seem.* Ask your subject question: *Who seem or seems?* You get no answer, so replace *who* with *what* and ask again: *What seem or seems?* The answer is *exhibits,* a plural subject that pairs with the plural verb form *seem.*

223. **V: were singing, broke; S: Matthew, I, voices. (Matthew and I were singing every single song until our voices broke from overuse.)**

Take each part of the sentence separately. The first blank offers two options in the past progressive tense, *was singing* and *were singing.* Ask your subject question: *Who was or were singing?* The answer is *Matthew and I,* a plural subject because you have two people. Therefore, you need the plural verb, *were singing.* Onward to the second part of the sentence: *Who broke?* The answer is *voices broke.* There you go: You have two verbs, *were singing* and *broke,* and three subjects, *Matthew, I,* and *voices.* By the way, *broke* is the past-tense verb form for both singular and plural subjects. Convenient, right?

224. **V: Have; S: you. (Have you any extra icing for my birthday cake?)**

The verb *to have* has two forms in the present tense: *has* and *have.* When you ask the subject question *who has or have?* the answer is *you have.* Is *you* singular or plural? You have no way of knowing, and it doesn't matter. The pronoun *you* may be singular or plural, depending upon context. Either way, it matches with *have.*

225. **V: crawl; S: chipmunks. (Through the dark, damp tunnel crawl the chipmunks, eager to reach the picnic tables.)**

The subject in this sentence is in an unusual spot, after the verb instead of before. No worries: Just ask the usual question: *Who crawl or crawls?* The answer is *chipmunks,* a plural, which must be matched with the plural verb form *crawl.*

226. **V: is, is; S: ham and cheese, salad. (Ham and cheese is my favorite sandwich, but salad is a more nutritious choice.)**

When foods form one dish or sandwich (peanut butter and jelly, for example, or rice and beans), the dish or sandwich is considered one, singular item. Therefore, when you ask *what is or are?* to find the answer for the first blank, your answer is *ham and cheese,* a singular subject that takes a singular verb, *is.* When you ask the same questions for the second blank, you get *salad is* — both singular forms.

227. **V: is; S: problem. ("Your problem is 17 unexcused absences," commented the teacher as she explained why the student was scheduled for detention.)**

This sentence revolves around a form of the verb *to be,* a linking verb that acts as a sort of "equal sign" in the sentence. If you were writing this sentence as a math problem, you'd have "problem = absences." You may notice that the first part of the "equation" is singular *(problem)* but the second part is plural *(absences).* So which one governs the verb? The first one. In this type of sentence, location is everything.

228. **V: influences, vote; S: Politics, senators. (Politics influences much of the debate on that issue, but the senators from that state always vote according to their consciences.)**

The word *politics* appears to be plural because it ends in the letter *s.* However, it's singular. Therefore, you should pair it with the singular verb form *influences.* In the second blank, your choices are *votes* and *vote.* Ask your question: *Who vote or votes?* The answer is *senators vote* — a plural subject-verb combination.

229. **V: is going; S: John. (John, not his friends, is going to attend the ceremony.)**

The expression *not his friends* is a distraction in this sentence. Notice the commas surrounding it? Imagine that you can lift the expression out of the sentence. Now your task is easier. The choices for present progressive include *is going* and *are going.* Time for your question: *Who is going?* The answer: *John is going.* The singular subject *John* matches the singular verb *is going.*

230. **V: offers, are; S: he, any. (Any of the solutions he offers to the panel are acceptable.)**

This sentence has two parts, one tucked inside the other. When you untangle them, the answer is easier to determine. The tucked-in part is *he (offers/offer) to the panel.* The outer part is *any of the solutions (is/are) acceptable.* In the tucked-in part, you have *he offers,* a singular subject and verb that you find with the usual questions *(Who offers or offer? He offers.* The singular subject *he* matches the singular verb *offers.)* In the outer portion of the sentence, the pronoun *any* is plural because the word it refers to *(solutions)* is plural. (Remember that *any* can be either singular or plural depending upon the word that it refers to.) Once you know that *any* is plural in this sentence, you can choose the plural verb *are* right away.

231. V: Is; S: House of Representatives. (Is the House of Representatives in session now?)

The *House of Representatives* is a single body — one thing. Therefore, pair it with the singular verb form *is* and you have a correct sentence.

232. V: comes; S: Most. (Most of the salt in those diets comes from natural sources.)

The pronoun *most* can be either singular or plural depending upon the word it refers to. In this sentence, *most* refers to *salt*, a singular word. Therefore, *most* is a singular subject that pairs nicely with the singular verb *comes*. If you selected *salt* or *diets* as subjects, you forgot one important fact: The object of a preposition can't be a subject. If you answered *most of the salt in those diets*, count your answer as correct because the true subject, *most*, is included with the descriptions.

233. V: are drooping; S: two, three. (Two or three of the plants with red leaves are drooping to the ground because of the drought.)

To crack this sentence, ignore the distractions — the prepositional phrases *of the plants* and *with red leaves*. Now ask your questions: *Who is or are drooping? What is or are drooping?* Your answer is *two or three*. The numbers *two* and *three* function as subjects here. They are plurals, so they need the plural verb *are drooping*.

234. V: seems; S: study. (The study of economics seems interesting, but I have never taken any courses about this subject.)

Cross off the prepositional phrase (*of economics*), which distracts you from the true subject-verb pair. Now focus on what's left: *the study (seems/seem) interesting. Study* is singular, so you need the singular verb form *seems*.

235. V: has been, expect; S: hours, I. (Two hours of homework has been my usual amount, but I expect to spend more time on my studies next year.)

When you speak about an amount of time, the amount is singular. Therefore, even though *two hours* appears to be plural, it's actually singular because it's *one* amount. Now ask the questions: *Who has been? What have been?* The answer is *two hours* or *hours*, which in this sentence is a singular subject and must pair with the singular verb form *has been*. The second part of the sentence is easy: *Who expect or expects?* The answer is *I expect*.

236. V: plays; S: girl, boy. (Every girl and boy in the kindergarten plays with the plastic blocks, not the wooden ones.)

The word *every* has the power to change the meaning of the sentence. No matter what follows it — even something that appears plural such as *girl and boy* — the word *every* creates a singular expression. Why? The logic is that *every* makes you consider the members of the group one by one. *Every* is not a pronoun and can't be a subject. Therefore, when you ask *who play or plays?* the answer is *girl and boy*, which is singular because the expression is preceded by *every*. Isn't English a strange language?

237. V: is, makes; S: girl, who. (That little girl is the only one of the dancers who makes friends easily.)

The first part of this sentence is easy. The subject, *girl,* pairs with the singular form *is.* The second portion is tricky, as are all sentences that refer to a group and a member of the group. These sentences contain the statements *the only one of the* (insert group name) or *one of the* (insert group name), followed by *who, which,* or *that.* The key is to think about the meaning of the *who/which/that* statement. In this sentence, the *who* statement is about making friends easily. When you apply your reading comprehension skills, you see that only one person is in that category. Therefore, *who* represents *girl,* a singular noun. Because *who* is singular, it requires a singular verb, *makes.*

238. V: is, looks; S: dollars, which. (A thousand dollars is too much to pay for that broken-down car, which looks like a rusty bucket.)

Amounts of money function as singular subjects, unless you're talking about the pieces of metal or paper that make up our currency. When you ask *what is or are?* for the first part of the sentence, the answer is *thousand dollars,* which looks plural but is actually singular. Therefore, you need the singular verb *is,* paired with the singular subject *dollars* or *thousand dollars.* (Either choice is fine.) Now check out the second part of the sentence. Ask the question *what look or looks?* The answer is the pronoun *which.* Because *which* refers to the singular noun *car,* it's a singular subject and needs the singular verb *looks.*

239. V: have, is; S: Ginger, aunts, landlord. (Neither Ginger nor her aunts have keys to the house, but the landlord is able to supply an extra set.)

The paired conjunctions (joining words) *neither/nor* follow a simple rule: The subject that is closest to the verb is the one to match. In this sentence, *aunts* is closer to the blank than *Ginger.* (Why focus on *Ginger* and *aunts?* Ask the question *who has or have?* The answer is *Ginger* and *aunts,* which are the subjects.) Because *aunts* is plural, you need the plural verb form, *have.* Moving to the second blank, your choices are *are, is,* and *am* — all present-tense forms of *to be.* Ask *who are? who is? what am?* and the answer is *landlord is.*

240. V: is selling, are; S: Shelby, that. (Shelby is selling me one of the cars that are energy efficient.)

This sentence contains two separate statements: (1) *Shelby is selling me one of the cars* and (2) *that are energy efficient.* The first portion of this sentence is easy: *Shelby* (singular subject) pairs with *is selling* (singular verb). The second portion of the sentence is harder. The key is the pronoun *that,* which begins a statement about energy-efficient cars. Your reading comprehension skills tell you that more than one car falls into the energy-efficient category, and *Shelby is selling one* of them. Because more than one car is energy-efficient, *that* is plural and pairs with the plural verb *are.*

241. his/Martin, they/players

The singular, masculine pronoun *his* refers to *Martin,* one male. The plural pronoun *they* (which can refer to men, women, or mixed groups) refers to the plural noun *players.*

242. her/Mary, their/Mary and uncle, his/uncle

The singular, feminine pronoun *her* refers to *Mary,* one female. The plural pronoun *their* refers to *Mary and her uncle* — a group of two. The singular, masculine pronoun *his* refers to *uncle.*

243. his/Shakespeare, their/readers

The singular, masculine pronoun *his* refers to *Shakespeare,* one male. The plural pronoun *their* (which can refer to men, women, or mixed groups) refers to the plural noun *readers.*

244. My/I, his/dog, I/no antecedent, it/bone

The personal pronoun *I* (as well as the plural *we*) refer to the person or people speaking, so you won't find an antecedent in the sentence for *I* (as in this sentence) or *we* (which doesn't appear in this sentence). The possessive pronoun *my* refers to the personal pronoun *I.* The singular, masculine pronoun *his* refers to *dog,* and the singular, neuter pronoun *it* refers to *bone.*

245. Whoever/no antecedent, it/window

The pronoun *whoever* refers to an unknown person or people. (That's a handy quality, as *whoever* works for both singular and plural situations!) You won't find an antecedent for *whoever* in the sentence. The singular, neuter pronoun *it* refers to *window.*

246. that/motorcycle, which/race

Both *that* and *which* can be singular or plural and masculine, feminine, or neuter, depending upon the antecedent. In this sentence, *that* is the *motorcycle* (so *that* is singular and neuter in this sentence) and *which* is the *race* (making *which* singular and neuter here).

247. None/programs, someone/no antecedent

The pronoun *none* can be either singular or plural and of any gender, depending upon the word it refers to. In this sentence, *none* refers to *programs.* It's plural and neuter in this context. *Someone* refers to an unknown person and has no antecedent.

248. who/John, his/John, mine/no antecedent

The pronoun *who* can be either singular or plural and either masculine or feminine, depending upon the word it refers to. In this sentence, *who* refers to *John,* as does the singular, masculine pronoun *his. Mine* refers to the speaker, who doesn't appear in the sentence, so *mine* has no antecedent.

249. What/no antecedent, you/no antecedent, I/no antecedent, everything/no antecedent

This sentence is full of pronouns, but not antecedents. The personal pronoun *I* refers to the speaker, just as *you* refers to the person being spoken to. *What* is an unknown quantity here; the reader or listener has no context. Similarly, *everything* is general and has no antecedent in the sentence.

250. **whom/dentist, her/Mary, them/teeth**

Mary trusted the *dentist,* so *dentist* is the antecedent of *whom. Her* refers to *Mary,* and *them* refers to *teeth.*

251. **it, her (Sara was delighted to receive the book and read it aloud to her friends.)**

The pronoun in the first blank refers to *book,* a singular neuter noun. Therefore, the pronoun *it* is correct. In the second blank, the singular, feminine, possessive pronoun *her* replaces *Sara's.*

252. **his, he, them (Gregory prepared three reports for his supervisor, but when he handed them in, the supervisor was not happy.)**

The masculine, singular, possessive pronoun *his* replaces *Gregory's,* just as the masculine, singular pronoun *he* takes the place of *Gregory.* For *reports* — a plural, neuter noun — you need *them,* a plural pronoun.

253. **we, they (Dora and I liked the dresses, but we decided they were too formal for the occasion.)**

The plural pronoun that includes the speaker is *we,* a good stand-in for *Dora and I.* In the second blank you need a plural, neuter pronoun — *they.*

254. **his, its (The company where his father works is expanding its business to Asia.)**

The singular, masculine, possessive pronoun *his* replaces *Arthur's.* In the second blank you need *its* to refer to the singular, possessive noun, *company's.* Did you choose *their?* That's a common error! Every company and business is singular and should match with *it* or *its,* not the plural pronoun *their.*

255. **their, it (The audience sat in their seats, patiently waiting for the performance to begin, but it was delayed.)**

This sentence is a little tricky. *The audience* appears to be singular, but it's actually a collective noun because an audience is made up of many different people. The audience can, as a whole, be seated, but once you mention *seats,* you have to think about the individuals, the component parts of the collective noun *audience.* With more than one individual, you need the plural, possessive pronoun, *their.* The second blank is simpler: The singular, neuter pronoun *it* works perfectly as a replacement for *performance.*

256. **our, they, it (Counting our votes is a simple task; they will ensure that it is done properly.)**

The plural, possessive pronoun *our* refers to a group that includes the speaker. Because *inspectors* is plural, you need a plural pronoun *(they).* The last blank calls for a singular, neuter pronoun, *it.*

257. **who, it (James, who loves football, plans to play it in college.)**

The relative pronoun *who* can be either singular or plural, and masculine or feminine. Here it relates the statement about James's love of football to the statement about James's college plans. (Relative pronouns relate; that's why they're called *relative.*) In the second blank, the singular, neuter pronoun *it* replaces *football.*

258. **his or her, I, them (Because neither of the athletes has his or her sneakers tied properly, I expect one of them to fall.)**

The pronoun *neither* is singular, so you need a singular, possessive pronoun here. You don't know whether the *athletes* are men, women, or one of each, so *his or her* works best in the first blank. The personal pronoun *I* refers to the speaker, and the plural pronoun *them* refers to *athletes*.

259. **his or her, her (Everyone in the restaurant wants his or her meal right away, but Chef Helen will cook at her own pace.)**

The pronoun *everyone* appears plural, but it's a singular word that must be matched by another singular pronoun. Because you don't know whether the diners are men, women, or a mixed group, *his or her* is best. The pronoun in the second blank refers to one woman *(Chef Helen),* so you need a singular, feminine pronoun, *her*.

260. **we, him or her (When a person wins a prize, we clap for him or her.)**

The plural pronoun *we* refers to a group including the speaker. In the second blank you need a singular form, but you don't know whether *a person* is a man or a woman. *Him or her* covers both possibilities.

261. **III. (The umpire found his glasses just in time for the playoffs.)**

In Sentence I *(Ellen and her sister thought she got a good grade), she* could refer to *Ellen* or *her sister*. *She* is too vague. In Sentence II *(The pitcher and catcher worked on his throwing speed), his* could refer to the pitcher's or the catcher's throwing speed, so *his* is also vague. In the last sentence, *his* has only one possible antecedent, *the umpire*.

262. **II. and III. (II. Joe and I hung our posters on the south wall. III. I hope you like the figs; I picked them myself.)**

In Sentence I *(The bowl was on the table with the green tablecloth; I washed it), it* is vague. The reader doesn't know whether *it* refers to the *bowl* or the *tablecloth*. In Sentence II, *our* clearly refers to *Joe and I*. In Sentence III, *them* clearly refers to *figs*.

263. **I. (He is tall and strong; those are attractive qualities.)**

In Sentence II *(Summer gives me more free time than winter, so I prefer it),* the pronoun *it* may refer to either season mentioned, so *it* is too vague. Similarly, in Sentence III *(When I slammed the vase into the wall, I broke it), it* may be either *the vase* or *the wall*. Not clear, and therefore not correct! Sentence I, however, is fine. *Those* refers to *qualities,* so the reader isn't confused.

264. **I. and II. (I. The boy Mary insulted walked away from her angrily. II. I love that horror film; there are five wonderfully scary monsters in it.)**

In the first sentence, *her* can refer only to *Mary*. In the second sentence, *it* refers to *film*. No confusion in Sentences I and II! In the last sentence *(Patrick wants to study law because his father is one),* the pronoun *one* has no antecedent. Patrick's father isn't *law;* presumably he's a *lawyer,* but *lawyer* isn't in the sentence. Without much needed clarity, Sentence III is wrong.

265. **III. (I read many modern novels, and I usually like them.)**

The pronoun *them* in Sentence III is clear; it refers to *novels*. Sentences I and II have problems. In the first sentence *(The tacks and nails from that store are very sharp, so I always buy them)*, *them* could be *tacks* or *nails* or both. In the second sentence *(The tacks covered all the seats, which were dangerous)*, *which* may be the *tacks* or the *seats*. Sentences I and II are unclear and therefore incorrect.

266. **II. and III. (II. The fish that Catherine bought had red spots on its tail. III. His grandmother introduced Mark to opera, and he loved it.)**

Check out Sentence I *(The library book has a stain on the cover, but I can't remove it)*: What can't *I remove* — the *stain* or the *book?* Because the reader doesn't know, Sentence I is wrong. In Sentence II, *its* refers to *fish*. Sentence II is clear and correct. In Sentence III, *it* refers to opera, and *his* and *he* refer to Mark. These pronouns are clear, so Sentence III is correct.

267. **I. and II. (I. The architect likes the new building, which was designed by his competitor. II. Gloria explained that she was late because her train left an hour past its scheduled time.)**

In Sentence I, the pronoun *which* clearly refers to *building*, and *his* refers to *architect*. In Sentence II, *she* and *her* refer to *Gloria*, and *its* refers to *train*. Everything's fine with these two sentences. Sentence III *(Charlie watches football and baseball games all day long and wishes he could be a professional at it)* has a problem, though. What does *it* mean? Watching sports? Playing them? *It* has no antecedent, so Sentence III is wrong.

268. **II. (The computer mouse I dropped broke into three pieces, but I glued them back together.)**

Sentence II has two pronouns: The *I* clearly refers to the speaker, and *them* refers to *pieces*. All correct! In Sentence I *(Georgina put one more card on top of the four she had fashioned into a little house, but it fell)*, what fell? The last *card* or the *house?* Because you can't determine the answer to that question, Sentence I is wrong. In Sentence III *(I did my homework in the middle of the night without a flashlight, which was a problem)*, *which* is unclear. The problem may be lack of sleep *(in the middle of the night)* or lack of light *(without a flashlight)*.

269. **III. (The government hopes to avoid war because of its high cost in both money and lives.)**

In Sentence I *(In the paper it says that war may break out within the next two days)* you have a double subject — *paper it*. Why repeat? Beginning the sentence with *The paper says that . . .* is clearer. Sentence II *(In an article in the paper it says that soldiers will report for duty tomorrow)* doesn't double up subjects as Sentence I does, though, because *article* and *paper* are objects of prepositions, not subjects. However, the second sentence has a different problem: *it* has no clear antecedent, because both *article* and *paper* are possible. (The correct version would be *An article in the paper says that soldiers will report for duty tomorrow*.) In the last sentence, *its* clearly refers to war. Only Sentence III is correct.

270.

II. and III. (II. The shades let in some light; they were translucent. III. Allowing some sunlight reduces the need for strong electric lights, which may not be efficient in energy use.)

In Sentence I (*The Yankee was a great hitter, but the other team's star was better at it*), *it* could refer to *batting,* if only *batting* were in the sentence. It isn't! Therefore, Sentence I is wrong. In Sentence II, *they* refers to *shades,* so that sentence is correct. Sentence III correctly pairs *lights* with *which*.

271.

S, O, S, O (As they built the shelter, the guides told us to watch carefully, in case we ever had to erect a hut like it.)

They is a subject pronoun, acting in this sentence as the subject of the verb *built. Us* is an object pronoun, which in this sentence serves as the indirect object of the verb *told.* (In case you're curious, the direct object is *to watch carefully.*) Next up is the subject pronoun *we,* which functions as the subject of the verb *had.* Finally, *it* is an object pronoun acting as the object of the preposition *like*.

272.

S, S, O, S (Doreen and I caught five fish yesterday, but she threw them back into the water because we don't like to eat salmon.)

I is a subject pronoun — specifically, the subject of the verb *caught. She* is also a subject pronoun, paired with the verb *threw.* Next you see an object pronoun, *them,* which is the direct object of the verb *threw.* Last but not least, *we* is a subject pronoun, acting as the subject of *do like.* (What happened to the negative? The contraction *don't* is actually *do not,* and *not* is an adverb, not part of the verb.)

273.

P, S, P (Lola is my friend; however, you are her enemy.)

This sentence has two possessive pronouns, *my* (attached to *friend*) and *her* (attached to *enemy*). The pronoun *you* is a subject pronoun in this sentence because it functions as the subject of the verb *are*.

274.

O, P, O, S (The flight attendant told him to turn off his computer and confiscated it when he refused.)

The pronoun *him* is an object pronoun functioning in this sentence as the indirect object of the verb *told.* (The direct object, if you care, is *to turn off his computer.*) *His* is a possessive pronoun attached to *computer. It* is an object pronoun, serving here as the object of the verb *confiscated.* Finally, the subject pronoun *he* is the subject of the verb *refused*.

275.

O, S, P (Al has placed Kerina and you at a lively table, but if you want to change seats, the choice is yours.)

The verb *has placed* has two direct objects in this sentence: *Kerina* (a noun) and the object pronoun *you.* Next you have a subject pronoun, *you,* which is the subject of the verb *want. Yours* is a possessive pronoun following the linking verb *is*.

276.

S, S, S, S (<u>I</u> know <u>it</u> was <u>she</u> on the phone because <u>I</u> always recognize voices.**)**

The first verb in this sentence is *know,* and the subject pronoun *I* is its subject. Then you run into a linking verb, *was.* Think of a linking verb as an equal sign in a math problem. What comes before and after a linking verb should be equal. Therefore, both *it* and *she* are subject pronouns. The first one, *it,* is the actual subject and the second, *she,* is the subject complement. Now you have another verb, *recognize. I* is the subject pronoun acting as the subject of *recognize.*

277.

P, S, S (Lulu's parents hate <u>her</u> adding an extra course because <u>they</u> think <u>she</u> is too busy already.**)**

Lulu's parents don't hate her. They hate that their daughter might add an extra course. Therefore, the *her* is attached to *adding* and is a possessive pronoun. (In technical grammar terminology, *her* is a possessive attached to the gerund *adding.*) *They* is a subject pronoun, acting as the subject of the verb *think. She* is also a subject pronoun, acting as the subject of the verb *is.*

278.

S, P, P (After Helen had examined the clothing thoroughly, <u>she</u> tried on a coat and declared, "<u>Mine</u> is more stylish and warmer," as she threw <u>his</u> away.**)**

The subject pronoun *she* is the subject of the verb *tried* in this sentence. Both *mine* and *his* are possessive pronouns here; *mine* refers to Helen's coat, and *his* to an unknown male. By the way, the possessive pronoun *mine* is the subject of the verb *is,* but it's possessive because it expresses ownership.

279.

P, O, P (<u>My</u> jumbo slice of cake didn't tempt <u>him</u>, perhaps because <u>yours</u> was dry and tasteless.**)**

The sentence begins with a possessive pronoun, *my,* which is attached to *jumbo slice of cake.* The object pronoun *him* is the direct object of the verb *did tempt.* (The contraction *didn't* is short for *did not,* but *not* is an adverb, not part of the verb itself.) The possessive pronoun *yours* acts as the subject of the verb *was,* but it's still possessive because it expresses ownership.

280.

P, P, O, S (The director loved <u>your</u> jumping in front of the runaway horse in the final scene, but <u>your</u> mom told <u>herself</u> not to look at the screen while <u>you</u> were in danger.**)**

The director doesn't love *you;* the director loves the *jumping.* The possessive pronoun *your* is attached to *jumping.* The next *your* is also possessive, attached to *mom.* Next up is the indirect object *herself,* an object pronoun. Finally, you have the subject pronoun *you* working as the subject of the verb *were.* (Are you wondering what the direct object of *told* is? The direct object of *told* is *to look,* an infinitive.)

281.

P, S, P, P (<u>Their</u> pitcher has a better record than <u>I</u>, but <u>my</u> team wins more games than <u>his</u>.**)**

The possessive pronoun *their* is attached to the noun *pitcher.* To figure out the next pronoun, you need to add an implied word: *do.* Tuck that word into the sentence and you have *than I do.* Now you see that the subject pronoun *I* is the subject of the verb *do.* You come across another possessive pronoun, *my,* which is attached to the noun *team.* Lastly, you have to add in some implied words again. Think of the sentence as ending with *than his team does. His* is a possessive pronoun attached to the noun *team.*

282. P, S, P (Give <u>your</u> food to <u>whoever</u> is hungry, even though <u>our</u> supply is low.)

The possessive pronoun *your* is attached to the noun *food,* just as the possessive pronoun *our* is attached to the noun *supply.* In between these two pronouns is *whoever,* a subject pronoun that serves as the subject of the verb *is* in this sentence.

283. O, S, S (Melissa, <u>whom</u> the proctor scolded for lateness, says <u>she</u> actually arrived earlier than <u>I</u>.)

The object pronoun *whom* is the direct object of the verb *scolded. She* is a subject pronoun, acting as the subject of the verb *arrived. I* is also a subject, though its verb, *did,* is implied; *earlier than I did* is the complete expression.

284. P, P, P (When <u>our</u> computer crashed, James shook <u>its</u> screen and yelled, "<u>Whose</u> program was running recently?")

This sentence has three possessive pronouns: *our* is attached to the noun *computer, its* is attached to the noun *screen,* and *whose* is attached to the noun *program.*

285. S, P, S (<u>I</u> won't go to the pool with <u>his</u> family because that cousin splashes <u>whoever</u> is nearby.)

The subject pronoun *I* is the subject of the verb *will go.* (Are you wondering where *will go* is in this sentence? The answer is inside the contraction *won't go,* which is short for *will not go.* Take away *not,* which is an adverb, and you have *will go.*) The possessive pronoun *his* is attached to the noun *family.* Finally you have the subject pronoun *whoever,* which is the subject of the verb *is.*

286. his, their, they (Scott and his fellow racewalkers swing their arms as they hurry to the finish line.)

The possessive pronoun *his* is equivalent to *Scott's,* a possessive noun. The plural possessive form *their* takes the place of the plural possessive nouns, *Scott's and the racewalkers'. They,* a subject pronoun, acts as the subject of the verb *hurry.*

287. she, her, she (Keith and she gave her nephew five crayons, because Pam always prefers to select the colors she likes.)

In the first blank you need a subject pronoun, *she,* which is the subject of the verb *gave.* The possessive pronoun *her* replaces the possessive noun *Pam's.* The subject pronoun *she* works nicely as the subject of the verb *likes.*

288. him, they, me (Woody saluted him before they bowed to the audience and thanked me for directing the play.)

You need an object pronoun for the first blank, and *him* functions properly there as the object of the verb *saluted.* Two people may be replaced by one plural pronoun, *they,* which functions as the subject of the verb *bowed.* In the last blank you need an object pronoun, *me,* which is the direct object of the verb *thanked.*

289. **He, I, they (He and I will order food for 100 people, in case they all come.)**

The subject noun *David* may be replaced by the subject pronoun *he.* You also need a subject pronoun to refer to the speaker, and *I* fits perfectly. (Did you choose *myself?* If so, you made a common mistake. The *-self* pronouns work only for emphasis, as in *I myself will do it,* or to express action that doubles back, as in *I asked myself why I was in such trouble.*) In the last blank the subject pronoun *they* replaces the subject noun *guests.*

290. **me, you, its (Everyone but me plays the guitar, but you understand the instrument and its construction too.)**

The word *but* is usually a conjunction — a joining word — but the first time you see it in this sentence, it's a preposition. Prepositions need objects, and *me* is an object pronoun. (If you selected *myself,* you made a common mistake. The *-self* pronouns work only for emphasis, as in *I myself will do it,* or to express action that doubles back, as in *I asked myself why I bother with grammar.*) *You* is the subject pronoun acting as the subject of the verb *understand.* In the third blank, go for the possessive *its.* The contraction *it's,* by the way, means *it is* and isn't a possessive pronoun.

291. **She, her, she, him (She and her favorite singer, Bob Cassino, have never met, but she thinks of him as a friend anyway.)**

You need a subject pronoun, *she,* to act as the subject of the verb *have met* and, in the third blank, as the subject of the verb *thinks.* In the second blank a possessive pronoun, *her,* is attached to *favorite singer.* In the last blank, the object pronoun *him* functions as the object of the preposition *of.*

292. **her, I, them (Amy Tan's novels provide Ira and her with many hours of pleasant reading, but I prefer the films and watch them often.)**

The first blank in this sentence calls for an object pronoun to act as part of the direct object, *Ira and her.* In the second blank you need a subject pronoun, *I,* to act as the subject of the verb *prefer.* Next up is another object pronoun, *them,* which is the direct object of the verb *watch.*

293. **she, they, me (Daniel and she weeded the garden together, but they hired me to mow the lawn.)**

In the first blank you need a subject pronoun *(she)* to act as the subject of the verb *weeded.* You also need a subject pronoun — this time, the plural *they* — to replace *Daniel and Pamela* as the subjects of the verb *hired.* Finally, the object pronoun *me* functions as the direct object of *hired.*

294. **We, they, our (We and the managers explain the insurance policy to clients whenever they request our help.)**

A group including the speaker may be represented by *we, us,* or *our.* In the first blank you need the subject pronoun, *we,* to act as the subject of the verb *explain.* In the second blank, the subject pronoun *they* acts as the subject of the verb *request.* Finally, the possessive pronoun *our* represents the speakers in the last blank.

295. **he, it, them (Did he hit it and run around them?)**

Questions are easy to figure out if you rearrange the words into statement format: ____ did hit ___ and run around ____. Now you can see that you need a subject for the verb *did hit*, so select the subject pronoun *he* for the first blank. *The ball* is a thing, so the pronoun *it*, which works as either a subject or an object, replaces *the ball*. Last, you need the object pronoun *them* to replace *the bases* and serve as the object of the preposition *around*.

296. **him, their, it (Seeing Laura and him pulling their wagon up the hill was impressive, because it was very steep.)**

The subject of the sentence *(seeing)* is a verb form used as a noun — a gerund. A gerund may have an object, and this one has two — *Laura and James*. The object pronoun *him* replaces *James* as the object of the gerund, *seeing*. For the second blank you need a possessive that refers to two people, and *their* is perfect. Next, you have the subject pronoun *it*, referring to *the hill* and acting as the subject of the verb *was*.

297. **him, I, ourselves (To satisfy him, Mr. Palgrove, Beth and I handed in an excellent paper that we wrote by ourselves, without extra help.)**

The blank after the infinitive *to satisfy* calls for an object, so select the object pronoun *him* to represent the teacher, *Mr. Palgrove*. In the second blank, place the subject pronoun *I* to represent the speaker and to act as the subject of the verb *handed*. Last, the pronoun *ourselves* substitutes for Beth and the speaker and acts as the object of the preposition *by*. Did you choose *us* for the last blank? If so, you fell into a trap. *Us* is an object pronoun, and you need an object of the preposition. However, because the pronoun refers back to the subject, the pronoun *ourselves* is more appropriate.

298. **they, who, him (Do they know the boy who designed the winning sailboat for him?)**

Questions are easy to figure out if you rearrange the words into statement format: _____ do know the boy _____ designed the sailboat for _____. As you see, you need a subject for the verb *do know*, so select the subject pronoun *they* for the first blank. Now you need a subject pronoun to act as the subject of the verb *designed*. One possibility is *he*, but then you end up with a run-on sentence, because two complete thoughts are stuck together: *Do they know the boy?* and *He designed the winning sailboat for Henry*. The solution is the pronoun *who*, which relates the statement about design to the question about knowing the boy. *Who* is a subject pronoun, perfect for the role of subject of the verb *designed*. Finally, insert an object pronoun, *him*, into the last blank to act as the object of the preposition *for*.

Did you choose *himself* for the second blank because you assumed that a word, *that*, was implied? Count yourself right, because this sentence makes sense: *Do they know [that] the boy himself designed the winning sailboat for Henry?*

299. **us, that, us (All of us students worried about the test that was scheduled for us.)**

In the first and third blanks you need an object pronoun *(us)* to act as the object of the prepositions *of* and *for*. The second blank is tricky. You could plug in *it* to represent *the test*, but then you'd have a run-on sentence, because two complete thoughts would be present: *All of us students worried about the test* and *the test was scheduled for us*. The pronoun *that* solves the problem, because it relates the statement about the students' worries to the statement about the scheduled test.

300. who, them, me (Everyone who borrowed bowling shoes must return them to me by 5 o' clock.)

The pronoun *who* relates the statement about borrowing shoes to the pronoun *everyone*. Because you need a subject for *borrowed*, opt for *who*, a subject pronoun. The second blank calls for an object pronoun, *them*, which is the direct object of the verb *must return*. Finally, you need an object pronoun, *me*, as the object of the preposition *to*.

301. she, I, we, her (It was she at the front desk; Peter and I are sure we recognized her.)

The linking verb *was* should always be followed by a subject pronoun — in this case, *she*. Next up is a compound subject, *Peter and I*. If you chose *myself*, you fell into a trap. The *-self* pronouns work only when the action expressed by the verb doubles back, as in *she told herself not to panic*. For the third blank, you need another subject pronoun for the verb *recognized*. *We* covers both *Peter* and the speaker. Finally, the object pronoun *her* functions as the direct object of the verb *recognized*.

302. its, it (When a stuffed toy loses its nose, it looks even more adorable.)

The possessive pronoun *its*, like all possessive pronouns, has no apostrophe. With an apostrophe, *it's* is a contraction of *it is* — not the meaning you want here. For the subject of the verb *looks*, opt for *it*, a handy singular pronoun that may be either a subject or an object. Why *it* and not *they?* The pronoun replaces a singular noun, *toy*, so a plural doesn't work here.

303. whose, he, it (Ken doesn't know whose chewing gum is stuck to the table, but he wants it removed.)

In the first blank you need a possessive form, and *whose* fills that need. If you chose *who's*, you confused the contraction (*who is = who's*) with the possessive (*whose*). In the second blank you need a subject pronoun to replace *Ken*, so *he* is perfect. Lastly, you need the singular pronoun *it* to replace *gum. It*, fortunately, works as either a subject or an object. No worries there!

304. who, him, his (Deborah, who is sitting in the second row, will watch him with great attention in case Bill forgets his lines.)

In the first blank you need a subject pronoun, *who*, to act as the subject of *is sitting*. In the second blank, go for the object pronoun *him* to act as the direct object of the verb *will watch*. Last, you need a possessive pronoun (*his*) to replace the possessive noun *Bill's*.

305. her, me, we (Please don't tell her and me any jokes while we are trying to concentrate.)

The first two blanks call for object pronouns, so *her* and *me* work well here as the direct objects of the verb *do tell*. (Why not *don't tell?* The contraction *don't* is actually *do not*, and *not* is an adverb, not a verb.) In the last blank you need a subject pronoun, *we*, to replace *Allison and I*. (The speaker is always *I*.) *We* acts as the subject of the verb *are trying*.

Answers
301–400

306. **its, my, I, your (The bus with its 20 passengers flew by my stop, so I was late for your barbecue.)**

> The bus is a singular thing, so the possessive pronoun *its* does the job in the first blank. You also need possessive pronouns for the second and last blanks. *My* always refers to the speaker, and *your* always refers to the person spoken to. The third blank calls for a subject pronoun, and *I* fits perfectly. (Did you pick *it's* or *you're* for the first and last blanks? Those words are contractions of *it is* and *you are,* not possessive pronouns.)

307. **its, its (Watson and Sons pays its employees too little compared to its competitors.)**

> A company is a singular thing, even when — as in the case of *Watson and Sons* — the name may appear plural. Therefore, you should select the singular possessive pronoun *its* for both blanks. (Did you pick *it's* or *they're?* Those words are short for *it is* and *they are,* not possessive pronouns.)

308. **he, she (Are Jason and he the funniest comedians in the show, or is she?)**

> Change this question to a statement and your choice is clearer: *Jason and _____ are the funniest comedians in the show, or _____ is.* The secret here is the linking verb *are.* Both sides of the linking verb require subject pronouns. Therefore, *Frank* becomes *he* and *Valerie* becomes *she.*

309. **himself, he, it (Jeff told himself that he would understand the question and write it quickly.)**

> When the action doubles back on the subject, a *-self* pronoun is justified. Such is the situation here: *Jeff told himself,* not someone else. Next up is a subject pronoun, *he,* that functions as the subject of the verbs *would understand* and *write.* Lastly, the neuter pronoun *it* represents the noun *essay.*

310. **her, he, me, he, me (Mack told the secret to Al and her before he told me, but he gave me more details.)**

> In the first blank you need the object pronoun *her* to act as the object of the preposition *to.* In the second blank, the subject pronoun *he* is the subject of the verb *told.* Now you need an object pronoun *(me)* to act as the object of the verb *told,* a subject pronoun *(he)* as the subject of the verb *gave,* and finally an object pronoun *(me)* for the verb *gave.*

311. **she, they, her (Jeremy is as nervous as she when they visit her parents.)**

> The secret to this sentence is that some of the words are understood, not stated. Add in the implied words, and your choice of pronouns is easier: *Jeremy is as nervous as Gloria is. Gloria* is the subject of the implied verb *is,* so you need a subject pronoun *(she)* to replace *Gloria.* Next you need a plural subject pronoun *(they)* to represent *Jeremy and Gloria.* For the last blank, the feminine, singular, possessive pronoun *her* replaces *Gloria's.*

312. my, her, me (Elizabeth hates my calling her "Liz" and has forbidden me to do so.)

This sentence contains what English teachers call a *gerund* — a verb form ending in *-ing* that is used as a noun. Before a gerund, you need a possessive form. You can forget about English-teacher terminology and solve this sentence with logic: Elizabeth doesn't hate *me;* she hates being called "Liz." The possessive pronoun *my* tilts your attention to *calling her "Liz,"* where it should be. Next you need an object pronoun, *her,* to act as the object of the gerund. (Gerunds, though they function as nouns, keep some of the properties of verbs, including the ability to have an object.) In the last blank, the object pronoun *me* is the object of the verb *has forbidden.*

313. who, its (Fran, who Charlie thinks should take a course in public speaking, is not open to its subject matter.)

This sentence contains several different ideas. Untangle them and the pronoun choices become easier. Start by pairing each verb with its subject. In this list, I've underlined the verbs in each idea: (1) *Fran is not open to the course's subject matter* (2) _____ *should take a course in public speaking* (3) *Charlie thinks.* Can you see that you need a subject for *should take?* Bingo: The subject pronoun *who* does the job. The second blank is simple; opt for the possessive pronoun *its* to replace the singular possessive noun, *course's.*

314. me, your, I (Between you and me, no one is happier about your getting a new puppy than I.)

The preposition *between* calls for an object pronoun, so *me* is the one you want. (*Between you and I* is a common expression, but it's also wrong.) For the second blank you need a possessive pronoun because the happiness is caused by *getting a new puppy,* not by a person. The possessive pronoun *your* shifts the attention of the reader or listener to the action. This construction is, in English-teacher terms, "possessive attached to a gerund." Now for the last blank. A word *(am)* is implied, but not stated in the sentence. The sentence, with that word added, explains that *no one is happier . . . than I am.* The subject pronoun *I* is the subject of the implied verb *am.*

315. you, whoever, he (Don't you think whoever wants to succeed should study harder than he?)

The person or people being spoken to are always referred to as *you,* which is conveniently correct for both singular and plural situations. When you refer to anyone in a group, you're in *whoever/whomever* territory. Here you need a subject for *wants,* so go for the subject pronoun *whoever.* To solve the third blank, add the implied verb *does* to the end of the sentence, which then reads *harder than _____ does.* Clearly you need a subject pronoun for the verb *does,* and *he* fills the gap.

316. I, whoever, my (Alex and I plan to read the article and respond to whoever has complaints about my work.)

The verb *plan* has a compound subject, *Alex and I.* (*I* is a subject pronoun and always refers to the speaker.) The next verb in the sentence is *has,* so you need a subject pronoun, *whoever,* to act as the subject of *has.* Did you choose *whomever* because you saw the preposition *to?* If so, you fell into a trap. True, *to* needs an object, but in this sentence its object is *whoever has complaints about my work.* The last blank is easy. The possessive pronoun *my* is attached to *work.*

Answers
301–400

317. he, its (The top students, Nick and he, will receive awards from the school, which always honors its scholars at the end of the year.)

The first blank is easy if you clear away some of the camouflage. Who *will receive awards? Nick and James will receive awards,* or, with the pronoun inserted, *Nick and he will receive awards.* The second blank refers to a singular, neuter, possessive noun *(school's),* which you can replace with *its.*

318. whoever, I, it (The letter tucked into the bottle began, "To whoever finds this bottle"; I read it eagerly.)

Your choices for the first blank are *whoever* and *whomever.* Because the sentence begins with the preposition *to,* you may be tempted to select the object pronoun *whomever.* Nope! The verb *finds* needs a subject, *whoever.* In case you're wondering about the object of the preposition: It's the entire clause, *whoever finds this bottle.* On to the second blank: Here you need the subject pronoun *I* to act as the subject of the verb *read.* The object pronoun *it* finishes the sentence, functioning as the object of the verb *read.*

319. I, she, who (The dancer and I believe that it is she who stole the salt shaker.)

In the first blank, the subject pronoun *I* acts as the subject of the verb *believe.* In the second blank, you need a subject pronoun *(she)* to act as a subject complement, because you have a linking verb *(is).* Finally, you need *who* to substitute for *Frances* in the last blank. *Who* is a subject pronoun, acting as the subject of the verb *stole.*

320. whomever, him, them (When Jason told you to ask whomever you like to work on the project with him, did you choose them?)

Break this question into parts to make your life easier. The first part is fine as it is, so direct your attention to the second part. The verb there is *like,* and the subject of *like* is *you.* You don't need a subject or a subject complement, so the answer can't be *whoever.* In fact, you need an object — *whomever.* The preposition *with* requires an object pronoun, so the singular, masculine, object pronoun *him* fits well here. Now look at the last part. Change it into a statement: *you did choose _____.* The verb is *did choose,* the subject is *you,* and the blank should be filled with an object pronoun, *them.*

321. III. (Have you eaten?)

The first question *(Have eaten?)* lacks a subject, and the second question *(Have you eaten)* has no endmark (a question mark). The third puts everything together correctly: a subject-verb pair *(you* is the subject and *have eaten* is the verb), a complete thought, and an endmark (a question mark).

322. None of the sentences

Each statement begins with a subject, *Boris,* but no verb pairs with Boris, so no statement is a complete sentence.

323. **I. (At the army museum, many exhibits caught our attention.)**

Sentence I is complete because it has a subject-verb pair (*exhibits* is the subject and *caught* is the verb). It also has an endmark (a period). Sentence II (*At the army museum, many exhibits caught our attention*) lacks an endmark, and Sentence III (*At the army museum, many exhibits catching our attention*) has a subject (*exhibits*) but no matching verb. The *-ing* form of a verb never functions as a verb unless a form of the verb *to be* is attached. Therefore, *many exhibits are catching our attention* would work, but not *catching* alone.

324. **II. (Balloons of all colors of the rainbow floated above us in the sky!)**

Sentence I (*Balloons of all colors of the rainbow above us in the sky!*) lacks a verb to pair with the subject, *balloons.* Sentence III (*Balloons of all colors of the rainbow floated above us in the sky*) has no endmark. Only Sentence II has an endmark and a subject-verb pair (*balloons* is the subject and *floated* is the verb).

325. **All of the sentences**

Although the subject-verb pair (*burglar came*) moves around in these three statements, it's present in every one. All three also end with periods and express a complete thought. Therefore, all are complete sentences.

326. **All of the sentences**

These three short sentences are all complete. You don't get many details, but you do get a complete statement, a true subject-verb pair (*I dance),* and an endmark.

327. **I. (Standing in the aisle, Charlotte scanned the audience, searching for an empty seat.)**

The first sentence has it all: a subject-verb pair (*Charlotte scanned),* a complete thought, and an endmark (a period). Sentence II (*Standing in the aisle, Charlotte scanned the audience and searched for an empty seat*) lacks an endmark. The third sentence (*Standing in the aisle, Charlotte, scanning the audience, searching for an empty seat*) has no true subject-verb pair. True, several verb forms are present in Sentence III, but all act as descriptions of *Charlotte.* None function as verbs.

328. **II. (The little dog chewed his food quickly and then ran off to play.)**

The first sentence (*The little dog, chewing his food quickly and then running off to play*) is a fragment, with no true subject-verb pair. *Chewing his food quickly and then running off to play* is a description, not a verb to match *dog,* the subject. The second sentence is perfect: It has a subject-verb pair (*dog chewed and ran),* a complete thought, and an endmark (a period). The third choice (*The little dog chewed his food quickly and then ran off to play*) lacks an endmark. Therefore, only Sentence II is complete.

329. **II. (Who is solving the puzzle?)**

The words are the same in each sentence, but only the second one expresses a complete thought because it makes sense as a question. As a statement (Sentence I: *Who is solving the puzzle.*) or an exclamation (Sentence III: *Who is solving the puzzle!*), the words leave you hanging. Only Sentence II is complete.

330. **I. and III. (I. Alan, having changed his clothes, was ready for the dance. III. Having changed his clothes, Alan was ready for the dance.)**

Sentences I and III have a true subject-verb pair *(Alan was)*, an endmark (a period), and a complete thought. Therefore, Sentences I and III are complete. Sentence II *(Having changed his clothes, Alan, ready for the dance)* has a subject *(Alan)* but no verb. By the way, *Having changed* is not a verb. That expression looks like a verb, but it doesn't pair with *Alan*. Instead, it describes *Alan*.

331. **III. (It was nice to meet you.)**

Sentences I *(Nice to meet you)* and II *(Nice meeting you!)* are common expressions, but only Sentence III has a true subject-verb pair *(It was)*. Therefore, only Sentence III is complete.

332. **I. and III. (I. The table fell over, but it didn't break. III. The table fell over but didn't break.)**

The first sentence employs a conjunction *(but)* to join two complete thoughts: *the table fell over* and *it didn't break*. The second sentence *(The table fell over, it didn't break)* tries to link these ideas with a comma. Nope! A comma isn't strong enough to join two complete thoughts. The last sentence uses a conjunction *(but)* to join two verbs *(fell, did break)* to one subject *(table)*. No problems there! Sentences I and III are correct.

333. **II. and III. (II. Miami has a warm climate, and Greenland is much colder. III. Miami has a warm climate, but Greenland is much colder.)**

Sentence I *(Miami has a warm climate, Greenland is much colder)* links two complete thoughts with just a comma, but a comma can't perform that function. Sentence II adds a conjunction *(and)*, so it's grammatically legal. Similarly, Sentence III adds the conjunction *but,* so it's also correct.

334. **I. and II. (I. Although she had reviewed the material thoroughly, Lisa was still nervous before her test. II. Lisa was still nervous before her test, although she had reviewed the material thoroughly.)**

In the first two sentences, you have a complete thought *(Lisa was still nervous before her test)* and an incomplete thought *(although she had reviewed the material thoroughly)*. Both are correct, regardless of the location of the incomplete thought. The third sentence *(She had reviewed the material thoroughly, Lisa was still nervous before her test)* has two complete thoughts: *Lisa was still nervous before her test* and *she had reviewed the material thoroughly*. No conjunction joins them, so the sentence is incorrect.

335. **I. and II. (I. Tomorrow Laura will hike two miles, or she will work out for an hour at the gym. II. Tomorrow Laura will hike two miles, and she will work out for an hour at the gym.)**

Sentence I links two complete ideas *(Tomorrow Laura will hike two miles* and *she will work out for an hour at the gym)* with a conjunction *(or)*. Sentence II links the same ideas with a different conjunction *(and)*. Both are correct. Sentence III *(Tomorrow Laura will hike two miles, she will work out for an hour at the gym)* relies on a comma to link the two ideas. Incorrect! A comma is not strong enough to join clauses (statements with *subject-verb* pairs).

336. **II. and III. (II. The baby cried for hours, and no one could quiet her. III. The baby cried for hours, because no one could quiet her.)**

In Sentence I *(The baby cried for hours, no one could quiet her)*, two statements *(the baby cried for hours* and *no one could quiet her)* are joined only by a comma — not a proper way to connect these ideas. The second and third sentences use conjunctions *(and* in Sentence II and *because* in Sentence III) to link these statements. Both are correct. Remember: A comma can't join clauses — a statement containing a subject-verb pair — but a semicolon or conjunction can.

337. **All of the sentences**

In Sentences I *(Before she met the ambassadors, the President examined their credentials carefully)* and II *(The President examined their credentials carefully before she met the ambassadors)*, the conjunction *before* links these two ideas: *she met the ambassadors* and *the President examined their credentials*. Both Sentence I and Sentence II are correct. Sentence III *(The President first examined their credentials carefully, and then she met the ambassadors)* uses the conjunction *and* to accomplish the same goal — also correct.

388. **I. (The can is full, so please empty it.)**

The conjunction *so* joins two ideas in Sentence I: *the can is full* and *please empty it*. Both Sentence II *(The can is full, you should empty it)* and Sentence III *(The can is full, please empty it)* try to connect these ideas with commas — an illegal joining.

339. **All of the sentences**

In Sentences I *(Although they had arrived late, the manager refused to shorten the team practice)* and II *(The manager refused to shorten the team practice, although they had arrived late)*, the conjunction *although* links two ideas *(they had arrived late* and *the manager refused to shorten the team practice)*. In Sentence III *(They had arrived late, but the manager refused to shorten the team practice)*, the conjunction *but* does the same job. All are correct.

340. **I. (Even though George has never studied French, he understands a few simple words.)**

In Sentence I, the conjunction *even though* makes a logical and grammatically correct connection between these two ideas: *George has never studied French* and *he understands a few simple words*. Sentence II *(George has never studied French, however, he understands a few simple words)* relies on an adverb, *however*, to link these ideas, but *however* may not perform that function without a semicolon between *French* and *however*. Sentence III *(George has never studied French, he understands a few simple words anyway)* uses a comma to join these ideas — another improper joining. Only Sentence I is correct.

341. **II. (Stamp collecting is a fascinating hobby, although it can be expensive.)**

Sentence I *(Stamp collecting is a fascinating hobby, it can be expensive)* attempts to link two complete sentences *(Stamp collecting is a fascinating hobby* and *it can be expensive)* with a comma — not proper English grammar. Sentence III *(Stamp collecting is a fascinating hobby, additionally it can be expensive)* tries to link these ideas with *additionally*, an adverb that may not join complete sentences. Only Sentence II employs a conjunction, *although*, to do the job, so Sentence II is the only correct choice.

342. II. and III. (II. Jim dropped the fragile vase; consequently, it shattered into a thousand pieces. III. Jim dropped the fragile vase, and consequently it shattered into a thousand pieces.)

The adverb *consequently* is long and appears important, but it's just an adverb and can't legally join two complete thoughts on its own. Therefore, Sentence I *(Jim dropped the fragile vase, consequently, it shattered into a thousand pieces)* is a run-on. Sentence II adds a semicolon, and III inserts a true conjunction *(and),* so both II and III are correct.

343. I. and III. (I. Penny turned off her phone, for she didn't want to be interrupted. III. Penny turned off her phone because she didn't want to be interrupted.)

In Sentence I, the conjunction *for* links two complete sentences *(Penny turned off her phone* and *she didn't want to be interrupted).* In Sentence III, the conjunction *because* performs the same function. Both of these are correct. Sentence II *(Penny turned off her phone, she didn't want to be interrupted)* attempts to link ideas with a comma, but a comma may not join complete sentences.

344. I. (I went to Vermont, where I met many skiers.)

In Sentence I, *where* relates the last word of the first idea *(I went to Vermont)* to the second idea *(I met many skiers).* This joining is legal. Sentence II *(I went to Vermont, there I met many skiers)* tries to link the ideas with *there,* and Sentence III *(I went to Vermont, I met many skiers there)* sends in a comma to do the job. Neither *there* nor a comma may properly combine these ideas.

345. III. (Jack's suit is old; he still looks good in it though.)

Nevertheless (as in Sentence I: *Jack's suit is old, nevertheless, he still looks good in it*) and *however* (as in Sentence II: *Jack's suit is old, however, he still looks good in it*) seem to be important, strong words — and they are! Unfortunately, neither is a conjunction and therefore neither may join two complete thoughts. Only Sentence III is grammatically legal, because the semicolon is powerful enough to link two complete thoughts.

346. All of the sentences

In Sentence I *(The mechanic checked the steering wheel, which was fine, but he said that the brakes were defective),* the conjunction *but* links two complete thoughts *(the mechanic checked the steering wheel, which was fine* and *he said that the brakes were defective).* Tucked inside each of those statements is still another statement *(which was fine* in the first half of the sentence and *that the brakes were defective* in the second half of the sentence). Those tucked-in statements are linked to the main idea by relative pronouns, *which* and *that.* Relative pronouns relate one idea to another, so everything is fine in Sentence I. Sentence II *(The mechanic checked the steering wheel, which was fine, and then he said that the brakes were defective)* relies on the conjunction *and* to join ideas, and Sentence III *(The mechanic checked the steering wheel, which was fine, although he said that the brakes were defective)* gives the joining job to *although,* another conjunction. Because the ideas in these sentences are joined by conjunctions, they are all correct.

347. **held the tray (Teresa held the tray as I placed the glasses on it.)**

The original statement is a fragment because there's no true subject-verb pair. Insert *held the tray* and you have *Teresa held,* a fine subject-verb match. Did you opt for *was holding?* That answer is also fine. If you selected *holds,* you're wrong, because the verb in the second portion of the sentence *(placed)* is in past tense, so a present-tense verb *(holds)* is inappropriate for the first part of the sentence.

348. **box. Their contributions fund (Generous donors drop coins in the box. Their contributions fund scholarships.)**

The original statement is a run-on — two complete ideas jammed together without a proper conjunction or a semicolon. You can make two sentences, placing a period after *box* and capitalizing *their* to correct the error. You can also insert a semicolon between *box* and *their* or insert a conjunction, such as *and.*

349. **Who likes ice cream?**

The original lacks an endmark, and only a question mark makes sense. With a period or an exclamation mark, you have an incomplete idea.

350. **No change**

The original is a command directed to *Margaret.* No change is needed because the sentence has a subject-verb pair, *you* (understood but not stated) and *place.* All complete and correct! Direct address words, by the way, can roam around. *Margaret* may appear at the beginning, middle, or end of the sentence without creating any problems.

351. **The dictionary rested (The dictionary rested on a shelf in the corner.)**

The original statement lacks a subject-verb pair. Change *resting* to *rested* and you're all set, because the subject *dictionary* pairs well with the verb *rested.* You can also pair *dictionary* with *was resting, rests, will rest,* and *has rested.*

352. **relaxing, but my aunt prefers (I find knitting relaxing, but my aunt prefers embroidery.)**

The two complete thoughts in the original *(I find knitting relaxing* and *my aunt prefers embroidery)* can't be connected with a simple comma. A semicolon or a conjunction such as *but* properly links these ideas. You can also correct the original by making two sentences, placing a period after *relaxing* and capitalizing *my.* Another possible correction is to use the conjunction *although* or *even though* before *my aunt.*

353. **were covered (Those mountain peaks were covered with snow even in the summer.)**

The original appears to have a matching subject-verb pair, but *mountain peaks* aren't performing the action *(covered),* so *covered* is a description, not a verb. Insert *were* to create a passive-voice verb, and the subject-verb pair works: *mountain peaks* (subject) *were covered* (verb). The passive verb allows the subject to receive the action. If you chose *are covered,* you're also correct.

354. **No change**

The subject-verb pair here is *Mattie went*. The underlined portion is just part of a description — what English teachers call a participle, to be exact — that supplies more information about *Mattie*. No change is needed.

355. **lot; be sure (Park the truck in the lot; be sure to lock it.)**

The original improperly joins two complete ideas (both commands with the same implied subject, *you*) with a comma. Nope! Change the comma to a semicolon and you're fine. You can also place a period after *lot* and begin a new sentence by capitalizing *be*. Another possibility is to insert a conjunction (*and,* for example) before *be*.

356. **There were a pen and pencil on the desk in the corner of the living room.**

The original has no verb. An easy correction is to add *there were*. Now the subject of the sentence is *pen and pencil* and the verb is *were*. (Surprised? *There* is an adverb, not a subject noun.) You can correct this sentence in other ways, too. For example, you might insert *lay* or *were* before *on the desk*. The present-tense verb *are* works also.

357. **performs better in the annual talent show? (Which performs better in the annual talent show?)**

The original sentence lacks an endmark, and only a question mark creates a complete thought.

358. **Accepting an internship, Bert always plans (Accepting an internship, Bert always plans his next career move, which will lead him to success.)**

The original begins with a descriptive verb form (a participle), which gives you more information about *Bert*. The problem is that the original lacks a verb to pair with *Bert*, not just to describe him. Change *planning* to *plans* and you're fine. You could also change *always planning* to *always planned* or *was always planning* or *is always planning*.

359. **No change**

The original sentence has everything it needs — a subject-verb pair *(hose sprays),* a complete thought, and an endmark.

360. **side, which highlights (Picasso's statue has a gently curved side, which highlights the grain of the marble.)**

The beginning of the original sentence is fine, but the underlined portion lacks a matching subject-verb pair. The pronoun *which* is the subject, but *highlighting* is a description. Go for *highlights*. Other possible corrections are *side, which is highlighting* and *side, which highlighted.*

361.

No change

The underlined portion of the sentence appears to be incomplete because no subject appears and you have only a partial verb. However, the rules of grammar allow you to imply a subject in one portion of the sentence, so long as the subject that appears in the other portion of the sentence is the same as the implied subject. You're also allowed to imply part of the verb. Here, the implied words between *while* and *swimming* are *Harriet was*. The subjects match, so this one is fine as it is. You could also choose *Harriet swam* and end up with a correct sentence.

362.

ADJ, ADV, ADJ (The <u>green</u> scarf slipped <u>off</u> her <u>bare</u> head.)

What kind of *scarf*? A *green scarf*. *Green* is an adjective describing the noun *scarf*. Where did the *scarf slip*? It *slipped off*. *Off* is an adverb describing the verb *slipped*. What kind of *head*? A *bare head*. *Bare* is an adjective describing *head*.

363.

ADJ, ADV, ADV (Put these <u>shiny</u> cups <u>below</u> because I may use them <u>later</u>.)

What kind of *cups*? *Shiny cups*. *Shiny* is an adjective describing the noun *cups*. *Put where*? *Put below*. *Below* is an adverb describing the verb *put*. *May use* when? *May use later*. *Later* is an adverb describing the verb *may use*.

364.

ADJ, ADV, ADJ, ADJ (<u>Good</u> journalists <u>still</u> cover <u>important</u> stories, not <u>sensational</u> gossip.)

What kind of *journalists*? *Good journalists*. *Good* is an adjective describing *journalists*. *Cover* when? *Cover still*. *Still* is an adverb describing the verb *cover*. What kind of *stories*? *Important stories*. *Important* is an adjective describing the noun *stories*. What kind of *gossip*? *Sensational gossip*. *Sensational* is an adjective describing the noun *gossip*.

365.

ADJ, ADJ, ADV, N (<u>Five</u> <u>tiny</u> mice curled up and squeaked <u>softly</u> when they sensed <u>danger</u>.)

How many *mice*? *Five mice*. What kind of *mice*? *Tiny mice*. *Five* and *tiny* are adjectives describing the noun *mice*. *Squeaked* how? *Squeaked softly*. *Softly* is an adverb describing the verb *squeaked*. *Danger* is neither an adjective nor an adverb. It's a noun, not a description.

366.

ADJ, ADJ, ADJ, ADV (The <u>escaped</u> prisoners, <u>tired</u> and <u>hungry</u>, <u>eventually</u> surrendered.)

What kind of *prisoners*? *Escaped prisoners*. *Escaped* is an adjective describing the noun *prisoners*. *Tired* and *hungry* also describe *prisoners*, even though these words appear after that noun, not before (the usual spot for adjectives). *Surrendered* when? *Surrendered eventually*. *Eventually* is an adverb describing the verb *surrendered*.

367.

ADJ, ADV, ADJ, ADJ (Your <u>school</u> shoes are <u>too</u> <u>tight</u>, so we must buy a <u>larger</u> size.)

What kind of *shoes*? *School shoes*. *School* is an adjective describing the noun *shoes*. Ask the same question, and you also get the answer *tight*. *Tight* is an adjective describing the noun *shoes*. *Tight* is located after the linking verb *are* because it completes the meaning of the subject-linking verb pair: *shoes are tight*. Now ask another question: How *tight*? *Too tight*. *Too* is an adverb describing the adjective *tight*. Next up: What kind of *size*? *Larger size*. *Larger* is an adjective describing the noun *size*.

368. **ADJ, ADJ, ADJ, N (When Luke sounded <u>hoarse</u>, his <u>trusted</u> <u>voice</u> coach gave <u>him</u> honey and lemon.)**

Sounded is a linking verb, and every statement with a linking verb needs something to complete the meaning. In this sentence, ask *Luke sounded* what? *Hoarse. Hoarse* is an adjective describing *Luke.* Now ask: What kind of *coach?* You get two answers — *trusted coach* and *voice coach. Trusted* and *voice* are both adjectives describing the noun *coach.* The last underlined word, *him,* is a pronoun functioning as an indirect object. It's neither an adjective nor an adverb.

369. **ADJ, N, ADJ, ADJ (<u>Identical</u> twins are <u>playing</u> <u>one</u> role in that <u>Broadway</u> play.)**

What kind of *twins? Identical twins. Identical* is an adjective describing the noun *twins. Playing* is neither an adjective nor an adverb. In this sentence, *playing* functions as part of the present progressive verb, *are playing.* How many *roles? One role. One* is an adjective describing the noun *role.* What kind of *play? Broadway play. Broadway* is an adjective describing the noun *play.*

370. **ADJ, ADJ, ADV, ADV (A <u>vacant</u> building, <u>unguarded</u>, may attract squatters who live <u>there</u> <u>illegally</u>.)**

What kind of *building? Vacant building. Vacant* is an adjective describing the noun *building.* The *building* is also *unguarded,* so *unguarded* is another adjective describing *building,* placed after the word it describes instead of in front — the usual location for an adjective. *Live* where? *Live there. There* is an adverb describing the verb *live. Live* how or under what conditions? *Live illegally. Illegally* is an adverb describing the verb *live.*

371. **ADJ, ADV, ADV, ADJ (Be <u>smart</u>. Drive <u>defensively</u>, and you'll arrive <u>safely</u> and enjoy a <u>lovely</u> vacation.)**

This sentence begins with a command based on a linking verb, *be.* After a linking verb, you need a word to complete the idea. Ask the usual question, *be* what? *Be smart. Smart* is an adjective describing the understood subject of *be, you.* (The command is actually *You be smart,* but the *you* is implied.) Next up is another command, *drive.* Ask, *drive* how? *Drive defensively* and *safely. Defensively* and *safely* are adverbs describing the verb *drive.* Now examine *lovely.* It looks like an adverb because it ends in *-ly,* as many adverbs do. However, *lovely* isn't attached to *enjoy. Lovely* doesn't tell you how, when, where, or why you'll *enjoy a vacation.* Instead, *lovely* expresses what kind of *vacation* you'll have if you *arrive safely.* Therefore, *lovely* is an adjective describing the noun *vacation.*

372. **ADJ, ADJ, N, ADV (The <u>production</u> crew is <u>responsible</u> for setting the props on stage <u>before</u> the curtain <u>first</u> rises.)**

What kind of *crew? Production crew. Production* is an adjective describing the noun *crew.* After the linking verb *is, responsible* gives you more information about the *crew.* Therefore, *responsible* is also an adjective describing the noun *crew. Before* sounds like an adverb because it refers to time, and adverbs may express when an action or state of being occurred. However, in this sentence *before* links two ideas (clauses, in grammatical terms) — *the production crew is responsible for setting the props on stage* and *the curtain first rises. Before* functions as a conjunction in this sentence, not as an adverb. Turn your attention to the last underlined word. *Rises* when? *Rises first,* or, *first rises. First* is an adverb describing the verb *rises.*

373. ADV, ADJ, ADV, ADJ, ADJ, ADJ (Chef John is <u>justly</u> <u>famous</u> for his use of <u>extremely</u> <u>fresh</u> ingredients and <u>fast</u> preparation of <u>complicated</u> dishes.)

The linking verb *is* alerts you to the fact that you need a completion for the statement that the verb *is* appears in: *Chef John is* what? *Famous. Famous* is an adjective describing *Chef John.* How *famous? Justly famous. Justly* is an adverb describing the adjective *famous.* What kind of *ingredients? Fresh ingredients. Fresh* is an adjective describing the noun *ingredients.* How *fresh? Extremely fresh. Extremely* is an adverb describing the adjective *fresh.* What kind of preparation? *Fast preparation. Fast* is an adjective in this context because it describes the noun *preparation.* (In another context, *ran fast,* for example, the word *fast* may be an adverb, describing a verb — in this example, *ran.*) Last one: What kind of *dishes? Complicated dishes. Complicated* is an adjective describing *dishes.*

374. pleased, local, national (The reporter was pleased to see his local story attract national attention.)

The adjective *pleased* completes the meaning of the subject-linking verb pair, *reporter was. Local* is an adjective describing the noun *story,* and *national* is an adjective describing the noun *attention.*

375. common, bad, social (Are common electronic devices bad for social connections?)

The adjective *common* describes the noun *devices,* just as the adjective *social* describes the noun *connections.* To fill the middle blank, take a look at the linking verb, *are.* You need something to complete the subject-linking verb pair, which in this sentence is *devices are. The devices are bad. Bad* is an adjective describing *devices.*

376. deep, cool, immediately (Wading into deep waters, Ron felt cool immediately.)

The adjective *deep* describes the noun *waters. Cool,* another adjective, describes *Ron.* It follows and completes the subject-linking verb statement, *Ron felt.* The adverb *immediately* explains when *Ron felt cool.*

377. new, energetically, well (Ben strummed his new guitar energetically but not well.)

Two adverbs tell you how *Ben strummed* — *energetically* and *well.* (Yes, the sentence states that *Ben strummed* not *well,* but you should ignore *not* because you weren't asked about that word.) An adjective, *new,* describes the noun *guitar.*

378. large, smoothly, good (The large delivery van runs smoothly, so its contents remain in good condition.)

The adjective *large* describes the noun *van* (or *delivery van,* if you prefer). How does the van run? *Smoothly,* an adverb that describes the verb *runs. Good* is an adjective describing the noun *condition.*

379. loyal, loudly, seriously (Our show's loyal audience protests loudly whenever the network seriously threatens to cancel it.)

The adjective *loyal* describes the noun *audience.* The adverb *loudly* describes the verb *protests.* (*Protests* how? *Protests loudly.*) *Seriously,* another adverb, describes the verb *threatens.*

380. **extremely, generous, minimal (Jackson's gift was extremely generous, even though he considered the donation minimal.)**

This sentence is easy if you begin with the middle blank. The adjective *generous* follows the linking verb *was* and completes the meaning of the subject-linking verb statement — *gift was generous.* Okay, how *generous? Extremely generous. Extremely* is an adverb describing the adjective *generous.* Lastly, the adjective *minimal* describes the noun *donation.*

381. **happy, surely, controversial (Dave feels happy because the voters surely agree with his position on the controversial issue.)**

The linking verb *feels* in this sentence is followed by the adjective *happy,* which describes *Dave* (the subject). In the second blank, the adverb *surely* describes the verb *agree.* In the last blank, the adjective *controversial* describes the noun *issue.*

382. **nicely, overly, rough ("Play nicely," exclaimed the overly strict babysitter, but the children continued their rough games.)**

The adverb *nicely* describes the verb *play,* and the adverb *overly* describes the adjective *strict.* (How *strict? Overly strict.*) In the last blank, the adjective *rough* describes the noun *games.*

383. **really, unusual, rare (It's really unusual for an amateur to discover such a rare fossil.)**

The contraction *it's* expands to the subject-linking verb pair, *it is.* Any statement with a linking verb needs a completion, and in this case you have an adjective, *unusual.* Now ask, "How *unusual?*" The answer is *really unusual.* The adverb *really* describes the adjective *unusual.* Last, you have an adjective, *rare,* describing the noun *fossil.*

384. **hard, low, sadly (Mina worked hard, but the low grade she sadly read on her paper did not reflect her efforts.)**

The word *hard* may be either an adjective or an adverb. *(Hardly,* on the other hand, is an adverb meaning *scarcely* or *barely.)* In this sentence *hard* is an adverb describing how Mina *worked. Low* is an adjective describing her *grade,* and *sadly* is an adverb telling you how she *read.* By the way, *lowly* is also an adjective, even though it ends with the usual adverb letters, *-ly.* However, the adjective *lowly* means "humble" or "low status."

385. **badly, promptly, gentle (Children who behave badly should be scolded promptly and then given a chance to improve with the gentle guidance of their caretakers.)**

The adverb *badly* describes the verb *behave,* and the adverb *promptly* describes the verb *scolded.* The adjective *gentle* describes the noun *guidance.*

386. **Ripe, sweet, bitter (Ripe plums taste sweet, but fruit picked too soon may be bitter.)**

The adjective *ripe* describes the noun *plums.* Next up is the linking verb, *taste,* which must be followed by an adjective to complete the meaning of the subject-linking-verb expression, *plums taste.* The adjective *sweet* works well here, describing *plums.* The last portion of the sentence has another linking verb, *may be,* paired with the subject, *fruit.* Thus you need another adjective, *bitter,* to describe *fruit.*

387.

rapidly, sharply, first (Walk rapidly down the hall and turn sharply when you reach the first door on the left.)

The adverb *rapidly* describes the verb *walk,* just as the adverb *sharply* describes the verb *turn. First,* an adjective, describes the noun *door.*

388.

bad, insultingly, important (I feel bad that I spoke insultingly to my most important client.)

The verb *feel* is a linking verb, so the subject-verb statement needs something to complete the meaning. In this sentence you need the adjective *bad,* because that word describes the person speaking, *I* (the subject). (To feel *badly* refers to your ability to feel — how sensitive your fingers are, for example.) In the second blank, the adverb *insultingly* explains how *I spoke.* Because you're describing a verb, you need the adverb. In the final blank, the adjective *important* describes the noun *client.*

389.

merry, sad, nervous (Eileen appeared merry at the party, but afterwards she sounded sad and nervous.)

The linking verbs *appeared* and *sounded* are both completed by adjectives: *merry, sad,* and *nervous.* The first *(merry)* describes the subject of *appeared (Eileen),* and the second pair *(sad, nervous)* describes the subject of the verb *sounded (she).*

390.

wicked, uncomfortable, short (Anything wicked makes us feel uncomfortable, at least for a short time.)

The adjective *wicked* describes the pronoun *anything.* (Yes, adjectives may follow the words they describe, though the usual position is in front.) The linking verb *feel* should be followed by an adjective, because *uncomfortable* describes the pronoun *us,* not the manner in which someone *feels.* Finally, the adjective *short* describes the noun *time.*

391.

certainly, patiently, fun (It's certainly true that young children often wait less patiently for their turns to play fun games.)

In this sentence, the adverb *certainly* describes the adjective *true.* (How *true? Certainly true.*) You also need an adverb to describe how children wait — less *patiently.* Finally, the adjective *fun* describes the noun *games.*

392.

widely, surely, dismal (The widely seen broadcast was surely helpful to the show's dismal ratings.)

The adverb *widely* describes the adjective *seen,* in the same way that the adverb *surely* describes the adjective *helpful.* The adjective *dismal* describes the noun *ratings.*

393.

suddenly, firmly, politically (The senator suddenly interrupted to declare firmly that she was politically neutral.)

The adverb *suddenly* describes the verb *interrupted,* just as the adverb *firmly* describes the verb *declare.* For the last blank, opt for *politically,* an adverb that describes the adjective *neutral.*

394. **an, an, a (an apple, an orange, a banana)**

The article *an* precedes *apple* and *orange* because those words begin with vowel sounds. *A* precedes *banana,* because *banana* begins with a consonant.

395. **a, a, an (a card, a printer, an outdoor trip)**

The article *a* precedes *card* and *printer* because those words begin with consonant sounds. *An* precedes *outdoor trip* because *outdoor* begins with a vowel sound.

396. **a, an, a (a bicycle, an old-fashioned girl, a modern woman)**

The article *a* precedes *bicycle* and *modern woman* because those words begin with consonants. *An* precedes *old-fashioned,* which begins with a vowel sound.

397. **an, a, a (an everyday dish, a light, a history)**

The word *everyday* begins with a vowel, so it is preceded by *an.* Both *light* and *history* begin with consonants, so they are preceded by *a.*

398. **an, an, an (an amusing story, an unusual incident, an original song)**

The first word in each of these expressions *(amusing, unusual, original)* begins with a vowel sound, so the article *an* precedes each one.

399. **an, a, an (an initial impression, a very happy child, an additional payment)**

The words *initial* and *additional* begin with vowel sounds, so the article *an* should precede those words. *A* precedes *very happy child* because *very* begins with a consonant.

400. **a, an, a (a historic occasion, an important dictionary, a telephone)**

The word *historic* begins with a consonant, so it should be preceded by *a.* Surprised? A very long time ago, *historic* was pronounced differently, as if it began with a vowel. Therefore, you may hear people say *an historic occasion,* but the more modern expression is *a historic occasion.* The article *an* should precede *important dictionary,* because *important* begins with a vowel sound. *A* precedes *telephone,* which begins with a consonant.

401. **an, a, a (an herb garden, a fir tree, a balcony)**

The word *herb,* in American usage, has a silent *h,* so in America it's preceded by *an.* (In Britain, the *h* is pronounced, so *a* is correct.) Both *fir tree* and *balcony* begin with consonants, so they're preceded by *a.*

402. **an, an, an (an orphan, an adventure, an e-mail message)**

All three of these expressions *(orphan, adventure, e-mail message)* begin with a vowel sound, so all three should be preceded by *an.*

403. **I. and II. (I. self-cleaning oven; II. best-dressed list)**

The words preceding *oven* and *list* each form a single description, so I and II are correct. *Blue pens* (in Phrase III: *package of blue-pens*) should not be hyphenated, because *blue* describes *pens*.

404. **I. and II. (I. recently passed law; II. brown-eyed boy)**

Recently describes *passed,* so no hyphen is needed there. Phrase I is correct. *Brown-eyed* forms one description of *boy,* so the hyphen should be present. Phrase II is correct. Because *poorly* describes *expressed,* no hyphen is needed. Phrase III *(poorly-expressed idea)* is incorrect.

405. **III. (sixth-grade math)**

Is Phrase I *(third base coach)* referring to the third coach the manager sent to stand near a base, or is it the coach at third base? Without the hyphen, the meaning is unclear, and I is wrong. (Two meanings are possible: The *third-base coach* stands near third base; the *third base-coach* is the manager's choice after his first two selections have left the game.) The adverb *very* never appears in a hyphenated expression, so Phrase II *(very-shallow water)* is wrong. Only with Phrase III do you have a winner. *Math* is described by one phrase, *sixth-grade.*

406. **I. (nine-year-old kid)**

Three words *(nine, year, old)* form one description of *kid,* so *nine-year-old* is correct. In Phrases II *(constantly-changing world)* and III *(nearly-enough candy),* the first word is an adverb describing an adjective — a situation that doesn't call for a hyphen. Therefore, II and III are incorrect.

407. **All of the phrases**

In the first phrase *(tension-relieving exercise),* two words, *tension* and *relieving,* form one description of *exercise.* In the second phrase *(a job well done),* the description follows the noun *(job)* it's describing, so *well done* isn't hyphenated. In Phrase III *(newly formed committee),* the adverb *newly* describes *formed,* so it's not hyphenated either. Every phrase is correct.

408. **None of the phrases**

In the first expression *(three-blind mice),* each description of *mice (three* and *blind)* is separate, so no hyphen is needed. In the second and third expressions *(very-happy puppy* and *less-valid argument), very* and *less* describe the adjectives that follow them *(happy* and *valid).* Therefore, they shouldn't be hyphenated. All the phrases are wrong.

409. **All of the phrases**

Ordinary expressions such as *elementary school, Yankees baseball,* and *book review* aren't hyphenated, even when they precede the word described. All the phrases are correct.

410. **I. and III. (I. more interesting story; III. extremely difficult problem)**

The words *more* and *extremely* are both adverbs describing the adjectives they precede *(interesting, difficult)*. No hyphen is needed for either of these phrases. You do, however, need a hyphen for *red-haired* in Phrase II *(red haired ape)*, because those words create a single description for *ape*.

411. **II. (language-proficiency test)**

Phrase I *(annual-dental exam)* doesn't need a hyphen because each word *(annual, dental)* describes *exam* separately. *Language* and *proficiency*, on the other hand, form one description of *test*, so you need a hyphen there. *Mostly* describes *boring*, so no hyphen is called for in the third phrase *(mostly-boring material)*. Only Phrase II is correct.

412. **zookeeper**

The prepositional phrase *with a long broom* describes *zookeeper*. The phrase answers an adjective question: Which one? (In other words, Which *zookeeper? A zookeeper with a long broom*.)

413. **sneezed**

One of the adverb questions is "where?" So, where did Clara sneeze? *Into her handkerchief*. That prepositional phrase describes the verb *sneezed*.

414. **soared**

The prepositional phrase *above the clouds* tells you where the kite *soared*. Therefore, it describes the verb *soared*.

415. **author**

Which *author? The author of the mystery series*. The prepositional phrase *of the mystery series* describes the noun *author*.

416. **lay**

Lay where? *Lay over the scratched floor. Over the scratched floor* is a prepositional phrase describing the verb *lay*.

417. **Monica**

The verbal *(sliding her finger around the bowl)* gives you more information about *Monica*. Although the phrase resembles a verb, it doesn't function as a verb in this sentence. The real verb is *did realize*.

418. **puppets**

The clause *which belonged to my grandmother* gives you information about *puppets*, answering this question: Which *puppets?*

419. researched

The clause *Before Dennis applied for a scholarship* indicates when *he researched* the topic. Therefore, the description applies to the verb, *researched*.

420. Sheltering

The prepositional phrase, *beneath their mother's arms,* tells you where the twins sheltered. Therefore, it describes the verbal *sheltering*.

421. one

How many photos did Shirley take of the famous monument? *Only one. One* is an adjective, telling you how many. *Only* emphasizes that number, *only one,* so *only* describes *one*.

422. boy

Which *boy? The boy who cried wolf. Who cried wolf* is a description of the noun *boy*.

423. were

The description *although sometimes she seemed to benefit from too many coincidental clues* explains under what conditions the stories *were fun to read about.* "Under what conditions?" is a question you ask to find any sort of adverb description, and adverbs describe verbs. The verb *were* is described by the underlined adverb clause.

424. water

Which *water? Water flowing through the cracks in the foundation.* The underlined verbal describes *water*.

425. discussed

Where did the manager discuss the price of the new uniforms? *At his meeting.* Did you stumble over *last night?* Those words explain when the manager discussed the price, just like *at his meeting. At his meeting* doesn't describe *last night.* It's attached to the verb, *discussed*.

426. an hour

Nearly is an adverb, describing (and limiting) the amount of time Tom was *stirring the sauce.* Not *an hour,* but *nearly an hour.* If you answered *hour,* your answer is also correct, as you zeroed in on the important word, *hour*.

427. dropped

The underlined expression is missing a couple of words — an implied subject *(lumberjack)* and verb *(was)*. Add those into the sentence, and you see that an expression containing the subject, *lumberjack,* doesn't describe the subject that does appear in the sentence (also *lumberjack*). Instead, the underlined expression tells you when the *lumberjack dropped a few logs. While carrying wood* describes the verb, *dropped*.

428. everything

What do you mean by *everything*? *Everything* the *supervisors* do? Think? Feel? No, just *everything their supervisors say.* The underlined expression, which is a clause, describes (and clarifies the meaning of) the pronoun *everything*.

429. David, puppy

What were *David and his puppy* doing? The verb in the sentence tells you that they *knocked over a lamp and two tables.* But *knocked* is the verb in the sentence, not a description. What else were *David and his puppy doing?* They were *rolling together in a mock fight.* This extra information is a description and doesn't form a matching subject-verb pair. Because it's extra information about *David and his puppy,* the underlined verbal describes *David* and *puppy*.

430. traveled

Why did *I* travel? *To see my family. To see my family* is a verbal (specifically, an infinitive) describing the verb *traveled*.

431. Receiving

This one is tricky. An introductory verb form, by the rules of proper English, must describe the subject of the sentence, which in this case is *principal*. However, the underlined words aren't an introductory verbal. They're part of a verbal phrase. In fact, they tell you why the action of *receiving* took place. Therefore, the underlined words describe *receiving*.

432. II. (The ruby earrings that I wore to the dance rested on the nightstand next to my bed.)

The key description here is *that I wore to the dance.* You have to place that description near the word it describes. Logic tells you that the description applies to *earrings.* In Sentence II, the description follows *earrings.* In Sentences I *(The ruby earrings rested on the nightstand next to my bed that I wore to the dance)* and III *(The ruby earrings rested on the nightstand that I wore to the dance next to my bed),* it appears elsewhere. Only Sentence II is correct.

433. I. and II. (I. The crosstown bus filled with holiday shoppers inched slowly through heavy traffic. II. Filled with holiday shoppers, the crosstown bus inched slowly through heavy traffic.)

Keep your eyes on the description *filled with holiday shoppers.* Logically, it applies to *bus.* Sentences I and II place it just after and just before *bus,* so both are correct. Sentence III *(The crosstown bus inched slowly through heavy traffic filled with holiday shoppers)* moves it to the end of the sentence — where it improperly describes *traffic.* The *traffic* may be the result of holiday shopping, but it isn't *filled with holiday shoppers. The crosstown bus* is.

434. **II. (Elena has only three children, though she had hoped for a larger family.)**

The key word here is *only,* which describes the word it precedes. The intended meaning of the sentence is *only three,* not more. Sentence II expresses that idea. In Sentence I (*Elena only has three children, though she had hoped for a larger family*), *only* applies to *has* — not a logical expression. Similarly, in Sentence III (*Elena has three children, though she had only hoped for a larger family*) *only* describes *had hoped.* Elena presumably has done more in her life than have children (Sentence I) and hope (Sentence III). She has probably done many things! Only Sentence II is correct.

435. **II. and III. (II. George's unnecessary scowling alarmed people. III. George's scowling alarmed people unnecessarily.)**

What's unnecessary in this statement? The *scowling* or the fact that people were *alarmed?* In Sentence I (*George's scowling unnecessarily alarmed people*), you can't tell which meaning the writer wants to express. Sentences II and III are clear, though different. In II, the *scowling* is *unnecessary.* In III, he alarmed *unnecessarily.* Both II and III are correct.

436. **I. (Tracy and the cat licking fur curled up on the couch.)**

Who's *licking?* Not *Tracy. The cat!* The description, therefore, must be close to *cat.* Because the description follows *cat* only in Sentence I, only Sentence I is correct. The placement of the description in Sentence II (*Tracy and the cat curled up on the couch licking fur*) means that the *couch* is grooming. Sentence III (*Licking fur, Tracy and the cat curled up on the couch*) is even more disturbing, because in that sentence, Tracy is *licking fur.*

437. **II. (The letter in Alice's mailbox said that she had won the lottery.)**

The description *in Alice's mailbox* applies to *letter,* not to where *Alice . . . won the lottery* (as in Sentence I: *The letter said that she had won the lottery in Alice's mailbox* and Sentence III: *The letter said that in Alice's mailbox she had won the lottery*). Only Sentence II places the description near *letter,* so only Sentence II is correct.

438. **III. (He drove the car that he bought last year down the highway.)**

The description *that he bought last year* describes *car* and must be next to that word. Only Sentence III places the description in that spot, so only III is correct. Sentences I (*He drove the car down the highway that he bought last year*) and II (*That he bought last year, he drove the car down the highway*) miss the mark.

439. **II. and III. (II. Although the lobby renovation is taking longer than expected, we are sure that when it reopens in September, everyone will like the new floor tiles from Greece. III. Although the lobby renovation is taking longer than expected, when it reopens in September we are sure that everyone will like the new floor tiles from Greece.)**

In Sentence I (*Although the lobby renovation is taking longer than expected, we are sure that everyone will like the new floor tiles from Greece when it reopens in September*), *Greece* is reopening in September. Because you can't close a country, Sentence I is wrong. In Sentences II and III, the description *when it reopens in September* applies to *the lobby.* Those sentences are logical and correct.

440.

II. (II. My hands were slippery, and the dishes fell, breaking into a thousand pieces.)

What broke *into a thousand pieces?* Not *my hands,* but *the dishes.* Only Sentence II places the description near *dishes,* where it belongs. In the other two choices, *my hands* are broken. That situation may be possible, but not *a thousand pieces!* Logic tells you to rule out Sentences I *(My hands, breaking into a thousand pieces, were slippery, and the dishes fell)* and III *(Breaking into a thousand pieces, my hands were slippery, and the dishes fell).*

441.

II. and III. (II. She won with almost 500 votes; the loser received 410. III. With almost 500 votes, she won; the loser received 410.)

Almost limits the number of votes (500) that the victor received. Because *almost* applies to 500, it must precede that amount, as it does in Sentences II and III. *Almost* is misplaced in Sentence I *(She almost won with 500 votes; the loser received 410).*

442.

I. and II. (I. The highway boundary, painted white, was visible even at night. II. Painted white, the highway boundary was visible even at night.)

The *boundary* is *painted white,* as Sentences I and II say. Sentence III *(The highway boundary was visible even at night, painted white)* has the *night painted white* — illogical and wrong.

443.

III. (Because Harry is on a diet that emphasizes fruit and vegetables, he bought ice cream just once a month.)

Just applies to the frequency of Harry's indulgence in ice cream, which is *once a month.* Therefore, *just* must precede *once a month,* as it does in Sentence III. *Just* is placed incorrectly in Sentences I *(Because Harry is on a diet that emphasizes fruits and vegetables, he just bought ice cream once a month)* and II *(Because Harry is on a diet that emphasizes fruit and vegetables, he bought just ice cream once a month).*

444.

II. and III. (II. Running into the woods, Jack avoided the mugger who was standing still and pointing a gun. III. Jack, running into the woods, avoided the mugger who was standing still and pointing a gun.)

Logic tells you that if the mugger is *standing still and pointing a gun, the mugger* can't also be *running into the woods.* Sentence I *(Jack avoided the mugger who was standing still and pointing a gun, running into the woods)* expresses that meaning, so it's wrong. Sentences II and III give the run to *Jack,* so they are correct.

445.

II. and III. (II. During the class, Eleanor told me the teacher was boring. III. Eleanor told me the teacher was boring during the class.)

In Sentence I *(Eleanor told me during the class the teacher was boring)* the description *during the class* may apply to either *told* or *was.* Because it's unclear, Sentence I is incorrect. Sentence II clearly expresses the idea that *Eleanor told me* something *during the class.* Sentence III goes in the other direction, explaining that *the teacher was boring during the class.* Because they are clear, Sentences II and III are correct.

446. **II. and III. (II. When you're dealing with unreasonable people, making decisions causes arguments quickly. III. When you're dealing with unreasonable people, making quick decisions causes arguments.)**

In Sentence I *(When you're dealing with unreasonable people, making decisions quickly causes arguments)*, *quickly* is between *making* and *causes*. The description may refer to either action, so the sentence is unclear — and wrong. Sentences II and III express clear meanings. In II, the arguments pop up fast. In III, the warning is about *quick decisions*. Sentences II and III are correct.

447. **III. (The nanny checked on the child lying asleep in her crib.)**

Who's *lying asleep? The child*. But in Sentences I *(Lying asleep in her crib, the nanny checked on the child)* and II *(The nanny, lying asleep in her crib, checked on the child)*, the *nanny* is asleep because the description is in the wrong place. Only Sentence III places the description after *child*, where it belongs.

448. **I. and II. (I. The house Agnes once visited sold for a million dollars. II. The house Agnes visited sold for a million dollars once.)**

In Sentence III *(The house Agnes visited once sold for a million dollars)*, *once* is between *visited* and *sold*. You can't tell which meaning the writer intends. Sentence I clearly states that *Agnes once visited*. Sentence II gives the price the house sold for *once*. Sentences I and II are clear and correct.

449. **III. (Testifying for the defense, Mr. Jones gave a compelling account of what he had witnessed.)**

When a sentence begins with a verb form acting as a description, the subject must be the person performing that action. Only in Sentence III is *Mr. Jones testifying*, so only Sentence III is correct. Sentences I *(Testifying for the defense, the eyewitness account from Mr. Jones was compelling)* and II *(Testifying for the defense, Mr. Jones's eyewitness account was compelling)* have the *account* doing the testifying.

450. **II. and III. (II. The commissioner explained with a slide presentation the environmental impact of mining. III. With a slide presentation, the commissioner explained the environmental impact of mining.)**

Slide presentations are powerful, but you can't *mine* with them as Sentence I *(The commissioner explained the environmental impact of mining with a slide presentation)* implies. Instead, you *explain* with them. Sentences II and III express the idea that the commissioner used a *slide presentation* as he *explained the environmental impact of mining*. That's the meaning you want, and that's your answer.

451. **I. (The tattoo artist injected ink into the client's upper arm, which was thickly muscled and hard to draw on.)**

What's *thickly muscled and hard to draw on?* Not the *tattoo artist*, as Sentence II says *(Thickly muscled and hard to draw on, the tattoo artist injected ink into the client's upper arm)*, or the *ink*, as Sentence III states *(The tattoo artist injected ink, thickly muscled and hard to draw on, into the client's upper arm)*. The *arm!* Because Sentence I places the description near *arm*, it's correct.

452. **neater, less neat, neatest, least neat**

More neater is wrong because you never combine *more* and *-er*. The others are correct. The one-syllable word *neat* adds *-er* and *-est* to create the comparative and superlative forms. All regular negative comparisons use *less* and *least*.

453. **closer, less close, closest**

The word *close* may be either an adjective (*close* call) or an adverb (come *close*). It forms comparisons with *-er* or *-est*. All regular negative comparisons use *less* and *least*.

454. **more beautiful, most beautiful, less beautiful**

Three-syllable words such as *beautiful* generally use *more, most, less,* and *least* to form comparisons, not *-er* or *-est*.

455. **scarier, scariest, least scary**

Two-syllable words such as *scary* often add *-er* or *-est* to form comparisons. When the base word ends with a consonant-*y* combination (in this case, *-ry*), you generally change the *y* to *i* before adding *-er* or *-est*. Never double up, adding these syllables as well as *more* or *most*. All regular negative comparisons use *less* and *least*.

456. **less competent, least competent**

All regular negative comparisons use *less* and *least*. Never double up, adding *-er* and *-est* along with *less* or *least*.

457. **prettier, prettiest, less pretty**

When a short word ends in a consonant-*y* combination, you generally change the *y* to *i* before adding *-er* or *-est*. Such is the case with *pretty*. All regular negative comparisons use *less* and *least*.

458. **more softly, most softly, less softly**

Many adverbs, such as *softly,* use *more, most, less,* and *least* to form comparisons.

459. **faster, fastest, less fast, least fast**

Fast may be either an adjective (*fast* car), or an adverb (drive *fast*). Like many single-syllable words, the comparative and superlative forms rely on *-er* and *-est*. All regular negative comparisons use *less* and *least*.

460. **tall, taller, less tall**

The single-syllable adjective *tall* forms comparisons with *-er* and *-est*. All regular negative comparisons use *less* and *least*.

461. **more rapidly, most rapidly, less rapidly, least rapidly**

Like many adverbs, *rapidly* forms comparisons with *more, most, less,* and *least*.

462. **more concerned, less concerned, most concerned, least concerned**

The two-syllable word *concerned* relies on *more, most, less,* and *least* to form comparisons.

463. **more nimbly**

Most adverbs ending in *-ly* form comparisons with *more, most, less,* and *least*. Never double up, adding both *-er* and *-est* to a form already containing *more, most, less,* or *least*.

464. **merrier**

The adjective *merry* forms comparisons with *-er* and *-est*. Because it ends in a consonant-*y* combination (in this case, *-ry*), you change the *y* to *i* before adding *-er* or *-est*. Never double up, adding both *-er* and *-est* to a form containing *more, most, less,* or *least*.

465. **more loudly, most loudly**

The adverb *loudly* forms comparisons with *more* and *most*.

466. **less curved, least curved, most curved**

The adjective *curved* forms comparisons with *more, most, less,* and *least*.

467. **friendlier, friendliest**

Friendly is an adjective, even though it ends with the usual adverb syllable, *-ly*. To form the comparative and superlative forms, change the *y* to *i* and add *-er* and *-est*. Never double up, adding both *-er* and *-est* to a form containing *more, most, less,* or *least*.

468. **more artificially, most artificially, less artificially, least artificially**

The four-syllable adverb *artificially* forms comparisons with *more, most, less,* and *least*.

469. **None of the choices**

Surprised? Despite all those vampire films and novels, *dead* is an absolute state. You either are or you aren't *dead*. No comparisons allowed!

470. **better, best**

Comparisons with the adjective *good* or the adverb *well* are irregular. The comparative form is *better,* and the superlative is *best*. To make a negative comparison, use *worse* or *worst*.

471. **more, most**

Much forms comparisons irregularly. *More* and *most* are the comparative and superlative forms. The negative comparisons are *less* and *least*.

472. worse, worst

Bad is an irregular adjective when it comes to comparisons. Use *worse* or *worst*.

473. None of the choices

A trick question! *Unique* is an absolute that can never be compared. The word means "one of a kind." The fact that many people say *more unique* doesn't make that expression correct. Something is either *unique* or not. No degrees of *uniqueness* exist.

474. better, best

The adverb *well* forms comparisons irregularly. The comparative and superlative forms of *well* are *better* and *best*.

475. more nearly perfect

Yes, it's true that the Founding Fathers of the United States talked about "a more perfect union," but if grammar experts had been involved, they would have said "a more nearly perfect union" instead. Why? *Perfect* is an absolute. You can approach that state, but once you're there, you can't be compared.

476. worse

The adverb *badly* forms comparisons irregularly, never employing *more* or *most*. You go from *badly* to *worse* and then to *worst* as you intensify the degree of badness. To move in the opposite direction, subtracting intensity, steer clear of *less badly* or *least badly;* opt for *better* or *best* instead.

477. happier than her sister (Alice is happier than her sister.)

The original comparison is incomplete. Hearing only the underlined words, you have no way to figure out whether *Alice is happier than a clam* or *Alice is happier now that she's no longer in jail* or whatever.

478. No change needed

Although the comparison isn't spelled out in the original sentence, the meaning is implied. *Peter* lost his salary when he quit. Because the meaning is clear, the original needs no change. Did you opt for *poorer than he had been?* Those words also create a good comparison, but their addition isn't necessary.

479. more famous than any other (George Washington may be more famous than any other President of the United States.)

George Washington, for those of you who slept through history class, was a President of the United States. The original compares him to the group as if he were not a member of that group. Insert *other* and you place George in the group of presidents, where he belongs.

480. **as (This allergy season is as bad as last year's season.)**

The expression *equally as* isn't proper English. Drop *equally* and you're fine. If you truly want to include *equally,* you can say, *equally bad compared to.*

481. **more freckles (Compared to his brother, Levi has more freckles.)**

When you compare two elements (in this case, *Levi* and *his brother*), go for the comparative form, which you usually create with *-er* or *more.*

482. **No change needed**

Loud functions as either an adjective or an adverb. In this sentence, it's an adverb describing *snored.* Because you're considering *Darian* in a group of five, the superlative form, *loudest,* does the job.

483. **less (Dmitri Smith and his wife Alicia Alvarez are both dentists, but Alicia earns less.)**

Only two people are being compared here, so the comparative form, *less,* is what you need.

484. **the curviest tail of all birds (My parakeet Robbie has the curviest tail of all birds.)**

The original sentence is incomplete. You know that Robbie's tail is curved, but you have no basis for comparison until you add *of all birds.*

485. **less than her friend Bob does *or* less than she likes Bob (Veronica likes Archie less than her friend Bob does *or* Veronica likes Archie less than she likes Bob.)**

The original sentence is vague. Does Veronica like Archie less than she likes her friend Bob? Or does Veronica like Archie less than her friend Bob likes Archie? Either is possible. The original sentence needs clarification.

486. **more important than any other (The invention of the touch screen was more important than any other technological innovation of that year.)**

The *touch screen* is a *technological innovation,* but the original sentence removes it from that group. Insert *other* and you solve the problem by placing the *touch screen* in the group of *technological innovations.*

487. **than most modern novelists' books (Ending on page 1,000, that Victorian novel is longer than most modern novelists' books.)**

A thousand pages is a lot, but people old enough to write novels are longer than, say, the 6-inch thickness of a 1,000-page book. In other words, the original compares a book to people, but you really want to compare a book to other books.

488. **No change needed**

The comparison, at first glance, appears incomplete, but it's actually implied. Fred looks *dumber* than he would if he were not so *nervous and self-conscious* and had he tried to avoid looking *dumb.*

489. incomparable (After examining 50 antique statues, the curator said that the one from Mesopotamia was incomparable.)

The word *incomparable* means "cannot be compared" or "unique." Therefore, you can't use *incomparable* in a comparison.

490. No change needed

Two states of being are compared in this sentence: how Elizabeth Bennet is and how she thinks she is. Because you're comparing two things, the comparative form, *less self-aware,* is correct.

491. than any other fruit ("Oranges are juicier than any other fruit," exclaimed Ann as she bit into a freshly picked piece.)

The original sentence compares *oranges* to *any fruit.* However, *oranges* are *fruit.* Insert *other* to place *oranges* inside the group.

492. less comprehensible than Alicia's (Julia's accent is less comprehensible than Alicia's.)

The original sentence compares *accent* to a person *(Alicia).* You should compare one *accent* to another. By changing *Alicia* to *Alicia's, accent* is implied *(less comprehensible than Alicia's accent).*

493. round, as is (A circle that is 2 inches in diameter is round, as is one with a 4-inch diameter.)

Round is an absolute. Either something is *round* or it isn't. No comparisons allowed!

494. the messiest in the neighborhood (Marcy loaned money to her friend, whose house is the messiest in the neighborhood.)

A neighborhood contains more than two houses, so the superlative form, *messiest,* is called for here.

495. less efficient than (Henry's strategy for achieving a perfect score on the SAT was less efficient than mine.)

Two things are being compared in this sentence: *Henry's strategy* and *mine.* The comparative form, *less efficient than,* is appropriate for this sentence.

496. the worst one (Of all the minutes in a day, the baby had to pick the worst one to fall asleep!)

Picture this scenario: Your kid is in the aisle seat of a plane, and after screaming for the first two hours of the flight, he falls asleep. At that exact moment the guy in the window seat needs the restroom. In terms of grammar, you're comparing one minute to the other 1,439 in the day, so the superlative form, *worst,* is proper here.

497. **as heavy as, perhaps even heavier than (My suitcase is as heavy as, perhaps even heavier than, yours.)**

The rule on double comparisons is simple: Each comparison must be complete. In the original sentence, *as heavy* is part of a comparison. Add *as* after *heavy* and the comparison is complete: *as heavy as.* The second comparison, *heavier than,* is already complete.

498. **No change needed**

Three people appear in this sentence: *George, Mac,* and *Nelson.* Nevertheless, the comparative form *(better)* is appropriate here because of the words *either/or.* With *either/ or,* you're comparing *George* to *Mac* first and then *George* to *Nelson.* In other words, you're making two separate, two-person comparisons. No change is needed.

499. **curlier than Anthony's (Sidney's hair, before his recent trip to the salon, was curlier than Anthony's.)**

In the original sentence you're comparing *Sidney's hair* to *Anthony* — a person! Unless Anthony curls up like a pretzel, the comparison is illogical. Change *Anthony* to *Anthony's* or to *Anthony's hair* and the sentence makes sense.

500. **No change needed**

Here you compare two people — *the two union representatives.* To compare two elements, the comparative form *(more effective)* is correct.

501. **as bright as, if not brighter than (This lamp is as bright as, if not brighter than, all the others in my house.)**

The rule on double comparisons is simple. Each must be complete. In the original sentence, *as bright* is part of a comparison. Add *as* after *bright* and the comparison is complete: *as bright as.* The second comparison, *brighter than,* is already complete.

502. **I, Thanksgiving, Mary's (I celebrate Thanksgiving with my family at Mary's house.)**

The personal pronoun *I* is always capitalized, as are the names of holidays *(Thanksgiving)* and people *(Mary).*

503. **The, President, Fowler (The ambassador told President Fowler that war was avoidable if both countries signed the treaty.)**

The first word of a sentence is always capitalized. A title preceding and attached to a name is capitalized; all proper names are capitalized. Titles without names *(ambassador,* in this sentence) generally aren't.

504. **Yesterday, Peter, God (Yesterday Peter expressed his belief that God is present at all times.)**

The first word of a sentence is always capitalized, as are proper names *(Peter,* in this sentence). Traditionally, references to a deity are capitalized.

505. Recently, Professor, Smith (Recently Professor Smith, dean of faculty, revised the requirements for promotion to department head.)

The first word of a sentence is always capitalized, as are proper names (*Smith*, in this sentence). A title preceding and attached to a name (*Professor*) is capitalized; titles following names (*dean of faculty*, in this sentence) or not attached to names (*department head*) generally aren't capitalized.

506. The, African, American (The display of African-American art at the museum drew huge crowds; more than 50 artists were represented.)

The first word of a sentence is always capitalized. Ethnic backgrounds that refer to countries are capitalized.

507. Did, Aunt, Elizabeth, Grandma, Grandpa (Did you know that Aunt Elizabeth always invites Grandma and Grandpa to her son's birthday party?)

The first word of a sentence is always capitalized, as are proper names (*Elizabeth*) and the titles that precede them (*Aunt*) or that function as names (*Grandma, Grandpa*). When a relationship word doesn't function as a name (*her son*, in this sentence), the relationship word (*son*) isn't capitalized.

508. Louise, Smith, Medico, Incorporated, Vice, President, Ellis (Louise Smith, chief of operations at Medico Incorporated, introduced Vice President Ellis to the staff.)

The first word of a sentence is always capitalized, as are proper names (*Louise, Smith, Ellis*). Company names (*Medico Incorporated*) are also capitalized. Titles preceding and attached to a name (*Vice President*) are capitalized. Titles following a name (*chief of operations*) are generally written in lowercase.

509. Conchetta, President, United, States (Conchetta, a distant cousin, recently met the President of the United States.)

Proper names (*Conchetta*) are always capitalized. Titles appearing without names (*President of the United States*) are capitalized only when the office referred to is of the highest national or international importance. Unimportant words in a title (*of, the*) are in lowercase. Family relationships (*cousin*) are in lowercase unless the relationship substitutes for a name.

510. A, Ballocco's, Italian, Specialties (A famous grocery, Ballocco's Italian Specialties, has both a website and a physical store.)

The first word of a sentence is always capitalized. The name of a business (*Ballocco's Italian Specialties*) is capitalized. Were you confused about the official name of the business? The commas are a clue, as they set off the name from the rest of the sentence.

511. The, Lord (The preacher explained in detail how to worship the Lord.)

The first word of a sentence is always capitalized. References to a deity traditionally are capitalized. A title without a name (*preacher*) should be in lowercase.

512.

The, General, Rodriguez (The district attorney gave me five pages of testimony from the principal prosecution witness, General Rodriguez.)

The first word of a sentence is always capitalized, as are proper names *(Rodriguez)*. Titles preceding and attached to a name *(General)* are capitalized. Titles without a name attached *(district attorney, witness)* are generally written in lowercase.

513.

His, Polish, Aunt, May (His Polish girlfriend taught Aunt May and me how to dance the polka, playing many songs suitable for that type of dance.)

The first word of a sentence is always capitalized. References to ethnicity *(Polish)* are generally capitalized, as are proper names *(May)* and titles preceding and attached to them *(Aunt)*. In this sentence, *polka* is clearly identified as a type of dance, not the name of a specific song or choreographed routine, so *polka* should be written in lowercase.

514.

One, Secretary-General, United, Nations, Dag, Hammarskjold, Nobel, Peace, Prize (One famous Secretary-General of the United Nations, Dag Hammarskjold, received the Nobel Peace Prize in 1961.)

The first word of a sentence is always capitalized. Titles of the highest national or international importance *(Secretary-General)* are capitalized even when they don't precede a name. Proper names *(Dag Hammarskjold)* are capitalized, as is the name of a specific organization *(United Nations)* or award *(Nobel Peace Prize)*.

515.

Janice, Jones, God, His (Janice Jones, treasurer of our religious study group, asked for a moment of silence to praise God and His works.)

The first word of a sentence is always capitalized. Proper names *(Janice Jones)* are capitalized. Traditionally, all references to God, including pronouns *(His)*, are capitalized. Titles following a name *(treasurer of our religious study group)* are generally written in lowercase.

516.

The, Greek, American, Archbishop, Kerakalos, Greek, Historical, Society (The annual Greek-American parade takes place tomorrow, according to Archbishop Kerakalos, the head of the Greek Historical Society.)

The first word of a sentence is always capitalized. References to ethnicity *(Greek-American)* are generally capitalized, as are proper names *(Kerkalos)* and titles preceding and attached to them *(Archbishop)*. The specific name of an organization *(Greek Historical Society)* is also capitalized.

517.

How, European, International, League, Ice, Hockey (How many non-European hockey players participate in the International League of Ice Hockey, the organization that oversees the schedule and salaries?)

The first word of a sentence is always capitalized. Ethnicities *(European)* are generally capitalized, but the prefix *non-* is not. The name of an organization *(International League of Ice Hockey)* is capitalized, except for unimportant words such as *of*.

518. **My, Jeffrey, O., Phelps, Oscar, Best, Supporting, Actor (My favorite film star, Jeffrey O. Phelps, won the Oscar for Best Supporting Actor.)**

The first word of a sentence is always capitalized. Proper names, including middle initials, are capitalized. Because *Oscar* is the name of a famous award, it is also capitalized, as is the category, Best Supporting Actor.

519. **The, Daniel, Ellis, Department, Parks, Hurricane, Sandy (The mayor fired Daniel Ellis, a supervisor with the Department of Parks, after Hurricane Sandy.)**

The first word of a sentence is always capitalized, as are proper names *(Daniel, Ellis)*. The important words in a name of a department or organization *(Department, Parks)* are capitalized. The name of an important event *(Hurricane Sandy)* is capitalized.

520. **Her, Consolidated, Edison (Her brother worked for Consolidated Edison, which supplies electricity to the city, until 2012, when he retired with the rank of vice president.)**

The first word of a sentence is always capitalized. The name of a company *(Consolidated Edison)* is capitalized. Titles not attached to a name *(vice president)* are not capitalized, unless the position is of the highest national or international importance.

521. **Does, Mother, Uncle, Bill, Alabama (Does Mother know that Uncle Bill just left for Alabama, where he will run for senator?)**

The first word of a sentence is always capitalized, as are proper names *(Bill, Alabama)* and the titles attached to them *(Uncle)* and titles used as names *(Mother)*. Titles not attached to names *(senator)* are generally not capitalized.

522. **My, French, Tunisia, Africa (My French teacher is from Tunisia, a country in Africa where that language is widely spoken.)**

The first word of a sentence is always capitalized. References to countries and the names of continents *(French, Tunisia, Africa)* are also capitalized.

523. **When, Alan, Monday, December (When Alan was a sophomore, he spent every Monday in December working on a mural for the school cafeteria.)**

The first word of a sentence is always capitalized, as are proper names *(Alan)*. Capitalize the days of the week *(Monday)* and the months of the year *(December)*. Don't capitalize years in school *(sophomore)*.

524. **Last, Marian, Every (Last winter Marian said, "Every snowy day is a treasure.")**

The first word of a sentence is always capitalized, as are proper names *(Marian)*. *Every* rates a capital because the first word in a quotation with a speaker tag (in this sentence, *Marian said*) is capitalized. Seasons of the year *(winter)* are written in lowercase.

525. **Lucy (Lucy loves her history class, but she excels in science and math.)**

The first word of a sentence is always capitalized, and this one is also a proper name — another reason for a capital letter. School subjects, unless they are also the names of countries or languages, aren't capitalized.

526.

In, Introduction, Biology, Nuclear, Physics (In the spring you should take Introduction to Biology instead of Nuclear Physics.)

The first word of a sentence is always capitalized. Capitalize the important words in the names of courses *(Introduction, Biology, Nuclear, Physics)*. Don't capitalize seasons *(spring)*.

527.

Lou (Lou thinks that sandals are "light and airy.")

The first word of a sentence is always capitalized, and this one is also a proper name — another reason for a capital letter. Don't capitalize the first word of a quotation that is tucked into the sentence without a speaker tag, such as *Lou said*.

528.

To, Rocky, Mountains, I (To reach the Rocky Mountains, I drove west for three days last summer.)

The first word of a sentence is always capitalized. You should also capitalize the names of specific geographical places *(Rocky Mountains)*. *The* is not part of the name of most places, by the way. The personal pronoun *I* is always capitalized. Don't capitalize directions *(west)* or seasons *(summer)*.

529.

Ruining, April (Ruining the entire month, April 15th is the deadline for filing tax returns for each year.)

The first word of a sentence is always capitalized. Capitalize the name of a month, but not the generic terms *month* and *year*.

530.

I, Jean, I ("I invest in fine art," remarked Jean, "because I like to support local artists.")

The personal pronoun *I* is always capitalized, as are proper names *(Jean)*. The second half of an interrupted quotation isn't capitalized, so *because* should be in lowercase.

531.

Joe, Tribeca, Manhattan, Midwest (Joe lives in Tribeca, a neighborhood in Manhattan, but he's originally from the Midwest.)

Proper names of people *(Joe)* or places, including neighborhoods *(Tribeca)* and areas *(Manhattan, Midwest)*, are capitalized. The generic word *neighborhood* should be written in lowercase.

532.

Having, Johnny (Having gobbled up my french fries, Johnny then wiped his greasy fingers on my best egyptian cotton towels.)

The first word of a sentence is always capitalized, as are proper names *(Johnny)*. In this sentence, don't capitalize *french* or *egyptian*. When those words refer to the country or language, they are capitalized. As part of common phrases *(french fries, egyptian cotton)*, they should be in lowercase.

533.

The, Love, Song, Benny, Jenny (The Love Song of Benny and Jenny)

The first word of every title and subtitle should be capitalized. Here you have no subtitle. You should also capitalize the important nouns *(Love, Song, Benny, Jenny)* and verbs, as well as pronouns, adjectives, and adverbs (though none are present here). Don't capitalize unimportant words *(of, and)* unless they begin the title or subtitle.

534. Penicillin, An (Penicillin: An examination of the safety and effectiveness of a common antibiotic)

> In sentence style, popular for scientific papers, only the first word of the title and subtitle and any proper names are capitalized.

535. Superbug, Snakefeet, Fish, Teeth, A, History, Three, Rock, Bands (Superbug, Snakefeet, and Fish Teeth: A History of Three Rock Bands)

> The first word of every title *(Superbug)* and subtitle *(A)* should be capitalized. You should also capitalize the important nouns *(Snakefeet, Fish, Teeth, History, Bands)* and verbs, as well as pronouns, adjectives, and adverbs *(Three, Rock)*. Don't capitalize unimportant words *(and* and *of,* in this title) unless they begin the title or subtitle.

536. Serafina, My, Love, How, Two, Star-Crossed, Lovers, Met, Their, Fate (Serafina My Love: How Two Star-Crossed Lovers Met Their Fate)

> All the words in this title are important, so all are capitalized. Did you notice that both words of a hyphenated form are capitalized? It's *Star-Crossed,* not *Star-crossed.*

537. Traffic, An (Traffic circulation patterns: An analysis of driver choice from 2005–2015)

> In sentence style, used for scientific papers, only the first word of the title and subtitle and any proper names are capitalized.

538. Hospital, A (Hospital sanitary practices: A guide for administrators)

> In sentence style, used for scientific papers, only the first word of the title and subtitle and any proper names are capitalized.

539. You, Get, More, You, Pay, Bargaining (You Get More than You Pay for by Bargaining!)

> The first word of the title is always capitalized, as are all nouns, pronouns, adjectives, adverbs, and verbs *(You, Get, More, You, Pay, Bargaining)*. Unimportant words — conjunctions such as *than* and prepositions such as *for* and *by* — should be in lowercase.

540. Basil, An (Basil: An invasive crop or helpful newcomer?)

> In sentence style, used for scientific papers, only the first word of the title and subtitle and any proper names are capitalized.

541. Are, You, Listening, A, Musician's, Memoir, Auditory, Education (Are You Listening? A Musician's Memoir of an Auditory Education)

> The first word of the title and subtitle are always capitalized *(Are, A)* as are the nouns, pronouns, adjectives, adverbs, and verbs *(You, Listening, Musician's, Memoir, Auditory, Education)*. Unimportant words (prepositions and articles such as *of* and *and*) aren't capitalized unless they lead off the title or subtitle.

542. ham, eggs, bacon, cereal, milk, and toast

> Every item in the list except for the last one *(toast)* is followed by a comma. *Note:* The comma before *and* is optional.

543. **drizzle, hurricane, hail, sleet, and rain**

Every item in the list except for the last one (rain) is followed by a comma. *Note:* The comma before *and* is optional.

544. **No commas needed**

Two items joined by *and* should not be separated by commas.

545. **No commas needed**

Surprised? When conjunctions (*and,* in this list) separate every descriptive word (*vanilla, chocolate, strawberry*), no commas are needed. *Ice cream* is one food, which is described by *vanilla and chocolate and strawberry,* so a comma should not be placed between *ice* and *cream.*

546. **slid, teetered, and fell flat**

The three verbs (*slid, teetered, fell*) form a list. A comma is required between *slid* and *teetered.* The comma preceding *and* is optional. The last word, *flat,* describes *fell* and is not part of the list. Therefore, it's not separated by a comma from the word it describes.

547. **the dirty, ripped, faded shoes**

When a list of descriptions precedes the word they describe, the descriptive words are separated by commas. No comma separates an article *(the)* from the first description *(dirty)* or the last word on the list *(faded)* from the word it describes *(shoes).*

548. **three blind, noisy mice**

Numbers and articles, such as *three* in this list, are generally not separated from the list by a comma. No comma separates the last word on the list *(noisy)* from the word it describes *(mice).*

549. **a constantly changing, mysterious personality**

Articles, such as *a* in this list, are generally not separated from the list by a comma. No comma separates the last word on the list *(mysterious)* from the word it describes *(personality). Constantly* describes *changing,* so it forms one description. No comma should be inserted between two words that form one description.

550. **my oldest, kindest friend and her extremely strict parents**

This short list has two basic elements, *friend* and *parents.* No comma should be placed before *and* in a two-item list. *Friend* is described by the list *my oldest kindest.* No comma ever separates a possessive pronoun (such as *my* or *her*) from the list it appears in. *Oldest* and *kindest,* on the other hand, should be separated by a comma. No comma may appear after *kindest* and *strict* because you can't separate a preceding description from the word it describes (*friend* and *parents*). Finally, no comma belongs between *extremely* and *strict,* because *extremely* describes *strict.*

Answers
501–600

551. **became angry, went to the boss, and vented his passionately held beliefs**

On a basic level, this is a three-item list *(became, went, vented)*. Each item is separated by commas, with an optional comma preceding *and*. The possessive pronoun *his* should never be set off by commas. *Passionately* describes *held,* so those words shouldn't be separated by a comma either.

552. **algebra, which I hated; geometry, which I loved; and calculus, which I enjoyed**

The three items in this list, at their most basic, are *algebra, geometry,* and *calculus.* Each of these items carries a description. The descriptions *(which I hated, which I loved, which I enjoyed)* are properly divided from the word they describe by commas. Therefore, semicolons are needed to separate the three items on the basic list. Semicolons emphasize the separation between items on the list when commas are present within the items.

553. **your penetrating, unusually creative mind**

Possessive pronouns, such as *your* in this list, aren't separated from the list by a comma. Don't place a comma after *unusually* because *unusually* describes another item on the list *(creative),* not *mind.* In a sense, *unusually creative* is one element of the list. The final word of the description, *creative,* should not be separated from the word it describes.

554. **Peter Walsh, her former sweetheart; Richard Dalloway, her husband; Hugh Whitbread, an old friend**

Semicolons help to separate items in a list when the items contain commas, clarifying where one item begins and another ends. Without semicolons, the reader can't tell how many items you're discussing — whether, for example, *Peter Walsh* and *her former sweetheart* are the same person or two people, one named and one not. The three people in this list are, therefore, separated by semicolons. The description of each person is separated from the name by a comma.

555. **No commas needed**

This list of verbs has only two elements: *sealed* and *mailed.* Don't separate two elements on a list with a comma. Did you stumble over *crucially important?* In that expression, *crucially* describes *important.* Don't separate the word described from its description.

556. **five sides, equal in length, width, and height**

Sides has two descriptions — one before *(five)* and one after *(equal).* The preceding description *(five)* should not be cut off from the word it describes by a comma. The description that follows *sides,* however, is set off by a comma. Now examine the words that come after *equal.* They form one description. *In length, width, and height* is a prepositional phrase describing *equal.* The elements of the list *(length, width, height)* are separated by commas. *Note:* The comma before *and* is optional.

557. No commas needed

Which *plant* are you talking about? You don't know until the identifying information *(that has drooping leaves)* is supplied. Because the information is essential, no commas surround it.

558. No commas needed

The sentence clearly states that not all football players favor different equipment. (The quarterback disagrees.) Only those players *who are injured* want a change. The information supplied by *who are injured* is essential identification and should not be set off by commas.

559. Street, place (The corner of Second Avenue and Fifth Street, where the accident took place, now has a stoplight.)

By the time you get to the description *(where the accident took place)*, you already know which corner you're discussing — *Second Avenue and Fifth Street.* Therefore, the description is nonessential and should be set off from the rest of the sentence by commas.

560. No commas needed

The statement about *five siblings* tells you that Alice has more than one cousin. Therefore, which one are you talking about? *Alice's cousin* is too general, so the name *(Charles)* is essential and should not be set off from the rest of the sentence by commas.

561. ceiling, cracks (My bedroom ceiling, which has three long cracks, will be repaired next week.)

You start off knowing that the sentence is talking about *my bedroom ceiling.* Therefore, the information following ceiling *(which has three long cracks)* is extra information and should be set off from the rest of the sentence by commas.

562. No commas needed

The house is a general statement. You can't tell which house until the identifier, *I grew up in,* shows up. Because the information is essential, no commas should surround it.

563. Johnny, cars (Johnny, playing with his toy cars, was not old enough to drive a real vehicle.)

You know the name of the person discussed in the sentence *(Johnny)*, so the fact that he's *playing with his toy cars* is extra information, not essential. Extra information should be set off from the rest of the sentence by commas.

564. chloride, salt (Sodium chloride, better known as salt, is a flavorful addition to most meals.)

The chemical name identifies the ingredient; the phrase *better known as salt* is helpful — but nonessential — information and should be surrounded by commas.

565. No commas needed

Which *toddler* didn't want to leave? In real life, all of them. In grammar, though, you can't tell until the toddler is identified as *playing in the sandbox*. Because the information is essential, no commas are needed.

566. board, Smith (The chairman of the board, Mr. Smith, resigned yesterday.)

The title *chairman of the board* identifies the person you're discussing, so the name (*Mr. Smith*) is extra information and is set off by commas.

567. No commas needed

Which law? You don't know until you learn more from the phrase *enacted at midnight*. As essential identification, the phrase isn't set off by commas.

568. blue, color (The office decorated in blue, our state color, displays paintings with patriotic themes.)

Which office? Who knows? You don't, until you read the identifier (*decorated in blue*). The identifier adds essential information, so you don't want to separate it from *office*. The description, *our state color,* is not essential because you already know that you're talking about the color *blue*. Therefore, *our state color* should be set off by commas from the rest of the sentence.

569. o'clock, rings (Six o'clock, when my alarm rings, is the time I jump onto my exercise bike and pedal for an hour.)

The time is identified (*six o'clock*), so *when my alarm rings* is extra information that should be set off by commas.

570. No commas needed

Which *cheerleader?* You don't know until you read the identifying information (*who doesn't concentrate*). Identifying information isn't set off by commas.

571. No commas needed

To understand this sentence, you have to think of the first part with and without a comma. With a comma, the statement *I didn't join the club* is absolute. The speaker, *I,* is not in the club, and the information *because we're friends* is a reason. (Maybe the speaker is afraid to compete with the friend.) Without a comma, the speaker did join the club, but not *because we're friends* but rather because the speaker is *interested in its activities*. The second version makes more sense, so no comma sets off *because we're friends*.

572. salads, dill (The herb Debby sprinkles on most of her salads, dill, is easy to grow.)

This sentence presents two problems. Take them one by one. First, which *herb* are you discussing? You can't tell until you learn that it's what *Debby sprinkles on her salads*. Because that information is essential, no commas surround it. Second, the herb is identified as *dill*. You've already supplied one identifier (*Debby sprinkles on her salads*), so this one is extra and should be set off by commas.

573. **No commas needed**

> When did *Catherine* get the giggles? You don't know until you reach the clause *(as she told the story)*. The information is essential and isn't set off by commas.

574. **you (Sarah won't slap you, because she avoids violence at all costs.)**

> With a comma after *you*, the next bit of information is extra — just a reason why *Sarah won't slap you*. You may want to know the reason, but even if you don't, you don't have to brace for a slap. The fact that *she avoids violence at all costs* means that the first statement is absolute — no exceptions.

575. **made, *Caddyshack* (I have seen the funniest film ever made, *Caddyshack,* about 30 times.)**

> The *funniest film ever made* is a personal statement. You may select something else. Within this sentence, however, *the funniest film ever made* is enough to identify what the speaker is discussing — his or her opinion. Therefore, the name of the film is extra and should be surrounded by commas.

576. **play (Nearly every student of English literature loves Shakespeare's best play, *Hamlet*.)**

> *Shakespeare's best play* is considered adequate identification in this sentence, so the name of the play is extra information, set off by a comma from the rest of the sentence. Yes, you can argue that a reader may choose *King Lear* or *Romeo and Juliet* or another work as *Shakespeare's best play*. In the context of the sentence, though, the name isn't essential.

577. **Yes (Yes, I hate geraniums and roses.)**

> *Yes* serves as an introduction to this sentence and should be set off by a comma.

578. **Max, however (Max, however, would like to pilot a jet.)**

> The interrupter *however* should be set off by commas in this sentence. Place one comma after *Max* and another after *however*.

579. **Oscar (Oscar, I think you could become a superstar.)**

> In this sentence *Oscar* is being addressed. A direct-address word is always set off by commas from the rest of the sentence.

580. **door (Eloise closed the door, and then she locked it.)**

> When you have two complete sentences joined by a conjunction *(and)*, insert a comma before the conjunction.

581. **No commas needed**

> In this sentence you have one subject *(clerk)* matched by two verbs *(slapped, placed)*. No comma precedes the conjunction *(and)* in a subject-verb verb sentence.

582. room, Henry (Go to your room, Henry, before I lose my temper!)

In this sentence the speaker is talking to *Henry*. The word *Henry* is a direct-address expression and should be set off by commas — both before and after.

583. Oh (Oh, no one remembered to bring the ketchup or mustard!)

The introductory word *oh* should be separated from the rest of the sentence with a comma. No comma should divide the two items that *no one remembered — ketchup or mustard*.

584. Really, kitchen (Really, she's so elegant that I can't imagine her in a kitchen, laundry, or basement.)

The first word, *Really,* introduces the sentence but isn't attached to it grammatically. Separate it from the sentence with a comma. In the list of places the speaker imagines that *she* won't go, place a comma after *kitchen*. (The comma after *laundry* is optional.)

585. park (He walked two miles through the park, but he took a bus home.)

Two complete sentences are joined by a conjunction *(but)*. A comma should precede the conjunction.

586. spout (The itsy-bitsy spider went up the water spout, you know.)

Place a comma after *spout* to separate *you know,* which is a comment on the statement about the spider. Without the commas, *you know* appears to identify which *spout* the speaker is discussing — the *spout [that] you know*.

587. Nevertheless (Nevertheless, you must complete all your chores before you watch the playoffs.)

The introductory word *nevertheless* should be separated from the rest of the sentence by a comma.

588. broken, answer, therefore (Your calculator is broken, and your answer, therefore, is incorrect.)

First, you have two complete sentences joined by a conjunction *(and)*. You must place a comma before the conjunction. Next, you have to surround the interrupter, *therefore,* with commas.

589. way, Gloria, open (By the way, Gloria, your zipper is open, and so is your mouth.)

In this sentence you're dealing with three different situations. First, use a comma to separate the introductory phrase, *by the way,* from the rest of the sentence. Next, surround the direct-address name, *Gloria,* with commas. Finally, place a comma before the conjunction *(and)* that joins two complete sentences.

590. plane (Logging more than a thousand hours flying that plane, Albert is an expert pilot.)

An introductory verb form *(Logging more than a thousand hours flying that plane)* should be set off by a comma from the rest of the sentence.

591. beginners (Although it's too difficult for beginners, the course is great for advanced students.)

When an adverb clause (a subject-verb statement explaining how, when, where, why, or under what condition) begins a sentence, it is always set off from the rest of the sentence by a comma. In this sentence, *although it's too difficult for beginners* is an adverb clause.

592. Dora's, stars', girl's

Dora is a singular noun. Form the possessive by adding *'s*. *Stars* is a regular, plural noun. Form the possessive by adding an apostrophe after the *s*. *Girl* is a singular noun. Form the possessive by adding *'s*.

593. lamps', Robin's, pencils'

Lamps is a regular, plural noun. Form the possessive by adding an apostrophe after the *s*. *Robin* is a singular noun. Form the possessive by adding *'s*. *Pencils* is a regular, plural noun. Form the possessive by adding an apostrophe after the *s*.

594. lawyer's, peanuts', parakeet's

Lawyer is a singular noun. Form the possessive by adding *'s*. *Peanuts* is a regular, plural noun. Form the possessive by adding an apostrophe after the *s*. *Parakeet* is a singular noun. Form the possessive by adding *'s*.

595. child's, children's, boys'

Child is a singular noun. Form the possessive by adding *'s*. *Children* is an irregular, plural noun. Form the possessive by adding *'s*. *Boys* is a regular, plural noun. Form the possessive by adding an apostrophe after the *s*.

596. men's, rugs', dinosaur's

Men is an irregular, plural noun. Form the possessive by adding *'s*. *Rugs* is a regular, plural noun. Form the possessive by adding an apostrophe after the *s*. *Dinosaur* is a singular noun. Form the possessive by adding *'s*.

597. workbook's, french fries', women's

Workbook is a singular noun. Form the possessive by adding *'s*. *French fries* is a regular plural noun, even though it contains two words. Concentrate on the second word, *fries*, and follow the usual rule for regular, plural possessives, adding an apostrophe after the *s*. *Women* is an irregular plural, so add *'s* to form the possessive.

598. son-in-law's, deer's, Martin's

To form the possessive of a singular or plural hyphenated noun (*son-in-law*), add *'s* after the last word. *Deer* is a strange word because it serves as both the singular and plural. No worries: Just add *'s* as you do with any irregular plural to create a possessive form. *Martin* is a singular noun. Form the possessive by adding *'s*.

599. **buildings', brothers-in-law's, whose**

Buildings is a regular, plural noun. To form the possessive, add an apostrophe after the *s*. To form the possessive of a singular or plural hyphenated noun *(brothers-in-law)* add *'s* after the last word. Did you stumble over *whose? Who* is a pronoun and forms its possessive *(whose)* without an apostrophe.

600. **fish's, oranges', Ms. Jones's**

Fish may be either singular or plural, but either way you form the possessive by adding *'s. Oranges* is a regular, plural noun. Form the possessive by adding an apostrophe after the *s*. Strictly speaking, to form the possessive of a singular noun *(Ms. Jones)* ending in *s*, you should add *'s*. However, everyone except the most traditional grammarians accepts a simple apostrophe after the final *s* as a way to form the possessive. Therefore, *Ms. Jones'* is also a correct answer.

601. **don't, I'll, isn't**

The apostrophe replaces the letter *o* in the word *not* in *do not* and *is not*. In each expression, the remaining letters form one word *(don't, isn't)*. The apostrophe replaces *wi* in *I will*. The other letters form the contraction *I'll*.

602. **it's, they're, you've**

The apostrophe replaces the second letter *i* in *it is* and the letter *a* in *they are*. The remaining letters in each expression combine to form *it's* and *they're*. (Don't confuse these contractions with the possessive pronouns *its* and *their*.) Two letters drop out of *you have* — *h* and *a* — to form the contraction *you've*.

603. **he's, she was, we're**

The apostrophe replaces the letter *i* in *he is* and the letter *a* in *we are*. The remaining letters in each expression combine to form *he's* and *we're*. No contraction exists for *she was*. *(She's* is a contraction of *she is*, or, informally, *she has*.)

604. **won't, shouldn't, I'd**

The contraction of *will not* is irregular; instead of replacing letters and squeezing the remainders together, *will not* contracts to *won't*. *Shouldn't* is easier; just drop the *o* from *not* and make the remaining letters one word. Similarly — but with lots of dropped letters! — delete *woul* from *would* and you come up with *I'd* as a contraction of *I would*.

605. **hasn't, mustn't, why's**

Drop the *o* from *not* and compress the remaining letters to form the contractions *hasn't* and *mustn't*. Drop the *i* from *is* to create the contraction *why's,* as in this question: *Why's that grammar rule so hard?*

606. **can't, would've, she'd**

The negative expression *cannot* (which, by the way, is one word, not two) contracts to *can't.* To create the contraction of *would have,* drop the *ha* and make the remaining letters into one word *(would've).* Drop *ha* and compress the remainder to create the contraction *she'd,* short for *she had* or *she would.*

607. **might've, 'twas, doesn't**

To create the contraction *might've,* delete the letters *ha* and insert an apostrophe. The contraction *'twas,* which you hear mostly in poetry or old-fashioned writing, is short for *it was.* Drop the *o* from *not,* compress the remaining letters, and insert an apostrophe to create the contraction *doesn't,* short for *does not.*

608. **who'd, could've, how's**

Delete *woul* and insert an apostrophe to create the contraction *who'd,* which is short for *who would.* Drop *ha* from *have* and compress the remaining letters to form the contraction *could've* out of the expression *could have.* Delete the *i* from *is* and combine what's left with *how* to form *how's,* the contraction of *how is.*

609. **what's, let's, should've**

Delete *i* from *is* to form the contraction of *what is (what's)* and *u* from *us* to form the contraction of *let us (let's).* Drop the *ha* from *should have,* insert an apostrophe, and you have *should've,* the contraction of *should have.*

610. **'55, its, months (The class of '55 will celebrate its reunion in two months.)**

The number *19* is missing from *1955,* so you need an apostrophe to replace it. The possessive pronoun *its* doesn't have an apostrophe. *(It's* means *it is.)* Don't create a plural with an apostrophe; change *month's* to *months.*

611. **cameras, isn't (Jane bought two new cameras but isn't pleased with her purchase.)**

Don't create a plural with an apostrophe; change *camera's* to *cameras.* You need an apostrophe to form the plural of *is not (isn't).* Possessive pronouns, such as *her* in this sentence, don't have apostrophes.

612. **Don't, '12, dollars (Don't wait until 2018 to start saving; six years earlier, in '12, start to pile up dollars.)**

The contraction of *do not (don't)* needs an apostrophe. The apostrophe takes the place of *20* in the contraction *'12.* Don't create a plural with an apostrophe; change *dollar's* to *dollars.*

613. **should've, exams (They should've given us more time to take those exams.)**

The contraction *should've* is short for *should have.* Don't create a plural with an apostrophe; change *exam's* to *exams.*

614. **Bagels, 1909 (Bagels were very popular breakfast foods in 1909.)**

You don't need an apostrophe to create the plural noun, *bagels*. Because *1909* is complete, no apostrophe is needed there either.

615. **I'm, hours', Mary's (I'm tired of doing two hours' homework every night; Mary's assignments are easier.)**

The apostrophe takes the place of *a* in the contraction *I'm* (short for *I am*). Why *hours'*? Because the meaning of the phrase is *two hours of homework*. The apostrophe replaces *of*. Add *'s* to *Mary* to create the possessive form.

616. **Who'd, day's (Who'd work two weeks for only a day's pay?)**

The apostrophe signals the contraction *who'd,* which is short for *who would.* You need an apostrophe in *day's* because the apostrophe replaces *of (a day of).*

617. **No quotation marks needed**

The sentence doesn't quote Jane's exact words, so no quotation marks are necessary.

618. **"I stayed home to do the most boring math homework in the universe."**

Jeff explained is a speaker tag — a short phrase that identifies whose words are quoted in the sentence. The exact words from the script (*I stayed home to do the most boring math homework in the universe*) should be surrounded by quotation marks.

619. **"I'm glad I did,"**

The exact words that Jane spoke (*I'm glad I did*) must be surrounded by quotation marks. The comma precedes the closing quotation mark.

620. **"stupendous."**

The only word from Jane quoted in this sentence is *stupendous,* which should be surrounded by quotation marks. The period precedes the closing quotation mark.

621. **No quotation marks needed**

Jeff's words are paraphrased but not directly quoted, so no quotation marks are necessary.

622. **No quotation marks needed**

True, a couple of Jeff's words (*grade, the homework*) appear in the sentence. However, they aren't arranged the way they are in the script. Because they're paraphrased but not directly quoted, no quotation marks are necessary.

623. **"Were you there?"**

The quoted words (*Were you there?*) should be surrounded by quotation marks. Because the quotation is a question, the question mark must be attached to the quotation. Therefore, it precedes the closing quotation mark.

624. **"the most boring math homework in the universe."**

The only words in the sentence that come directly from the script are *the most boring math homework in the universe,* so only those words must be surrounded by quotation marks.

625. **"The heat wave will end on Saturday," the forecaster promised.**

The directly quoted words appear inside quotation marks. In Standard American English usage, the comma precedes the closing quotation mark.

626. **Mark screamed, "Let her go!"**

The first word of a quotation with a speaker tag (in this sentence, *Let*) should be capitalized, and the speaker tag *(Mark screamed)* should be followed by a comma. Because the quoted words are an exclamation, the exclamation point is attached to the quotation and should appear inside the quotation marks.

627. **Wilbur asked, "Did Christine take a taxi to the theater?"**

In Standard American English usage, the speaker tag *(Wilbur asked)* should be followed by a comma when it appears before the quotation. The quotation begins with a capital letter and is surrounded by quotation marks. Because the quoted words are a question, the question mark is attached to the quotation and should appear inside the quotation marks.

628. **Pilar was born in Ecuador, where, she says, "The weather is often hot and humid."**

The first word of a quotation in a sentence with a speaker tag should be capitalized. In this sentence, the speaker tag is *she says*. It is not part of the quotation and should not be preceded by a quotation mark. The only words inside the quotation marks are those that *Pilar* says: *the weather is hot and humid.* In Standard American English usage, the period precedes the closing quotation mark.

629. **Xavier eventually declared that his unusual name was "awesome."**

Only one word is quoted, and you have no speaker tag. (You may have thought that *declared* qualified as a speaker tag, but because it's followed by *that,* it's not a speaker tag.) No speaker tag means no capital letters for the quoted word (unless, of course, the quoted word is a proper name or the pronoun *I*). In Standard American English usage, the period precedes the closing quotation mark. **Note:** If you're quoting only one or two words, decide whether the words are distinctive, revealing character or mood. If so, place the word(s) in quotation marks. If the words are common and you have no special context, you can skip the quotation marks. Here, *awesome* tells you something about Xavier's personality, so quotation marks are appropriate.

630. **"I wonder where the birthday candles are," Grandma whispered, "and if we have enough."**

In this sentence the speaker tag *(Grandma whispered)* appears in the middle of the sentence. The second half of the quotation doesn't begin with a capital letter (unless, of course, it happens to be a proper name or the pronoun *I*) because it's a continuation of the first half of the quotation, not a new sentence. Commas set off the speaker tag. The first comma belongs, according to Standard American English usage, inside the closing quotation mark. The second follows the speaker tag. The period at the end of the sentence, also according to Standard American English usage, precedes the closing quotation mark.

631. No change

The only word underlined is *shopping,* so you know that the seller used that word in some context. However, the sentence has no speaker tag and *shopping* doesn't reveal anything special about character or mood, so no quotation marks are necessary.

632. Marisa explained that she was "completely exhausted"; she and Lola went home immediately.

The quoted words are tucked into the sentence and not introduced by a speaker tag. Therefore, you don't need a comma or a capital letter to set them off from the rest of the sentence. Semicolons appear after the closing quotation mark.

633. No change

The underlined words *(knife, pony)* came out of Henry's mouth (or pen or computer), but here they appear without a speaker tag or context. Also, they do not reveal anything about Henry's character or mood, so no quotation marks are necessary.

634. "When he learned to read, Daryl was five," declared Jordan, "not ten years old."

The speaker tag *(declared Jordan)* is in the middle of this quotation. It should be set off by commas. The first word of the second portion of the quotation should not be capitalized, unless it's a proper noun or the pronoun *I.* According to Standard American English usage, the first comma setting off the speaker tag belongs inside the closing quotation mark, as does the period at the end of the sentence.

635. Robbie explained, "The teacher thinks I am 'supersmart.'"

A quotation inside another quotation is surrounded by single quotation marks, in Standard American English usage. Because *supersmart* isn't preceded by a speaker tag, it isn't capitalized. The larger quotation *(the teacher thinks I am supersmart)* begins with a capital letter. The speaker tag *(Robbie explained)* is followed by a comma. The period at the end of the sentence appears before the closing quotation marks, as Standard American English usage requires.

636. "It is going to rain," Harry predicted. "The picnic will be postponed."

Did you have trouble with this one? The fact that words are quoted doesn't give you license to create a run-on sentence. End the sentence after *predicted,* which is part of the speaker tag, *Harry predicted.* Begin the second sentence with a capital letter. As Standard American English usage requires, place the commas at the end of the first quotation and the period at the end of the second sentence before the closing quotation marks.

637. Will said that the cheese smelled "funky": It had been in the refrigerator for more than a year.

The quoted word, *funky,* is unusual and tells you something about the speaker who chose it as a description. Therefore, *funky* should be surrounded by quotation marks. The colon follows the closing quotation mark. Because the sentence has no speaker tag and the quotation is in a clause beginning with *that,* no capital letters are needed. By the way, when you link two complete sentences with a colon, the second half of the statement begins with a capital letter.

638. According to the authorities, police officers were called "brave" and "heroic" by all who witnessed the daring rescue.

The two quoted words are tucked into the sentence, not labeled with a speaker tag. Therefore, the quoted words are surrounded by quotation marks but not capitalized.

639. In his first paper, "A History of the Stuart Family," Professor Milling explores the relationship between the Stuarts and their business partners.

According to Standard American English usage, the comma at the end of the title precedes the closing quotation mark.

640. Jacobs argues that the colonies "were motivated by a desire for freedom," not additional markets for their goods.

No capital letters are needed for the first word of a quotation not identified with a speaker tag (such as *he said, Adams declared,* and so forth). Nor does a comma introduce a quotation without a speaker tag. According to Standard American English usage, the comma at the end of the quotation precedes the closing quotation mark.

641. Rich's poem, "Diving into the Wreck," explores gender and other themes.

The title of a poem is set off by quotation marks. According to Standard American English usage, the comma at the end of the title precedes the closing quotation mark.

642. "Going to Savannah," a poem by Agnes Little, is on the reading list.

The title of the poem is set off with quotation marks. According to Standard American English usage, the comma after the title precedes the closing quotation mark.

643. The chorus's version of "You Are My Sunshine" relies on three-part harmony.

The title of this song is set off by quotation marks. No other punctuation is needed.

644. In homage to Shakespeare, the main character considers whether "to be truthful or not to be truthful" (line 23).

The citation in parentheses is part of the sentence but not part of the quotation, so it follows the closing quotation mark but precedes the period at the end of the sentence. Because the quotation is tucked into the sentence without a speaker tag (*Arthur said, Marlene claimed,* and so forth), no capital letters or commas are needed to introduce the quotation.

645. When she wrote "Killer Whales and Their Prey," Maxine Davis asserted that these animals are endangered (44).

The title of the paper should be enclosed in quotation marks. According to Standard American English usage, the comma precedes the closing quotation mark. The citation refers to a page number where Davis claimed that killer whales are endangered. It is part of the sentence, so it precedes the period.

646. **No change**

Because nothing is quoted and no title appears, no quotation marks are needed. The citation, in the style of the Modern Language Association, needs no punctuation.

647. **I. and II. (I. skiing, skating, complaining; II. to plant, to sow, to reap)**

In Line I, all the words are gerunds — verb forms that function as nouns. In Line II, all are infinitives (*to* + verb). In Line III (*going to sleep, waking up, ready for work*), you have two gerunds and then a description, *ready for work*. You don't need to know the grammar terms. Just listen to each list. You can hear that I and II match, but III doesn't. Therefore, I and II are parallel.

648. **II. and III. (II. keeps score, notifies the umpire, encourages the team; III. over the mountain, through the woods, to Grandmother's house)**

In Line I (*smart, creative, has immense energy*), you have two descriptions (*smart, creative*) and one verb-statement (*has immense energy*). No match there! In Line II, you have three verb-statements. Match! In Line III, you see three prepositional phrases. Another match. Only II and III are parallel.

649. **I. (Jane calculates, Artie summarizes, Peter plans)**

Line I has three subject-verb pairs, so it's parallel. Line II (*riding a bike, walking in the garden, to relax*) begins with two gerunds (verb forms that act as nouns) and ends with an infinitive (*to* + verb). Line II isn't parallel. Line III (*around the corner, sneaky as a fox, behind the fence*) has two prepositional phrases (*around the corner, behind the fence*) and one description (*sneaky as a fox*). Line III isn't parallel.

650. **I. and II. (I. came, saw, conquered; II. coming, seeing, conquering)**

The first line has three past-tense verbs, so it's parallel. Line II consists of three gerunds (verb forms used as nouns), so it's also parallel. Line III veers away from present tense (*come, see*) into past (*conquered*), so it isn't parallel.

651. **II. (jump, twirl, fall)**

Line I isn't parallel because it begins with two nouns (*silk, thread*) and follows with a description (*carefully sewn*). Line II has three verbs, so it's parallel. Line III has two past-tense verbs (*bought, sold*) and one -*ing* form (*ignoring*), so it isn't parallel.

652. **III. (Ringo plays the drums, Paul strums the guitar, I sing along)**

Line I (*sung by the Beatles, recording a hit song, performed by the school chorus*) has two past participles (*sung, performed*) and descriptions attached to them. It also has a present-tense -*ing* form (*recording*). Because the present and past are mixed together in this list, it isn't parallel. Line II (*heard everywhere, is popular, has many fans*) also mixes present (*is, has*) and past (*heard*), so it's not parallel either. Only Line III matches, with three present-tense, subject-verb pairs, so only III is parallel.

653. **I. (who needs a computer, that costs a fortune, which the store displays in the window)**

Line I has three dependent clauses (subject-verb statements that must attach to an independent clause in order to make sense), so Line I is parallel. Line II has two prepositional phrases *(in the basement, in need of cleaning)* and one noun with a description attached *(energy-efficient furnace)*. Line II isn't parallel. Line III includes one prepositional phrase *(with remote control)*, a past participle *(flanked by speakers)*, and a noun with descriptions attached *(sharp picture quality)*. Line III isn't parallel. Even without knowing the grammar terms, you can probably hear the mismatches.

654. **III. (because I said so, when the blizzard rages, after the game ends)**

Line I *(early opening, excellent service, committed to quality)* has two nouns with attached descriptions *(early opening, excellent service)* and a description — specifically, a past participle *(committed)*. Line I isn't parallel. Line II *(Lisa's spying on her neighbors, the detective tapping her phone, the judge hearing the case)*, at first glance, looks good because three people are paired with activities. However, examine the first of the three pairs. Instead of a noun, *Lisa*, you have a possessive, *Lisa's*. That little difference is important, because the verb form *spying* then functions as a noun because it's described by *Lisa's*. The other two elements are nouns *(detective, judge)* described by verb forms *(tapping, hearing)*. Line II isn't parallel. Line III includes three clauses, all dependent. (In other words, they can't stand by themselves as complete sentences.) Line III is parallel.

655. **I. and II. (I. a bulldozer piled up sand, the dump truck carted it away, the jackhammer broke the pavement; II. gliding, smoothing the ice, stopping by the fence)**

In Line I, all the statements are complete sentences. Line I is parallel. Line II is also parallel because three gerunds *(gliding, smoothing, stopping)* match. True, two of the three gerunds have descriptions attached. However, the descriptions don't matter. The important word, the gerund, does matter when you decide whether a list is parallel. Line III isn't parallel because it contains two nouns with attached descriptions *(soil rich in nutrients, endangered species of plants)*, and a simple prepositional phrase *(in the botanical garden)*.

656. **II. (buying a cottage, replacing the roof that was damaged in the storm, redecorating)**

Line I *(screamed, threw food, epic tantrum)* isn't parallel because two verbs *(screamed, threw)* don't match a noun *(tantrum)*. Notice that the descriptions here aren't an issue; only the core of each item (verbs and a noun) matters. Line II is parallel precisely because the important elements do match; *buying, replacing,* and *redecorating* are all gerunds. Ignore the attached descriptions and objects. Line III *(hid under a chair, away from other players, whispered)* includes two verbs *(hid, whispered)* but one prepositional phrase *(away from other players)*, so it's not parallel.

657. **II. and III. (II. why the card is wet, while it is raining lightly, before the monsoon ends; III. he had been told, he had been warned, he had been suspended)**

Line I *(as time goes by, if I applied to that college, before midnight at the latest)* isn't parallel because it begins with two clauses — statements containing subject-verb pairs — and ends with prepositional phrases *(before midnight at the latest)*. Line II consists of three dependent clauses (subject-verb statements that must attach to a complete thought in order to create a sentence). Line II is parallel. So is Line III, which contains three independent clauses (subject-verb statements that make sense by themselves).

658. **II. (the editor liked it, he praised the writing, reviewers went wild)**

Line I *(Mary wrote the chapter, she proofread it, the chapter was revised by her)* isn't parallel because the first two items are in active voice, in which the subject does the action *(Mary wrote, she proofread)* but the last is passive, in which the subject receives the action *(the chapter was revised)*. Line II (a writer's fantasy!) includes three independent clauses — subject-verb statements that make sense by themselves — all in active voice. Line II is parallel. Line III (a writer's nightmare!) includes two prepositional phrases *(on the remainder table, off the bestseller list)* and one clause *(the book tanked)*. Line III isn't parallel.

659. **I. and II. (I. the apple he picked, the grapes he harvested, the grass he mowed; II. stop, look, listen)**

Line I is parallel because every item contains a noun described by a clause (a subject-verb statement). Line II consists of three commands; it's parallel. Line III isn't parallel because two dependent clauses (subject-verb statements that don't make sense by themselves) — *while you cook, although the wedding is tomorrow* — are listed with an independent clause (a subject-verb statement that can stand alone) — *Henry irons the scarf.*

660. **II. (whoever is hungry, whatever you need, whomever I ask)**

Line I *(the puppy to watch, to take to the park, the kitten to cuddle)* isn't parallel because the first and third items have a noun *(puppy, kitten)* described by infinitives *(to watch, to cuddle)*. The middle item has no noun anchoring the descriptions, just an infinitive *(to take to the park)*. True, *park* is a noun. In this item, though, it's not being described. Instead, it's part of a description. Line II is parallel because it contains three dependent clauses (subject-verb statements that don't make sense by themselves). Line III isn't parallel because the first item *(when winter comes)* is a dependent clause, but the second and third items *(the snow piles up, the plow scours the streets)* are independent clauses, capable of standing alone.

661. **III. (tomorrow, yesterday, soon)**

Line I *(twist and shout, dance the night away, went to the movies)* isn't parallel because the first two items are commands, with *you* as an understood subject. The last is just a past-tense verb, *went*, with no subject. Line II *(the parrot with yellow feathers, the dog running away, a zoo is out of control)* has one independent clause *(a zoo is out of control)*, a subject-verb statement that makes sense by itself. Line II also has two nouns *(parrot, dog)* with attached descriptions, but no verbs. Therefore, Line II isn't parallel. Line III contains three adverbs and is parallel.

662. **go home (I would rather work in the library than go home.)**

The paired conjunction *rather than* may appear with both words together or with words in between. When the words are separated, check what follows *rather* and compare that to whatever follows *than*. The elements should match grammatically. Here, *work* precedes the conjunction, so *go* should follow. Because both are verbs, they create a parallel sentence.

663. **on looks (Style depends not only on looks but also on attitude.)**

After the second half of this conjunction *(but also)* you have a prepositional phrase, *on attitude*. To make the sentence parallel, you need a prepositional phrase after the first half of the conjunction, *not only*. *On looks* fits perfectly.

664. **too long (Oliver's supposed masterpiece was both tuneless and too long.)**

After the first half of the conjunction pair *(both)* you have a simple description — *tuneless*. So you need a simple description after the second half of the conjunction pair *(and)*. *Too long* is a simple description — that is, not a phrase or a clause — and makes the sentence parallel. If the first element has no verb form *(being or was,* for example), the second element shouldn't have one either.

665. **you will be either accepted (When you apply for a selective school, you will be either accepted or rejected; you won't know unless you try.)**

After the second half of the conjunction pair, *or,* you have a description, *rejected*. That's what you need after the first half of the conjunction pair, *either*. Rearrange the words so that *either* precedes *accepted* to make your sentence parallel.

666. **vegetables (Recipes in that cookbook contain meat rather than vegetables.)**

The paired conjunction in this sentence is *rather than* (which may appear together or with words in between). When *rather than* shows up together, compare what precedes it to what follows it. Here, *meat* precedes the paired conjunction, so *vegetables* should follow. Both are nouns and balance nicely.

667. **the general agreed (Both the soldiers and the general agreed, so the proposed change to the battle plan was accepted.)**

When you see the paired conjunction *both/and,* check what follows each half. After *both* you have a noun, *soldiers*. Therefore, you need a noun after *and: the general*. The verb *agreed* works with two subjects, *the soldiers and the general*.

668. **No change**

After the first half of the conjunction pair, *both,* you have a noun and some descriptions attached to the noun *(the patient's blood pressure)*. After the second half of the conjunction pair, you have the same grammatical element: *slower heart rate*. Perfectly parallel!

669. **careful (Mary was not only fair but careful to explain her decision to the contestants.)**

The paired conjunction *not only/but also* sometimes — but not always — drops the *also*. After the first half of the conjunction pair *(not only)*, a simple description *(fair)* appears. Place another simple description *(careful)* after the second half of the conjunction *(but)* to create a parallel sentence. You could also use the simple description, *also careful,* to complete the sentence.

670. **her co-workers' coffee break (Neither Jean's absence nor her co-workers' coffee break mattered, as no customers called.)**

After *neither* you have a simple noun and a possessive form *(Jean's absence)*. You need the same grammatical element after *nor; her co-workers' coffee break* fits perfectly and makes the sentence parallel.

671. **No change**

After the first half of the paired conjunction, *neither,* you have a verb *(explained)*. After the second half of the conjunction, *nor,* you need another verb *(cared)*.

672. **design (The film director will not only emphasize special effects but also design them herself.)**

After the first half of the paired conjunction, *not only,* you have a verb *(emphasize)*. After the second half of the paired conjunction, *but also,* you need a verb too: *design*. With that change, the sentence is parallel.

673. **plan (Participants in the study either have worked in a laboratory or plan to do so within five years.)**

After the first half of the paired conjunction, *either,* you have a verb *(have worked)*. After the second half of the conjunction, *or,* you need another verb *(plan)*. Don't worry about the change in tense; it's justified by the meaning of the sentence. Did you opt for *are planning?* That's correct also.

674. **Playing baseball (Playing baseball is as appealing to Suri as baking cookies.)**

The comparison in this sentence is created by *as . . . as.* The sentence compares *to play baseball* (an infinitive) with *baking cookies* (a gerund). Not parallel! Change the infinitive to *playing baseball* and both halves of the comparison match.

675. **walk (I would rather go to the movies than walk around the mall.)**

The comparison in this sentence comes from *rather . . . than.* After *rather* you have a simple verb, *go. Walking* doesn't match. Pair *go* with the simple verb *walk* and your comparison is parallel.

676. **No change**

Here *equal* creates a comparison. The terms *in height* and *in weight* match, so the comparison is parallel.

677. **because of his tracking mud (George's mother was upset with him more because of his lateness than because of his tracking mud on the kitchen floor.)**

The words *more . . . than* create the comparison. After *more* you have a prepositional phrase, *because of his lateness.* Therefore, you need another prepositional phrase after *than.* Did you opt for *to track mud?* That's not a prepositional phrase; it's an infinitive phrase, because *track* is a verb, not a noun acting as the object of a preposition. *Because of his mud tracks* or a similar phrase would also be correct.

678. **passive (That small dinosaur was probably more aggressive than passive.)**

The comparison is created by *more . . . than.* After *more* you see a simple description, *aggressive.* To balance the sentence and make it parallel, place a simple description, *passive,* after *than.*

679. **your scores (Are your scores on the real SAT as high as your scores on the practice test?)**

Two conjunctions, *as* and *as,* create the comparison between *scores* on two tests. The original sentence tries to balance *scores on the real SAT* (a noun with descriptions attached) with *what you got on the practice test,* a clause (a subject-verb statement). Nope! Not parallel. Change the second half of the comparison to *your scores,* and the sentence becomes parallel. The pronoun *those,* meaning *your scores,* would also work here.

680. **No change**

The sentence compares two ways to fill your stomach (and empty your wallet) — *eating at the diner* and *dining in a fine restaurant.* Two gerunds = one match. The sentence is parallel.

681. **for John (Spelling is easier for me than for John.)**

The sentence revolves around the word *than.* Just before *than* you have a prepositional phrase, *for me.* To make the sentence parallel, a prepositional phrase, *for John,* should follow *than* also.

682. **to prepare as much today as tomorrow (We have to prepare as much today as tomorrow.)**

What's being compared in this sentence is what *we have* to do on two different days. You can balance the comparison in a couple of different ways, but the shortest version moves the beginning of the comparison *(much)* to the spot preceding what's being compared *(today).* The second *as* then precedes the other element you're comparing *(tomorrow).*

683. **he locked (Pursued by a bear, Nicholas ran as fast as possible to the car, and then he locked the door.)**

The beginning of the sentence is in past tense. For no good reason, the original sentence changes from past tense *(ran)* to present *(locks).* Once you swap *he locked* for *he locks,* everything is in past tense and the sentence is parallel.

684. **you should turn off the valve (Before you disconnect the water pipe, you should turn off the valve.)**

The first part of the sentence is in active voice: The subject *(you)* does the action *(disconnect).* The second part of the sentence, in the original version, is passive. The subject *(valve)* receives the action *(should be turned off).* Change passive to active *(you should turn off the valve)* and the sentence is parallel. You can also say *turn off the valve* to make a parallel sentence.

685. **Traveling (Traveling in Sweden was relaxing; coming home was not.)**

The subject of the second half of the sentence is a gerund (the *-ing* form of a verb that functions as a noun). To match the second half, change the infinitive *to travel* to a gerund, *traveling*.

686. **he later examined her (Dr. Weber admitted the patient, Ms. Smith, to the hospital, and he later examined her.)**

The first half of the sentence is in active voice; the subject *(Dr. Weber)* performs the action *(admitted)*. In the original sentence, the second half shifts into passive voice, in which the subject *(the patient)* receives the action *(was examined)*. Reword the second half to make the verb active, and you're correct.

687. **actors must speak forcefully (They should capture the audience's attention right away, so actors must speak forcefully when the curtain rises.)**

The sentence begins with the plural pronoun *they.* Why shift to the singular term, *an actor?* If you begin with a plural, stay with a plural *(actors)* unless the meaning requires a change.

688. **rugs (The stage set has colorful lighting, costumes, curtains, and rugs.)**

Lots of things are *colorful* in this sentence, including *rugs.* You have no reason to break the pattern established by *colorful,* which is positioned to describe *lighting, costumes, curtains,* and *rugs.*

689. **cooled by a pond (Shirley smiled when she saw the backyard, which was bordered by daisies, shaded by oak trees, and cooled by a pond.)**

This backyard sounds nice! Every description on the list, except the underlined portion, is passive. In passive voice, the subject receives the action. So the yard *was bordered, was shaded,* and *was cooled.* Conveniently, the first *was* works for the whole list, so you don't need to repeat that word. (If you do, you have to use it for all three verbs, not just the first and third.)

690. **to learn new languages, and to visit foreign countries (To study other cultures, to learn new languages, and to visit foreign countries are worthwhile pursuits.)**

In a list of three infinitives (*to* + verb), you have two choices. You can let the first *to* work for all three *(to learn, study, and visit),* or you can repeat *to* in front of each item *(to study, to learn, and to visit).* What you can't do is place *to* in front of two terms and not the third — not if you want a parallel sentence.

691. **is convenient (Bicycle riding helps people become physically fit and is convenient too.)**

The original sentence consists of two complete thoughts linked by *and.* The first half is in third person, talking about *bicycle riding* and *people.* The second half shifts to second person, talking to *you.* The original isn't parallel because of the shift in person (from third to second). The easiest fix is to let *bicycle riding* be the subject of two verbs, *helps* and *is.* Now everything is in third person.

692. **include neither (Many dictionaries include neither slang words nor common texting abbreviations.)**

The original sentence pairs *not* with *nor*. All by itself, this pairing isn't a problem. However, after *not* you have a verb *(include)*. After *nor* you have a noun and attached descriptions *(common texting abbreviations)*. Now you're violating parallelism. Change the original to *include neither slang words nor common texting abbreviations*. Another possible correction is *include no slang words or common texting abbreviations*.

693. **An apple, a pear, and a banana (An apple, a pear, and a banana are in the fruit bowl.)**

A and *an* are articles. The first precedes words beginning with consonants, and the second precedes words beginning with vowel sounds. In the original sentence, *an* is the only article in front of three nouns *(apple, pear, banana)*. Two of those nouns begin with consonants, so *an* is out of place. Add the missing articles, and your sentence is parallel.

694. **they use social media too (Successful politicians greet each supporter in person, and they use social media too.)**

The first half of the sentence is in active voice (the subject does the action). The second half of the sentence is in passive voice (the subject receives the action). Change the passive voice to active, and the sentence becomes parallel.

695. **and prevention of (As a short-term solution for hurricane victims and prevention of future storm damage, this plan is excellent.)**

The first part of the sentence focuses on a noun *(solution)*, but then the sentence shifts to a prepositional phrase *(in prevention of)*. Stay with two nouns *(solution . . . and prevention)* and you're fine. Another correct sentence employs two phrases *(With a short-term solution for hurricane victims* and *in prevention of future storm damage)*.

696. **the student can submit (A current teacher must recommend a student applying for an honors course, or the student can submit an essay explaining why the workload will not be too challenging.)**

The first part of the sentence talks about *a student* — a singular term. Then the sentence shifts, with no good reason, to plural *(they)*. Both halves can be plural or both can be singular, but switching makes the sentence not parallel.

697. **streets, roads; each, every**

A *street* is a *road,* so these two words are repetitive. So are *each* and *every,* which both make the point that Mike never skips a day of jogging. You should cut one term from each pair (either *streets* or *roads,* for example).

698. **four-sided, square, shape**

A *square,* by definition, is *four-sided.* It's also a *shape.* To make the point, all you need is *square.*

Answers
601–700

699. **long, in length**

Long and *in length* make the same point, so choose one or the other.

700. **Totally, completely; circular, ring**

Totally and *completely* are synonyms, so you don't need both. The common definition of *ring* is *circular in shape,* so unless you add some strange variation (say, a *double ring* or a *boxing ring,* which is square), stick with *ring* alone.

701. **easiest, most carefree, with no effort**

Easiest, most carefree, and *with no effort* all express the same idea. One is enough! Did you trip over *ovens and other kitchen equipment? Ovens* are *kitchen equipment,* so that phrase without the word *other* would be repetitious. Including *other,* however, brings in the rest of the machinery in your kitchen — blenders, dishwashers, and so forth. Because *other* adds information, the phrase is not repetitious.

702. **In my opinion, I think; experienced emotionally, felt in my heart**

Each of these pairs expresses the same idea. Your *opinion* is what you *think.* What you experience emotionally is what you feel in your heart. Opt for one half of each pair to avoid repetition.

703. **No repetition**

Surprised? *Untreatable* is not a synonym for *fatal.* Some illnesses don't go away but don't kill you either, and the sentence clearly states that whatever Georgina has is fatal in most cases, but not all. Nor are *dismayed* and *frightened* synonyms. The first term refers to sadness and the second to fear. Finally, *retreated* is a movement, and *stayed* is lack of movement — not repetitive!

704. **No repetition**

Did you puzzle over *thorough* and *checking original papers as well as secondary sources?* True, someone who is *thorough* does perform those tasks. However, the phrase *checking original papers as well as secondary sources* gives details about the biographer's methods, explaining how he is *thorough.* Because the second phrase adds information, it's not repetitive.

705. **Attempting, tried; wire, wire walker; cross, other shore**

Attempting and *tried* are synonyms. If you're on a *wire,* you're a *wire walker.* (Either that or you're insane, but if 300 million people are watching, you're probably a professional!) If you're crossing Niagara Falls, you're clearly aiming for the *other shore*.

706. **popular, hit; small, that has 500 inhabitants**

When something is *popular,* it's a *hit.* The next pair is trickier. *Small* is a relative term. In Manhattan, a *small* building may have ten floors when it's compared to a skyscraper. In another context, a ten-floor structure may be the largest building in the area. In this sentence, though, cross out *small* and let the more specific term (*that has 500 inhabitants*) remain. The reader gets the information and can decide whether such a town is *small*.

707.

IV. (The ambition of the title character of *Macbeth* leads him to crime.)

The original sentence *(The title character in Macbeth is ambitious, and it is this ambition that leads him to crime)* repeats *ambitious* and *ambition*. Revision IV includes all the information of the original, which has 17 words, in 12 words. You may notice that Revisions I, II, and III are shorter than IV. However, something is lacking in each. In Revision I *(The title character, Macbeth, has ambition and leads him to crime)*, the subject of *leads* is *title character* — not the meaning you want. Revision II *(Leading to crime, the title character in* Macbeth *is ambitious)* has the same meaning because the introductory verb form, *leading*, describes the subject of the sentence *(title character)*. Revision III *(Ambition leads to crime in Shakespeare's* Macbeth*)* drops an important reference to the title character. Only IV does the job.

708.

I. (Fair and reasonable, Jill saw the advantages and disadvantages of both sides in every argument.)

Revision I cuts four words from the original *(Jill was always fair and reasonable, and she saw the advantages and disadvantages of both sides in every argument)* without sacrificing meaning. If it's *every argument, always* is implied. By turning *was always fair and reasonable* into an introductory description, you also save words. Revision II *(Jill was always fair and reasonable, and she saw each side's advantages and disadvantages)* is longer than Revision I and omits the idea of *argument*. Without that word, the sentence may discuss political or social advantages of siding with one or another group. Revision III *(Jill seeing the advantages and disadvantages of both sides in every argument fairly)* is a fragment, not a complete sentence. Revision IV *(Jill's fairness and reasonableness led her to see both sides)* may refer to a visit with two sides, not an evaluation of each argument.

709.

II. (Abraham Lincoln, one of the greatest presidents of the United States, was born in Illinois.)

Eight words shorter than the original *(It was this place, Illinois, that saw the birth of Abraham Lincoln, one of the greatest presidents who ever headed the United States)*, Revision II has all the information you need. The construction *it was this . . . that* is almost always unnecessary. Avoid it in your writing!

710.

I. (Fifi loves going to the park, where she plays with other dogs.)

Revision I of the original sentence *(Fifi, who is a dog, loves going to the park; the park is where she plays with other dogs)* is short and complete. Once you see *other dogs*, you don't have to label *Fifi* as a *dog*. Her identity is clear. Nor should you repeat *the park*. Revision II *(Fifi, who is a dog, loves going to the park and plays with other dogs)* isn't parallel because *going* and *plays* don't match. Revision III *(Fifi, who is a dog, loves going to the park with other dogs)* changes the meaning slightly, implying that Fifi travels to the park with other dogs. Maybe Fifi does, but the original sentence simply states that she *plays with other dogs* there. Revision IV *(Fifi, a dog who loves going to the park, plays with other dogs there)* drops the repetitive reference to *park* but unnecessarily labels *Fifi* as a *dog*.

711. **No change**

The original sentence *(When I asked Dr. Spencer about his training, he told me that he had studied at Oxford University in Britain)* doesn't need any revision. Revision IV *(Dr. Spencer trained at Oxford)* is tempting, isn't it? Only five words! The problem with IV, and with the other revisions (I: *Dr. Spencer told me that he had studied at Oxford University in Britain;* II: *Dr. Spencer studied at Oxford University in Britain;* and III: *Dr. Spencer told me that his studies took place at Oxford University in Britain*), is that some information is missing, and all of it may be relevant. For example, imagine that you visit Dr. Spencer and he blurts out, unasked, that he studied at Oxford. Is he defensive about his preparation for the job? Does he like to brag? Either situation is possible. If you ask, however, then his answer is simple courtesy. Similarly, you can't cut the identification of *Oxford* unless you're certain that the reader knows what you mean. Other institutions have the same name.

712. **IV. (Handcuffed, the burglars then demanded phone calls, lawyers, and immediate release.)**

If you're *handcuffed,* your *wrists* are *restrained.* You don't need to say this twice, as the original sentence does *(Handcuffed with their wrists restrained, the burglars then proceeded to demand phone calls, lawyers, and immediate release). Then proceeded* is also repetitious. All you need to write is *the burglars then demanded.* Revision IV is shorter, simpler, and better.

713. **III. (After 12 years in marketing, Edward was interested in a different career.)**

Revision III is half as long as the original *(After 12 years of experience at his previous jobs, all positions in marketing, Edward was interested in pursuing a different career path that wasn't marketing),* but it gets the job done. Revision I *(After 12 years of experience at his previous jobs, in marketing, Edward was interested in pursuing a different career path, not marketing)* states *different* and *not marketing* — both giving the same information. Revision II *(After 12 years of experience in marketing, Edward's previous job was due for a change)* has a misplaced description, with *Edward's job* having *12 years of experience.* Revision IV *(After 12 years of experience at his previous jobs, Edward was interested in a different career path outside of marketing)* states both *different* and *outside of* — repetitive phrases.

714. **II. (Smith Publishing employs many experts to eliminate errors in its science and math publications.)**

Once you read *Smith Publishing* in the original sentence *(Smith Publishing, which publishes some books that deal with science and math, employs many experts in science and math to check its publications and eliminate any errors),* you know that the company publishes. If *experts eliminate errors in its science and math publications,* that they are *experts in science and math* and that they *check* are implied. Revision II supplies all the information in half the space. All the other revisions (I: *Smith Publishing, which publishes some books about science and math, employs many experts in science and math to check its publications and eliminate any errors;* III: *Smith Publishing, publishing some books about science and math, employs many experts in science and math to check its publications;* and IV: *Smith Publishing, which publishes some books about science and math, employs many experts to check its publications and eliminate any errors)* contain unnecessary words.

715.

I. **(We were already seated when the conductor raised his baton and the orchestra began to play.)**

The original sentence reads: *We were already sitting in seats when the orchestra, all musicians, began to play at the direction of the conductor, who raised his baton to start the performance. Sitting in seats?* Seriously, where else can you sit? Okay, you can sit on the grass or on an exercise ball, but those are the exceptions. Don't bother placing the common meaning, *in seats,* in the sentence. Also, *the orchestra* is made up of *all musicians* — another common fact you don't have to mention. Finally, *began to play* and *start the performance* provide the same information.

716.

II. (*Oliver Twist,* **which some consider Charles Dickens's finest novel, focuses on a young boy forced to steal.)**

Revisions I (Oliver Twist, *considered Charles Dickens's finest novel, focuses on a boy who is not too old who is forced to steal*) and IV (Oliver Twist, *Dickens's finest novel, focuses on a boy who is forced to steal*) change the meaning of the original sentence (Oliver Twist, *which some consider Charles Dickens's finest novel, focuses on a young boy, not very old, who is forced to steal*) a little too much, because not everyone favors this novel as Dickens's *finest.* Revision III (Oliver Twist, *which some consider Charles Dickens's finest novel, focuses on a boy who is forced to steal*) cuts out the age factor, which also alters the meaning of the sentence. Revision II has everything, stated more concisely.

717.

III. **(The researchers hoped the new medication would make a difference during cell division.)**

The original sentence (*It was then, at the moment when the cell divided, that the researchers hoped that the new medication would make a difference*) repeats *then* and *at the moment* and *when the cell divided* — three comments about time. Opt for the most specific (*when the cell divided*), shorten it to *cell division*, and the whole sentence contracts.

718.

No change

This one is tricky. In the original sentence (*For four hours, quasars — high energy objects — were observed in that galaxy*), the material between the dashes is a definition of *quasars*. If your readers definitely know what quasars are, you don't need the definition. However, inserting a definition when you're explaining something is perfectly legitimate. The original sentence is fine.

719.

II. **(Unanimous votes rarely occur in that committee, because committee members hold strong but opposing views.)**

In Revision II, when the original sentence (*Unanimous votes do not (or when they do, only rarely) occur in that committee, the reason for this fact being that committee members hold strong but opposing views*) goes on a diet, it loses 13 words. Revision II is also better because it takes a stand. It doesn't start out in one direction (*do not occur*) and then waffle (*or when they do, only rarely*). No doubt about it, Revision II is best.

720. III. (Colles' fractures occur when the arm bone breaks near the wrist.)

The original sentence reads: *As I said before, Colles' fractures are fractures of the arm bone near the wrist.* *As I said before* is a sure sign that you're repeating yourself. Unless you're in conversation and you think the listener hasn't gotten the message, make your point once and move on. Another problem with the original is the repetition of *fracture*. Revision III takes care of both issues.

721. IV. (This novel presents important ideas that the reader should ponder.)

Consider the original sentence: *In this novel, the author discusses various themes and ideas, all very important concepts that the reader should ponder.* When you read a novel and discover ideas to ponder, you know that the author placed them there. (They didn't show up by accident!) *Themes* aren't exactly the same thing as *ideas,* but the two concepts are close, so select only one. (The simpler expression is *ideas,* but *themes* would be fine also.) Furthermore, once you have a plural *(themes* or *ideas),* *various* is implied. *Very* is sometimes a good word to intensify the meaning of the word it describes, but here *important,* all by itself, gets the point across. Cut out all those extras and you end up with Revision IV, half as long and twice as powerful as the original.

722. I. and III. (I. The brightly shining lamp is on the table next to the sofa. III. On the table next to the sofa is the lamp, which shines brightly.)

In Sentences I and III, the lamp, the table, and the sofa are in the correct positions — lamp on table, table next to the sofa. Sentence II *(Next to the sofa, the lamp is shining brightly on the table)* places *next to the sofa* far from *table;* in general, descriptions should be close to whatever they describe. Also, Sentence II implies that the lamp shines *on the table.* Probably the lamp does light up the table, but it most likely illuminates the room as well. Sentences I and III work, but II doesn't.

723. I. (The bus, which has 50 seats, is stuck in traffic.)

Sentence I properly inserts extra information into the sentence with a clause, *which has 50 seats.* Sentence II *(The bus of 50 seats is stuck in traffic)* misuses a preposition, *of.* The correct preposition for this situation is *with.* Sentence III *(The bus, it has 50 seats and is stuck in traffic)* incorrectly presents the subject, *bus,* along with a pronoun, *it.*

724. II. (The children's book contains many pictures of forests and mountains.)

Sentence I *(The book contains many pictures, and it shows forests and mountains, and it is for children)* is grammatically correct but very choppy. It sounds like a child's sentence; all its ideas are strung together with *and.* Sentence II consolidates three ideas with a possessive noun *(children's)* and a prepositional phrase *(of forests and mountains).* Sentence II is a winner! Sentence III *(The book of many pictures shows forests and mountains, intended for children)* misplaces a description. As written, the *forests and mountains* are *intended for children* — clearly not the intended meaning.

725. **III. (This container is for food scraps, which form compost to fertilize the garden.)**

Sentence I *(Food scraps form compost in this container fertilizing the garden)* says that *this container fertilizes the garden,* but the *compost fertilizes,* not *this container.* Sentence II *(In this container there are food scraps, and they form compost, and they fertilize the garden)* is more accurate but very wordy. Sentence III is more concise and conveys the correct information.

726. **I. and II. (I. The suitcase is heavy, but fortunately, it has wheels and I don't have to carry it. II. I'm glad I don't have to carry the heavy suitcase, which has wheels.)**

Sentence I includes all the ideas and expresses them nicely, because *fortunately* is a comment people make when they're *glad.* Sentence II is even more concise, though Sentence I is also okay. Sentence III *(The heavy suitcase has wheels, and I don't have to carry it, and I am glad about not carrying it)* strings together too many ideas with *and.*

727. **II. (When the sun came out, the temperature rose and the ice melted.)**

Sentence I *(The sun coming out, the temperature rising and ice melting)* isn't really a sentence at all; it's a fragment. Sentence II uses an adverb clause *(When the sun came out)* and two independent clauses *(the temperature rose, the ice melted)* to express these ideas fluidly. It's a winner! Sentence III *(The sun came out, so the temperature rose, so the ice melted)* repeats *so* and sounds immature.

728. **I. and III. (I. The suspenseful play made me gasp at times. III. The play was so suspenseful that I gasped at times.)**

Sentences I and III get the point across concisely. Perhaps you noticed that these two sentences don't bother stating *I saw the play.* Well, how can someone *gasp at times* without seeing the play? Don't state the obvious, unless you're sure the reader will misunderstand. Sentence II *(Seeing the play, which was suspenseful, was something that made me gasp at times)* is wordy and not a good choice.

729. **I. and II. (I. Because the air is dry, the plant needs water more often. II. In dry air, the plant needs water more often.)**

In Sentences I and II, statements about the air *(Because the air is dry* and *in dry air)* introduce the main idea *(the plant needs water more often).* Sentences I and II convey meaning efficiently and correctly. Sentence III *(Needing water more often, the air is dry for the plant)* mangles the meaning, because an introductory verb form *(Needing water more often,* in this sentence) attaches to the subject *(air,* in this sentence). Sentence III doesn't work.

730. **I. (Jonathan has many clients who trust him to handle their taxes.)**

Sentence I tucks a descriptive clause *(who trust him)* and an infinitive *(to handle their taxes)* into the sentence, making it concise and complete. Sentences II *(Jonathan, with many clients, is trusted by them to handle the taxes they have)* and III *(Handling their taxes, Jonathan has many clients, and they trust him)* are wordy.

731. **II. and III. (II. My boss likes to work on Saturdays because the office is empty and free of interruptions. III. My boss likes working on Saturdays in an empty office without interruptions.)**

Sentence I *(My boss, working on Saturdays, likes that the office is empty and that no one interrupts him on Saturdays)* is wordy, with two unnecessarily long clauses beginning with *that* and repetition of the phrase *on Saturdays.* Sentence II condenses the long clauses of Sentence I into simpler descriptions — *empty* and *free of interruptions.* Sentence III is even shorter, but the prepositional phrases *(in an empty office without interruptions)* get the job done.

732. **I. (At harvest time, some growers add artificial color to fruit and vegetables to satisfy consumer demand for such produce.)**

Sentence I uses the general term *produce* to replace *fruit and vegetables.* That's a great idea, because repeating the same phrase is boring and inefficient. Sentence II *(Because of consumer demand for brightly colored fruit and vegetables, some growers artificially add bright color to the fruits and vegetables when the fruits and vegetables are harvested)* uses the phrase *fruit and vegetables* three times! Sentence III *(Demanding bright colors for fruit and vegetables for consumers, some growers add the color artificially)* mistakenly says that the growers are *demanding,* not the consumers. Remember that an introductory verb form (such as *demanding*) must apply to the subject of the sentence, which is *growers* in Sentence III.

733. **III. (Smartphone applications, or "apps," are more advanced now than they used to be.)**

Sentence I *(The applications, also known as "apps," for smartphones are more advanced now than the apps were some years ago, being less advanced then)* ends with a completely unnecessary phrase, *being less advanced then.* It dangles at the end of the sentence, attached to nothing. Sentence II *(Being more advanced now, smartphones running better apps)* looks good at first glance, because it's concise, but the sentence isn't really a sentence at all; it's a fragment. Sentence III expresses all the ideas smoothly and correctly.

734. **I. and II. (I. A train running at high speed cannot stop suddenly. II. Running at high speed, a train cannot stop suddenly.)**

Sentences I and II neatly express all the ideas. Sentence I uses a description *(running at high speed)* after the word described *(train).* Sentence II places the description before the word described. Sentence III *(Sudden stops, they cannot happen for high-speed trains)* doubles up the subject *(stops, they),* so it doesn't work.

735. **II. and III. (II. Energy-efficient fluorescent bulbs decrease customers' electric bills. III. Fluorescent bulbs, being energy efficient, decrease customers' electric bills.)**

Sentence I *(Fluorescent bulbs are energy efficient, so they use less energy, and customers' electric bills are lower)* strings together three statements with *so* and *and.* Sentence I isn't terrible, but it's a little awkward. Sentences II and III, on the other hand, tuck in the idea of using less energy with an adjective *(energy-efficient)* in Sentence II and a verbal *(being energy efficient)* in Sentence III. Both II and III flow nicely and communicate all the information.

---

736.   **I. (Studying anatomy may help artists draw human figures.)**

So many words express the ideas in this question! Yet all those ideas boil down to something simple, *Studying anatomy may help artists draw human figures.* In other words, Sentence I. Sentence II *(To study anatomy, which some artists do, is that which helps artists when they draw human figures)* adds unnecessary words, as does Sentence III *(Studying anatomy, some artists when they are drawing human figures work better).*

---

737.   **All of the sentences**

Four short sentences in this question express the ideas, but Sentences I, II, and III do so more efficiently and smoothly. Sentence I *(Because mosquitoes don't fly well, especially into the wind, a fan can repel mosquitoes)* starts with an adverb clause and Sentence II *(A fan can repel mosquitoes because they fly poorly into the wind)* ends with one *(because . . . into the wind).* Sentence III *(Generating wind, a fan may repel mosquitoes, which don't fly well)* begins with the fan's role *(Generating wind)* and adds a descriptive clause at the end of the sentence *(which don't fly well)* to clarify how the fan affects the bugs. These three sentences are all different, but all are good.

---

738.   **I. (Programmed properly, computers can mimic musical instruments.)**

Sentence I is short, but it gets the job done. The introductory verbal *(programmed properly),* and the subject it's attached to *(computers)* cover the first two ideas, and the rest is a simple statement *(computers can mimic musical instruments).* Sentence II *(Programming different sounds on a computer results in musical instrument sounds)* contains repetition, and Sentence III *(To create sounds resembling musical instruments, computer programmers can do that)* has a vague pronoun *(that)* and an awkward structure.

---

739.   **I. and III. (I. Before the mirror cracked, it was Emily's favorite possession. III. Until it cracked, Emily's favorite possession was the mirror.)**

Both Sentence I and Sentence III start off with adverb clauses and move fluidly to Emily's preference for the mirror. Sentence II *(A favorite possession, Emily's mirror was cracking and then wasn't favored)* begins well but then awkwardly shifts from *was cracking* (an active-voice verb) to *wasn't favored* (a passive-voice verb). Shifting from active to passive isn't a good idea, unless you have no alternative — and you do!

---

740.   **I. (That Henry cheats is a disgrace.)**

Sentence I begins with an unusual subject, the clause *That Henry cheats.* This noun clause works perfectly with the rest of the sentence, which tells you that Henry's cheating is a disgrace. Sentence II *(Henry, cheating, is a disgrace)* expresses a different meaning, making *Henry* the disgrace, rather than the fact that he cheats. Sentence III *(To cheat is a disgrace for Henry)* is more accurate, but it's awkwardly worded.

741. **I. (After mishearing and misunderstanding a word, people eventually accept the "wrong" meaning as right.)**

Sentence I has it all, conveying the ideas with an introductory phrase *(After mishearing and misunderstanding a word)* and a concise statement about the evolution of language *(people eventually accept the "wrong" meaning as right)*. The quotation marks around *wrong,* by the way, signal that the *wrong meaning* isn't really *wrong.* The quotation marks are the equivalent of the expression *so-called,* as in *my so-called friend who stabbed me in the back.* Sentence II *(To mishear and to misunderstand a word, the meaning is accepted as right, even though it used to be wrong)* has a dangling description. No one is present in the sentence *to mishear and to misunderstand.* (When a sentence begins with an introductory verb form, the subject must be the person performing the action.) Sentence III *(Because people mishear and misunderstand a word, they accept mistakes and go from wrong to right)* is too vague.

742. **III. (Letter carriers, who want higher salaries, are on strike.)**

Letter carriers are people, so the pronoun *who* is better than *that* when you refer to them. Only Sentence III employs the proper pronoun.

743. **I. (Jim washed his shirt, but the stains made with permanent ink remained.)**

The description *made with permanent ink* is essential to the reader's understanding of the sentence. Therefore, it shouldn't be set off from the rest of the sentence by commas. Sentence I gets this point right, but Sentence II *(Jim couldn't remove the stains, made with permanent ink, from his shirt)* doesn't. Sentence III *(Made with permanent ink, Jim couldn't remove the stains from his shirt)* begins with a verb form, which, by grammar law, attaches to the subject *(Jim)*. *Jim* isn't made with *permanent ink,* so Sentence III is wrong.

744. **I. and II. (I. To see her grandmother, Charlotte visited Indianapolis. II. Charlotte visited Indianapolis to see her grandmother.)**

Sentences I and II use infinitive phrases *(to see her grandmother)* to explain why *Charlotte visited Indianapolis.* Infinitive phrases express Charlotte's reason in an efficient and interesting manner. Sentence III *(For seeing her grandmother, Charlotte visited Indianapolis)* starts off with an odd prepositional phrase *(For seeing her grandmother)* and isn't as fluid as Sentences I and II.

745. **I. and III. (I. Hurtling through the air, the football cleared the goalposts. III. Clearing the goalposts, the football hurtled through the air.)**

In Sentences I and III, introductory verb forms convey information. Both tell the reader that the football was in the air and went through the goalposts. Sentence II *(To hurtle though the air, the football cleared the goalposts)* implies a cause-and-effect relationship that isn't accurate; the football didn't clear the goalposts in order *to hurtle through the air.* In fact, the reverse is true.

746. **III. (A polished piece of writing, that essay will win a prize.)**

Sentence I *(The essay that is a polished piece of writing and that will win a prize)* isn't a sentence at all; it's a fragment. Sentence II *(Polished, the essay is a piece and writing and it will win a prize)* begins well, with the description *polished*. Then it strings ideas together in a childish way, using *and* twice. Sentence III starts off with an appositive (an equivalent) — *a polished piece of writing*. The rest of the sentence states simply and clearly that the *essay will win a prize*. Sentence III works well.

747. **III. (Having stayed up all night, Ben fought to keep his eyes open at work the next day.)**

A descriptive verb form usually expresses action that happens at the same time as the action expressed by the main verb in the sentence. However, once you add *having*, you place the action from the descriptive form before the main action. Ben's all-nighter took place first, so *having stayed up all night* is the form you want. Only Sentence III has that form, so only Sentence III is correct.

748. **I. (Wearing masks and odd clothes, no one at the costume party recognized anyone else.)**

The descriptive verb form in Sentence I, the present participle *wearing*, expresses action that happens at the same time as the action expressed by the main verb in the sentence. In this situation, the guests are wearing masks and costumes and they don't recognize anyone else. Everything happens at the same time. Sentence I is correct. *Having worn* and *had worn* don't work in this situation.

749. **I. and III. (I. To see Mount Everest, her goal, wasn't easy. III. Her goal, to see Mount Everest, wasn't easy.)**

In Sentences I and III, you have an appositive — an equivalent. The order is reversed, but both sentences equate *to see Mount Everest* and *goal*. Both I and III are excellent combinations of ideas. Sentence II *(Being her goal, seeing Mount Everest not being easy)*, on the other hand, isn't really a sentence. It's a collection of participles with no complete thought.

750. **II. (I want the book that has an index.)**

The descriptive clause *that has an index* identifies which book *I want*. Because it's essential, it shouldn't be set off by commas. Sentence I *(I want the book, that has an index)* is wrong, therefore, and Sentence II is right. Sentence III *(Having an index, I want that book)* has an introductory verb form, which, by the rules of grammar, must describe the subject. The speaker, *I*, doesn't have an index. The book does! Sentence III is wrong.

751. **II. (Having done the laundry yesterday, I think you should do it today.)**

Sentence I *(Doing the laundry yesterday, you should do it today)* has an introductory verb form, which, in proper grammar, describes the subject. However, *you* didn't do the laundry yesterday; the speaker *(I)* did. Sentence I is wrong. Sentence II works well because the helping verb *having* places the first statement about laundry (that the speaker did it yesterday) earlier than the second *(I think you should do it today)*. Sentence III *(The laundry done yesterday, you should do it today)* omits the speaker, so it doesn't make sense.

752. **II. and III. (II. On the bus, was he? III. Was he on the bus?)**

Sentence III is the common pattern for a question in English. Sentence II is a fine variation, but Sentence I *(On the bus, did he?)* isn't. The verb *did* makes no sense unless you add another verb, such as *travel*.

753. **All of the sentences**

Every sentence here expresses the same idea in proper English. Isn't it nice to see some interesting variations?

754. **I. and II. (I. Around the corner, just in time, came a police officer. II. Just in time, around the corner came a police officer.)**

The basic subject-verb pair *(police officer came)* is inverted in Sentences I and II and placed at the end of the sentence instead of in its usual spot, the beginning. No worries: Both sentences are correct. Sentence III *(Coming around the corner, just in time, a police officer)* lacks the subject-verb pair, so it's a fragment, not a real sentence.

755. **III. (Chinese food he loved, but Japanese food he avoided.)**

Sentence I *(Loving Chinese food, avoiding Japanese food)* lacks a subject-verb pair, and Sentence II *(Loved Chinese food, he avoided Japanese food)* incorrectly drops a verb form *(loved Chinese food)* at the beginning of the sentence. Sentence III changes the usual pattern (subject-verb-complement) by placing the complements first *(Chinese food, Japanese food)*. Sentence III is correct.

756. **I. and III. (I. Finished everything, have they? III. Have they finished everything?)**

Sentences I and III are acceptable ways of asking whether *they have finished everything*. Sentence II *(Everything finished, have they?)* doesn't work because the reader instinctively adds *is*, as in *everything is finished*. That expression doesn't match *they have*.

757. **II. (Creating perfect ice for hockey, Freon flowed through the pipes under the surface.)**

The key to this question is figuring out where everything is and then ensuring that the descriptions put everything in the proper place. You have a surface that's perfect for hockey and pipes under the surface. Freon flows through the pipes. Okay, now that you know what's where, check out Sentence I *(Creating perfect ice for hockey, through the pipes flowed Freon under the surface)*. The prepositional phrase *under the surface* is in the wrong spot; it should follow *pipes*, because the *pipes* are *under the surface*. In Sentence III *(Through the pipes Freon under the surface flowed, creating perfect ice for hockey)*, *Freon* again separates *pipes* and *under the surface*. Penalty box! Only in Sentence II is everything where it should be.

758. **III. (No goal was more important to him than winning a gold medal.)**

Sentence I *(His winning a gold medal, no goal more important to him)* has no true subject-verb pair, so it's a fragment. Sentence II *(Winning a gold medal, his goal, was more important to him)* has an appositive, *his goal*, which is the equivalent of *winning a gold medal*. However, the comparison is incomplete — *more important* than what? You can't tell, so Sentence II is incorrect. Sentence III equates *goal* and *winning a gold medal* with the linking verb *was*. This sentence is correct.

759. **All of the sentences**

The noun clause *that Jane's motives were pure* moves around in these three sentences, but in each it's correctly used. In Sentences I *(That Jane's motives were pure was all that mattered to Joe)* and II *(To Joe, that Jane's motives were pure was all that mattered)*, the clause is a subject. In Sentence III *(All that mattered to Joe was that Jane's motives were pure)*, it's a complement.

760. **I. (No matter what Agatha says, don't listen.)**

In Sentence I, the basic subject-verb pair is present *(you* [understood] = the subject; *listen* = the verb). The expression *no matter what Agatha says* explains the condition for listening (or not listening), so it's an adverb, in a fine spot. Sentence II *(Whatever Agatha says, it does not matter, don't listen)* is a run-on, with two complete thoughts improperly placed together *(it does not matter, don't listen)*. Sentence III *(Not mattering what Agatha says, don't listen)* begins with a verbal that doesn't make sense.

761. **I. (What he does, you don't have to do too.)**

The word *too* floats around in two of these sentences. It makes sense where it is in Sentence I, because it applies to *you*. In Sentence II *(Whatever he does, too, you don't have to)*, though, the *too* could apply to the first or the second statement. Because it's vague, Sentence II doesn't work. Sentence III *(You not having to do what he does)* is a fragment.

762. **I. (Breaking through the cloudy skies was a rainbow.)**

Sentence I inverts the usual subject-verb order, but everything is present. Sentence II *(A rainbow, breaking through the cloudy skies was)* improperly separates the subject *(rainbow)* from the verb *(was)* with a comma. Sentence III *(Was a rainbow breaking through the cloudy skies)* would be fine if it were a question, but as a statement, it's incomplete — and therefore incorrect.

763. **I. and II. (I. Whatever attracts attention, such as a feather-and-glue dress, she wants. II. Whatever attracts attention — a feather-and-glue dress, perhaps — she wants.)**

The core of Sentences I and II is the subject-verb pair, *she wants*. The direct object is the noun clause, *whatever attracts attention*. The *feather-and-glue dress* is extra information, giving you more information about *whatever attracts attention*. Because *feather-and-glue dress* is not essential, it's properly set off by commas (Sentence I) and dashes (Sentence II). Sentence III *(Wanting a feather-and-glue dress, attracting attention)* is a fragment, lacking a subject-verb pair.

764. **I. and III. (I. Moving to Lithuania, he experienced his ancestors' culture. III. He, moving to Lithuania, experienced his ancestors' culture.)**

Sentences I and III place the descriptive verb form, *moving to Lithuania*, where it belongs — attached to *he*. Sentence II *(His ancestors' culture moving to Lithuania he experienced)* attaches that description to *culture*, not the intended meaning.

765. I. (On the track, speeding along, the blue racing car stood out.)

Only Sentence I has a true subject-verb pair, *car stood*. The other two sentences *(Standing out, on the track the blue racing car, speeding along* and *Standing out and speeding along, the blue racing car on the track)* are fragments.

766. I. and II. (I. Of love he knew nothing. II. Nothing he knew of love.)

Sentences I and II have a basic subject-verb pair *(he knew)*. The complement *(nothing)* and prepositional phrase *(of love)* move around, but they make sense. Sentence III *(Knowing nothing, he of love),* on the other hand, doesn't make sense, so it's incorrect.

767. were uncovered (PV) (The ruins were uncovered early in 1912.)

The subject of the sentence, *ruins,* receives the action here, so *were uncovered* is a passive verb form.

768. were connected (PV), was constructed (PV) (France and England were first connected by high-speed trains when the Chunnel, a tunnel under the English Channel, was constructed.)

The subject of the first part of this sentence, *France and England,* receives the action, so *were connected* is passive. In the second half of the sentence, the subject *(tunnel)* receives the action, making *was constructed* a passive verb. Did you select *first?* That's an adverb, telling when the action happened.

769. blanketed (AV), found (AV) (Fog blanketed the area, but somehow Raymond found the path home.)

The subject, *fog,* performs the action in the first portion of this sentence, so *blanketed* is an active verb. In the second portion of the sentence, the subject *(Raymond)* performs the action. Thus *found* is also an active verb.

770. is working (AV), writes (AV), are (AV) (Carlos's poetry class is working hard; the poems he writes are imaginative.)

This is a short sentence packed with verbs. First you have *is working* — which explains what the subject, *class,* is doing. Because the subject performs the action, *is working* is an active verb form. Next up is *he writes.* The subject, *he,* does the action *(writes),* so *writes* is an active verb. The last subject-verb pair is *poems are.* The verb here is also active, because the subject *(poems)* is in the state of being expressed by the verb. Did you struggle with *imaginative?* It's an adjective, not a verb.

771. rejected (AV), representing (AV), says (AV), was trained (PV) (William rejected 30 applicants representing 16 schools because, he says, not one was properly trained.)

The first subject-verb pair is *William rejected. William* performs the action, so *rejected* is an active verb. The next verb form, *representing,* is a descriptive verb form (a participle). Although it doesn't function as a verb, it's active because what it describes *(applicants)* performs the action. Next up is *says,* an active verb because the subject, *he,* performs the action. The last verb is *was trained.* It's passive because its subject, *one,* receives the action *(was trained).*

772. **Played (PV), stunned (AV), pleased (AV) (Played at maximum volume, Doug's music stunned and pleased the crowd.)**

The descriptive verb form *played* is passive because it describes *music,* which receives the action. Both *stunned* and *pleased* are active, because their subject, *music,* performs those actions.

773. **Having been summoned (PV), was (AV) (Having been summoned to jury duty, Richard was absent from work last week.)**

The introductory verb form, *having been summoned,* describes *Richard. Richard* receives the action, so the verb form is passive. The second verb, *was,* is active, because the subject *(Richard)* exists in the state of being the verb expresses.

774. **terrified (AV), afflicted (AV), has been eradicated (PV) (Smallpox, which terrified and afflicted so many, has been eradicated.)**

The pronoun *which* stands in for *smallpox. Terrified* and *afflicted* are two active verbs because their subject, *which,* performs those actions. The next verb is *has been eradicated.* Its subject, *smallpox,* receives that action, so the verb is passive.

775. **The clerk stamped the letter after Louella had paid the postage.**

The passive verb *was stamped* changes to the active *stamped* once you make *clerk* the subject of the first part of the sentence. The second subject-verb pair *(Louella had paid)* is already active, as the subject performs the action.

776. **The smiling toddler blew out two candles.**

The passive verb *were blown* changes to *blew* when you make the subject *toddler.*

777. **No change**

The sentence has two subject-verb pairs, *umbrella did hit* and *wind whisked.* In both pairs, the subject performs the action, so both verbs are active.

778. **Isaac hopes that Governor Mary Smith will lower taxes when she takes over.**

The original sentence has one passive verb, *will be lowered.* Change that to *Governor Mary Smith will lower,* and the verb is active. Did you select a descriptive verb form, *taking office,* to change the sentence? That verb form would work only if the subject were *Governor Mary Smith,* not *Isaac* or *taxes.*

779. **Riders should wear helmets at all times during bicycle rides.**

The original sentence has a passive verb, *should be worn,* but you can't change the verb to active unless you supply someone to wear the helmets. The logical choice is *riders,* though *cyclists* or another noun could also work. If you tried to fix the sentence with a descriptive, introductory verb form *(riding,* for example), you need a subject who's doing the *riding (bicycle riders,* perhaps). Remember, a descriptive, introductory verb form describes the subject, and *helmets* can't ride! The problem with adding *bicycle riders* or *riders* is that you end up with an awkward, repetitive sentence, such as this one: *Riding a bicycle, riders should wear helmets at all times.* Your best choice is to avoid the descriptive verb form.

780. Passengers must check large suitcases before boarding, but some take them into the cabin anyway.

Must be checked is passive, so you have to reword the sentence so that *passengers* are checking their bags.

781. No change

This sentence has three subject-verb pairs, all active: *minutes had passed, we realized, she was*. No change is needed here.

782. No change

The sentence expresses a real possibility, so a subjunctive verb isn't necessary.

783. If I were a lottery winner (If I were a lottery winner, I would circle the globe on a first-class ticket. Unfortunately, I didn't win.)

The second sentence hammers home the point: The speaker *(I)* didn't win the lottery. Therefore, the *if* statement isn't true and requires the subjunctive verb, *were*.

784. If Marty had been promoted (If Marty had been promoted, he would have taken us to a fancy restaurant to celebrate. Instead, we treated him to a hot dog from the corner stand.)

Hot dog? Clearly, Marty did not receive a promotion. The *if* statement isn't true and requires the subjunctive verb, *had been promoted*.

785. is suspended (If Alex is suspended, he will miss at least 50 games; the commissioner will announce his decision tomorrow, and Alex will know his fate.)

This sentence expresses a real possibility, so no subjunctive verb is necessary. The second half of the sentence is in future tense, so present tense is best for the *if* statement.

786. No change

The *if* statement is at the end of the sentence here, but the same rules apply: Anna did *not* know how hungry her guests were, so the *if* statement has a subjunctive verb *(had known)*. The other statement requires the helping verbs *would* and *have* to place the action in the past, matching *had known* and *were,* verbs that also refer to the past.

787. Were Dmitri an accomplished magician (Were Dmitri an accomplished magician, he would pull a rabbit out of a hat. Because he's still learning, he can retrieve only a scarf from a baseball cap.)

Dmitri isn't an accomplished magician, so that part of the sentence needs a subjunctive verb, *were*. *If Dmitri were an accomplished* is another possible correction.

788. No change

This sentence begins with an implied *if* statement that isn't true. Sparky didn't get lost, so you need the subjunctive verb, *had gotten*.

789. **was (On the way to the used car lot, Lola made up her mind: If the convertible was in good shape, she would buy it.)**

You don't need subjunctive because the sentence presents a real possibility — a car that may be *in good shape* or not. The whole sentence is set in the past (*made* is a past-tense verb), so a simple past-tense verb, *was,* works here.

790. **Had the chef added seasoning (Had the chef added seasoning to that food, it would have tasted better and more diners would have eaten it.)**

The sentence clearly says that the chef didn't add seasoning, so you need subjunctive. *Had the chef added seasoning* contains the subjunctive verb *had added.* The *if* is implied, but stating *if* also works *(If the chef had added seasoning).*

791. **If Maddy answers (If Maddy answers the phone, hang up!)**

The sentence presents possibilities: *Maddy* or no one or someone else may answer. When a situation is possible, don't use a subjunctive verb. The second portion of the sentence is a command *(hang up),* and commands are always in the present. Opt for the simple present-tense verb, *answers.*

792. **No change**

This sentence has an *if* statement, but it doesn't present an *if/then* idea. Instead, it simply explains the clerk's question, which deals with a condition and consequently uses a conditional helping verb, *would.* The original sentence is fine as written.

793. **would've hit (If the pitcher had thrown a fast ball, the batter would've hit a home run.)**

The sentence presents a classic subjunctive situation. The *if* statement tells what didn't happen, and the other part of the sentence employs the helping verb *would.* The problem with the original is *of.* The contraction *would have* shortens to *would've,* which sounds like *would of.* The expressions *would of, should of,* and *could of* are never correct. Go for *would've* or *would have.*

794. **as if Jordan were (The mathematician spoke as if Jordan were his equal, but Jordan has trouble adding two and two.)**

Jordan isn't the equal of *the mathematician,* so the subjunctive verb *were* is necessary here. You may wonder about *as if.* That expression may introduce a subjunctive situation, just as *if* alone does. In this sentence *as if* fits the meaning of the sentence, so don't change it. The word *like,* by the way, never begins a subject-verb statement.

795. **No change**

The first part of this sentence expresses something that isn't true: Cary isn't 60. He's 30. *As though* can introduce a subjunctive statement (just as the more common word, *if,* does). One more grammar point: The word *like* never begins a subject-verb statement.

796. **he had bought (Dialing the repair shop, Johnny wishes he had bought the computer at a store, not at a flea market.)**

This sentence is another variation on the sort of untrue statement that calls for subjunctive. Johnny didn't buy the computer at a store, so the untrue statement needs the subjunctive formed with *had: he had bought.*

797. **Capitalize *American,* no change, capitalize *First***

American is part of the title, so it should be capitalized. (It also comes from the name of a country — another reason for a capital letter.) *Inventors* is fine as written, but *First* should be capitalized. In a bulleted list not composed of complete sentences, you may choose to capitalize or lowercase the first word of every item, but you must be consistent. (Of course, if a bullet begins with a proper name, you should capitalize the name even if other bullets begin with lowercase letters.) In this slide, the first two bullets are capitalized, so the third one must be also.

798. **No change, delete period after *expense,* change to *better attendance***

The introduction to this list is a complete sentence, so a colon (:) is perfect after *following.* Drop the period after *expense* because items in a list generally don't end with periods unless the items are complete sentences. *More employees can attend* must change because the other items in the list aren't complete sentences, so this one doesn't match. A good choice is *better attendance,* but any noun and attached description *(increased attendance),* for example, would work.

799. **Delete *served as,* capitalize *Vice President,* no change**

Two of the three items in the list are nouns, but the first item adds a verb *(served).* Because all the items should match, delete *served as.* The position titles *(Governor, Vice President, President)* are all important, and all should be capitalized, including both halves of the title *Vice President.*

800. **Capitalize *What,* change the period to a colon after *dance,* lowercase *music***

The first word of an introductory phrase (in this slide, *What*) should be capitalized. As an introduction to the list, *What we need for the annual dance* should be followed by a colon, not a period, because the bullet points don't complete the sentence started by the introduction. The items in the list aren't complete sentences, and the first two items in the list are in lowercase, so *music* shouldn't be capitalized.

801. **No change, no change, change to *fake engagement announcement for Pam and Steve (2010)***

When an introductory line ends with a linking verb (a form of the verb *to be*), don't place any punctuation after the verb. Items in a bulleted list, unless they are complete sentences, generally aren't capitalized, so *glue* is fine. The second bullet point is a complete sentence, but the first and third points aren't. All bullet points should match, so change the complete sentence to a noun and its attached descriptions — *fake engagement announcement for Pam and Steve (2010).*

802. **Delete quotation marks, change to *Thiamin, riboflavin, and other compounds are B vita-mins,* no change**

Don't place a centered title in quotation marks. The first item in this list, unlike the second and third items, begins with a verb but has no subject. Any change that includes a subject-verb combination (so long as it expresses the same meaning) is fine; one possible choice is *Thiamin, riboflavin, and other compounds are B vitamins.* The third bullet point is correct.

803. **No change, change the comma after *following* to a colon, change to *to hire***

The first word of an introduction should be capitalized, so *Goals* is correct. Delete the comma after *following* and replace it with a colon. The first two bullet points are infinitives (*to* + the verb), so the third bullet point should be an infinitive (*to hire*) also.

804. **Enclose *Diving into the Wreck* in quotation marks, no change, no change**

The title of a slide generally contains no quotation marks, unless something in the title needs quotation marks for another reason. In this slide, the poem title requires quotation marks. The bullet points are all nouns with attached descriptions, and none are capitalized. All are fine as written.

805. **Change to *Stradivarius violins are expensive because of,* no change, no change**

In this slide you don't have a title; you have an introductory statement. Only the first word (and proper names) are capitalized in this sort of situation. No punctuation follows *because of,* given that the sentence isn't complete. The bullet points complete the sentence, so they must begin with lowercase letters. Each point must make sense when it is inserted into the introductory statement. All the bullet points meet this standard. Here's one example: *Stradivarius violins are expensive because of their limited numbers.*

806. **No change, lowercase *research,* lowercase *check***

You don't have a title for this slide, only an introductory statement. No punctuation follows *must,* because you haven't finished the sentence. The bullet points complete the sentence, so they must begin with lowercase letters (*research, check*). Each point must make sense when it is inserted into the introductory statement. ***Note:*** Super-strict grammarians punctuate bullet points that complete the introductory statement with semicolons after every item except the last one, which ends with a period. Many modern style manuals ignore this practice and omit the semicolons and period.

807. **Add *these features* and a colon after *features,* no change, change to *More than 90% of users approve of the app.***

The introductory statement isn't a complete sentence, but two of the bullet points are. Mismatch! Change the introductory statement to a complete sentence, and you're fine. You may choose to add *these features,* but any similar expression would do. Because you have a complete introductory sentence, you need a colon before the list. The third item changes, because in the original slide, it's incomplete. This answer is just one way to create a complete sentence. If you were thinking of a different sentence expressing the same idea, no problem!

808. **No changes to underlined material**

Shocked? This is a correct slide, just to keep you on your toes. The introductory statement isn't a complete sentence, so you need no punctuation after *for*. The bullet points are all nouns and attached descriptions, and all begin with lowercase letters. Yup, everything here is correct.

809. **Change to *Useful Arts and Crafts Materials*, change to *Glue sticks (any brand)*, change to *Felt and fabric scraps***

The centered title should be in "headline style," with all the important words capitalized. You don't have to capitalize items in a bulleted list, but if you capitalize some, you have to capitalize all. Therefore, *Glue* and *Felt* are fine. These bullet points aren't titles, though, so the words inside each item should be lowercase, except, of course, for proper nouns.

810. **Delete colon after *are*, no change, no change**

The introductory statement isn't a complete sentence, and it ends with a linking verb. Don't use any punctuation after a linking verb — ever! The other bullet points are fine, because each completes the thought the introductory statement begins. ***Note:*** Superstrict grammarians punctuate bullet points that complete the introductory statement with semicolons after every item except the last one, which ends with a period. Many modern style manuals ignore this practice and omit the semicolons and period.

811. **Delete colon after *Measures*, no change, change to *Use only disposable equipment*.**

Punctuation follows a centered title only in rare instances, such as when the title is a question and you need a question mark. The first two items in the bulleted list are commands *(Wash, Use)*, so the third item should be a command also *(Use)*.

812. **Insert a colon after *following*, place the parentheses after *Mystic Pizza*, delete the last bullet point**

The introductory statement is a complete sentence, so you need a colon after *following*. The second, third, and fourth bullet points are film titles; don't break the pattern with the first bullet point. If you move the parenthetical information after the title, the list is more uniform. (You can also delete it entirely.) The last bullet point is unnecessary, because the introductory statement says *include* and doesn't pretend to offer a complete list.

813. **No changes to underlined material**

The phrase "the famous writer" is surrounded by commas because it adds information about *Sam Smith*. When the bullet points are quotations, the speaker tag *(said)* in the introductory statement is followed by a comma. All the bullet points are properly capitalized and punctuated.

814. **Capitalize *Sources*, no change, delete the last bullet point**

The two little words here don't make sense as an introductory statement, but they work as a title. Capitalize both words *(Revenue Sources)*. The first three bullet points match; they're all nouns with attached descriptions. The fourth bullet point is a sentence and therefore a mismatch. (In grammar terms, it's not parallel.) If you delete the last bullet point, all the remaining bullet points are nouns. What about the *20% increase?* If you truly needed that information in the slide, you could place it in parentheses after the noun, making the last bullet point more specific by specifying the revenue source *(alumni gifts,* for example) and adding *20% increase* in parentheses after the source of additional funds.

815. **II.**

The key rule of writing — in any medium — is clarity. Only Option II *(walk?)* is clearly a request. Options I *(walk today)* and III *(Want to walk)* may be read as commands or statements about the message writer — not the intended meaning. Did the lowercase *w* and the absence of a subject bother you? Because this is a message between friends, the rules of capitalization and complete sentences can be ignored.

816. **III.**

Okay, most teachers would prefer a text saying *Please let me know how Susie's grades turned out this semester.* Most teachers would also like to win the lottery. Because texts are hard on your thumbs and everyone is busy, broken grammar rules are fine as long as the person receiving the text understands what the sender is saying. Option I *(grades good)* may be a statement of the parent's opinion. Option II *(Grades?)* may be an inquiry about a missing report card. Only Option III *(grades good?)* lets the teacher know what the parent wants — the teacher's opinion on the child's performance.

817. **II.**

In Option I, the subject line is blank. The subject line of an e-mail should communicate the topic of the message; otherwise, the person who receives the message will probably delete it unread. Option III has no spacing between *Dear Customer* and the message or between *Sincerely* and the message. Nor is there a space between *Sincerely* and the sender's identification. Option II properly spaces the parts of the message and includes a subject line.

818. **I. and III.**

If you want a book contract, you have to show that you can write. Option I *(This recipe for tomato stew needs a hint of dates)* is formal and correct. Option III *(Add a hint of dates to this tomato stew and wow!)* is informal but also acceptable. Option II *(This recipe 4 tomato stew needs a hint of d8s)* substitutes numbers for sounds *(4* instead of *for, d8s* instead of *dates).* Nope. In a blog, let real words rule.

819. **II. and III.**

Option I *(no   writing paper by herself)* is unclear. The history teacher may be saying that he's seen *no writing by herself* (by the student in question) or answering *no, [she's] writing the paper by herself.* The extra space between *no* and the rest of the message isn't enough to clarify the meaning. Option II *(no, writing paper by herself)* includes a comma, and Option III *(No. Writing paper by herself)* a period. These punctuation marks separate the *no* and clarify the important point — that the student is doing her own work. True, Options II and III don't follow all the grammar rules, but the teacher and counselor are equals. Bending the rules a bit when you're writing to someone of the same rank is acceptable in instant messages, as long as the meaning is clear.

820. **III.**

You can argue on this one, because out there somewhere is a grandfather who understands texting abbreviations such as *(G2G – got to go* and *ttyl – talk to you later).* However, those grandfathers are pretty rare. When you text to someone who outranks you in age or status (and a grandfather fits both categories), use Standard English, as Option III *(I have to go, Gramps. I'll talk to you later)* does.

821. **II.**

Option I assumes that the person who receives the message will realize that the subject line is the entire message. Option III is annoying. Capital letters are useful, but an entire message in capital letters comes across as a shout — a bad-mannered, hard-to-read shout. Stick with Option II, which could perhaps be more diplomatic but is fundamentally correct.

822. **III.**

If you want readers to take you seriously, you have to take yourself seriously — and follow at least some of the rules for Standard English. In Standard English, *gr8* isn't a proper substitute for *great,* so Option I *(gr8 CGI in the crashing planet sequence)* is out. Option II *(great CGI in the crashing planet sequence)* is better, but because the website is for general readers, not film buffs, the abbreviation for *computer generated imagery (CGI)* may be confusing. Option III (great special effects in the crashing planet sequence) substitutes *special effects* — much more comprehensible and therefore the best choice.

823. **I.**

Option I has an informative subject line, a respectful message, and an appropriate closing *(Sincerely).* It's a winner! Option II sounds as if it comes from the 19th century. It's too long and flowery for a busy employer. Option III almost, but not quite, makes the grade. The subject line is far too vague. Is it a job the company is doing for Maria Anderson, or one of perhaps several job openings at the firm? Don't gamble that the recipient will understand what your message is about!

824. **I. and III.**

Yes, you can — with your bff (best friend forever) — use shorthand when you text or send an instant message. You can also break the rules of capitalization, spelling *(your* instead of *you're),* and punctuation. As always, the only nonnegotiable quality is clarity. Option I *(omg I cant believe it)* employs a common abbreviation *(omg = oh my God* or *oh my goodness). Lol,* from Option III *(lol your joking),* is also a commonly accepted way to say *laughing out loud.* You may have been tricked by Option II *(idnbi),* which uses a made-up abbreviation *(idnbi* means *I do not believe it).*

825. **I.**

Presumably Mr. Smith worked hard on his article, so he deserves a courteous reply. Only Option I falls into that category. Besides, other readers disregard rants and look for comments with an actual point.

826. **All of the options**

If you're the boss, you have the freedom to be informal. Option I *(FYI: Breaks can be 10 minutes tops)* uses a commonly accepted abbreviation, *FYI (For Your Information).* Options II *(breaks now 10 mins long and no more)* and III *(10 min breaks only)* break the rules of Standard English, but they're clear and therefore okay — for the boss! If your writing will travel up the power ladder, be more cautious.

827. **2, 3, 1 (2. You do not comprehend the situation. 3. You don't understand what happened. 1. You just don't get it.)**

Expression 2 is the most formal, with no contractions (such as *don't,* which you see in Expression 3) and the somewhat sophisticated word *comprehend.* Expression 3 is correct but a little more relaxed, with the contraction *don't* and *what happened* instead of *the situation.* Expression 1 includes slang: *to get it* means *to understand.* Slang is always very informal.

828. **1, 2, 3 (1. I provide herein; 2. I enclose; 3. Here's)**

Expression 1 uses an old-fashioned, totally formal word, *herein.* Expression 2 is more modern and less formal. Expression 3 is a contraction *(here's* is short for *here is).* The contraction makes this expression the least formal of the three.

829. **1, 3, 2 (1. Don't worry about that issue. 3. Forget it, please. 2. Hey, don't flip out!)**

All three of these statements attempt to reassure the listener or reader. Expression 1 is the most formal, with a complete sentence including a dignified phrase, *that issue.* Expression 2 employs slang *(flip out = get upset),* as well as the informal greeting, *hey.* Somewhere in the middle is Expression 3, which attaches *please* to a complete sentence.

830. **1 and 3, 2 (1. does not exercise; 3. never exercises; 2. total couch potato)**

Expressions 1 and 3 are Standard English, on the same level of formality. Expression 2 is slang. (A *total couch potato* is someone who never gets off the couch.) Expression 2 is the least formal.

831. **3, 2, 1 (3. I will meet you later today. 2. See you later. 1. C U L8R)**

Expression 1 uses texting abbreviations *(C = see, U = you, L8R = later)* and is the least formal writing possible. Expression 2 is closer to proper English, but the subject and part of the verb *(I will)* are implied rather than stated. Expression 3 is correct and complete — the most formal of the three.

832. **3, 1 and 2 (3. I apologize. 1. My bad. 2. Oops! Sorry.)**

I apologize is grammatically correct and proper for all occasions. Expressions 1 and 2 are less formal because they include slang *(my bad = my mistake,* understood as an apology, and *oops,* an expression admitting an accident or error).

833. **1, 3, 2 (1. Does this interest you? 3. Are you in? 2. r u in?)**

Expression 1 has no contractions or slang, so it's formal. Expression 3, on the other hand, uses a shortened form of the expression — close to slang. *Are you in?* means *Are you interested?* and is conversational. The least formal is Expression 2, which uses texting abbreviations, *r (are)* and *u (you).*

834. **3, 2, 1 (3. pursuant to your request; 2. in reference to your request; 1. about your request)**

Pursuant to your request begins with an unusual word. *(Pursuant* comes from the same root as *pursue,* which means *follow.)* Because Expression 3 is probably familiar only to the read-the-dictionary-for-fun types, it's the most formal. Expression 2 takes it down a notch, because *in reference to* is more common (though still correct). Expression 1 is the least formal.

835. **2 and 3, 1 (2. In response to your question; 3. To answer your question; 1. You had to ask!)**

Expression 1 is obviously the least formal, with a slightly joking tone. Expressions 2 and 3 are formal without being stuffy.

836. **1 and 3, 2 (1. the child under discussion; 3. the child we are discussing; 2. the kid we're talking about)**

Expressions 1 and 3 are grammatically correct and have no contractions or slang. They're on the same level of formality. Expression 2 includes *kid,* a slang term for *child,* as well as the contraction *we're.* It's the least formal of the three.

837. **I. (Would you please write a letter of recommendation?)**

A teacher has more power than a student, and so does anyone who's doing you a favor. Statement II *(You get me. Wanna write for me? —* which a student actually sent!) is too informal. Statement III *(r u ok to write 4 me?)* is never acceptable in an e-mail, text, or instant message to anyone other than a close friend.

838.

I. and II. (I. Your vacuum stinks. I want my money back now! II. The vacuum doesn't work, so I want a refund.)

Statement I is rude, but it does get the point across. (Courtesy, of course, is always best, but grammatically this one works.) Statement II conveys the message more politely. It too is fine. Statement III (*Vacuum = busted. Refund = mine*) probably won't be taken seriously by a manufacturer. (Would you send money to someone who uses this sort of language?)

839.

All of the statements

Because Lily and Anthony are close friends, they probably text each other often and understand these abbreviations. Grammarians usually hate such shortcuts, but realists know abbreviations and shortened words convey meaning — and they aren't going away anytime soon. For those who don't text, *2G2BT* means *too good to be true*, *rly* means *really*, *r u sure* means *are you sure*, and *4 real* means *for real*.

840.

III. (The marketing is fine, but the neighborhood is questionable.)

Because the supervisor is present, the speaker should steer clear of slang such as *epic* (impressive, great), *sketchy* (borderline, not quite safe or correct) and *whassup* (a short form of *What's up?* or *What's going on?*). The third statement is fine.

841.

I. and II. (I. Saturday okay with you? Maybe the beach? Or the playground? Could be fun. II. How about I take the kids to the beach or the playground on Saturday for a fun afternoon?)

Parents are peers, so conversational English, which you see in Statements I and II, is fine. Statement III (*Would it be permissible for me to take our children on an excursion this Saturday, perhaps to the beach or to the playground, so that they can amuse each other for a while?*) is far too formal and stiff. A parent on the receiving end of Statement III would dress the kid in a tuxedo and send him out in a limo — if the parent let him go at all! Inappropriately formal language sometimes masks intention or meaning and may raise suspicions, even though none are warranted.

842.

II. and III. (II. What's the problem, Officer? III. Is there a problem?)

When a cop is ordering you around, he or she has more power. Statement I (*You gotta problem?*) is for peers, not the traffic patrol. Statements II and III are sufficiently formal for the situation.

843.

I. and II. (I. get me file asap; II. need file now)

When a boss speaks to an assistant, the boss has more power and can break the rules of conventional grammar, as long as the intended meaning is clear. The first and second statements are okay, assuming the assistant knows which file the boss wants. (*ASAP* is a common acronym meaning *as soon as possible*. It's safe to assume that most people understand it.) Statement III (*file – now*) doesn't have enough information. Does the boss want the assistant to file something away for the boss, work on the file, or bring it to the boss? More than one meaning is possible, so Statement III isn't acceptable.

844. **II. (Tell me your date of birth and social security number.)**

The acronyms *DOB* and *SSN* aren't universally understood. Similarly, *your social* may be mystifying. Only Statement II is completely clear.

845. **I. (ATM card no good. What to do?)**

Daughters and mothers are in the same family, so informality is fine, as long as the mother understands the daughter's message. *ATM* – short for *Automated Teller Machine* — is a commonly used acronym and more likely to be comprehensible than the long version. Statement I works, as it explains the situation. Statement II *(ATM no good. ??),* however, is vague. Is one particular machine broken, or is the card faulty? Two different possibilities exist, with two different remedies — go to a different ATM or call the bank and find out what's wrong with the card. Statement III *(ATM?)* is even foggier. The question may be *Can I go to an ATM? Where is an ATM? How do I use an ATM?* or something else.

846. **I. and III. (I. war b/c border wasn't where it s/b; III. border wrong, so war)**

Class notes are personal. The person who takes the notes has to understand what they mean. Class notes are also fast, because you're trying to capture speech, and speech is always faster than writing or typing. If you don't develop a system of abbreviations (*b/c* for *because* and *s/b* for *should be* are useful ones), you'll miss the teacher's next point while you're recording the previous statement. That's why Statement II *(They went to war because the border was drawn where it should not have been)* is wrong; it's just too wordy and inefficient.

847. **II. (We will file Form 112 after you send the "Explanation of Benefits" statement you received from your Primary Care Physician (your doctor).)**

Many fields create specialized terms, particularly the military and the insurance industry. That's fine if you're an insider, but if you're not, good luck understanding what they're trying to tell you. Statement I *(Don't expect us to file Form 112. You didn't supply a copy of the EOB from your PCP)* begins clearly, but then it lapses into acronyms *(EOB* and *PCP).* It also sounds harsh — not the tone a business should use with a client. Statement II spells out *EOB (Explanation of Benefits)* and *PCP (Primary Care Physician),* throwing in *your doctor* for those who are still confused. Statement II is excellent — clear and matter-of-fact. Statement III *(No 112 until we get the EOB from PCP)* assumes way too much knowledge of insurance jargon and lacks even a shred of courtesy.

848. **I. (Speak louder, please.)**

When you're dealing with people whose English is minimal, stay away from expressions that use language creatively, not literally. Statements II and III don't work in this situation because *sound off* and *kick it up a notch* (which both request an increase in volume) fall into the "creative" or "figurative" category. (Can you imagine a guide wondering where to kick?) Also, the speaker doesn't know the tour guide, presumably, and Statements II and III may be interpreted as rude; neither includes *please.* Statement I is clear and polite, a good combination for any tourist and, in fact, for any person.

849.

II. (she said yes wedding in july)

Parents usually know their children well, and the vast majority don't care about format or grammar when they're receiving important news. However, unless they're mind readers or have advance knowledge of the proposed proposal, Statements I *(she said yes)* and III *(Wedding in July)* are too vague. *She said yes* to what? Dinner? A visit with the parents? *Wedding in July* is better, but even this one could be clearer. Statement II gets the job done nicely.

850.

I. and III. (I. Spoke with Jacobs. Deal's OK with him. III. Re Jacobs: deal's okay with him.)

A customer usually merits your most formal writing, but if the customer wants something fast (and this one does), a condensed message is actually better than a drawn-out statement. Statements I and III give the facts — and the impression that the broker rushed the message to the customer as rapidly as possible. Both are better than Statement II *(I had a chance to speak with Mr. Jacobs, as you asked. I called him immediately, as you were in a rush. He indicated that the deal is fine with him),* which meanders toward meaning.

851.

II. (Important vote at tonight's meeting. Please attend.)

E-mail should never be used for communications you would like to keep private. In Statements I *(Tomorrow we should all call in "sick," if that's how the vote turns out at the meeting tonight)* and III *(We're getting the flu tomorrow, depending on tonight's vote),* the union representative hints at a planned strike. Those e-mails could lead to a court case. Statement II is more neutral and less likely to appear as evidence.

852.

I. and III. (I. moving <u>to</u> a new house; III. <u>it's</u> a shame)

The preposition *to* in Expression I correctly tells you where the *moving* is headed *(to a new house). There* indicates place, not ownership, so Expression II *(putting on <u>there</u> shoes)* should say *their shoes,* not *there.* The contraction *it's* means *it is,* so Expression III is correct.

853.

III. (<u>accept</u> the offer)

Expression I *(taking <u>you're</u> time)* is incorrect because *you're* means "you are." Here you need the possessive, *your.* Expression II *(thinks <u>two</u> much)* should be *too much,* to show excessive *thinking. (Two* is a number.) Only Expression III is correct, because *accept* means "agree."

854.

I. and III. (I. <u>you're</u> right, not wrong; III. everyone <u>except</u> Tom)

You're means "you are," which fits nicely into Expression I. The contraction *it's* means "it is," but you want the possessive *its* in Expression II *(a dog and <u>it's</u> bone).* Expression III excludes *Tom,* a proper meaning of the preposition *except.*

855.

III. (<u>it's</u> raining)

Expression I *(<u>too</u> books, one on the shelf and one on the desk)* is wrong because you need the number, *two.* Expression II *(<u>you're</u> right foot)* is also incorrect; *you're* means "you are," but here you need the possessive *your.* Expression III is right because *it's* is short for "it is."

856. **I. (no one <u>except</u> for Henry)**

Expression I properly uses *except* to remove *Henry* from the group defined as *no one*. Expression II *(<u>there</u> meeting us later)* requires *they're*, short for *"they are,"* not *there* ("a place"). Also incorrect is Expression III *(<u>too</u> the mall),* which should read *to the mall,* indicating direction.

857. **I. and II. (I. me <u>too</u>; II. <u>it's</u> my turn)**

Expression I correctly includes *too,* which in this case means "also." Expression II is right as well, because *it's* is short for "it is." Expression III *(every activity <u>accept</u> swimming)* doesn't work because the appropriate word is *except,* which separates *swimming* from a group of other activities.

858. **II. (bicycle losing <u>its</u> wheel)**

Expression I *(<u>you're</u> wallet)* requires a possessive, *your,* not a contraction *(you're,* short for "you are"). Expression II also requires a possessive, but this time you have one: *its.* Expression III *(<u>to</u> people who form a lovely couple)* refers to a number, so the word you want is *two.*

859. **I. and II. (I. styling <u>your</u> hair; II. in <u>their</u> neighborhood)**

Expressions I and II appropriately use the possessive forms *your* and *their.* Expression III *(<u>to</u> young for that toy)* mistakenly substitutes a preposition, *to,* for *too,* which means "overly."

860. **II. (<u>your</u> first job)**

Expression I *(sitting over <u>their</u>)* should include *there,* a place, instead of *their,* a possessive. Expression II properly employs the possessive *your.* Expression III *(whether <u>its</u> true or not)* needs the contraction *it's (it is),* not the possessive *its.*

861. **I. and II. (I. <u>exception</u> to the rule; II. college <u>acceptance</u>)**

An *exception to the rule,* Expression I, refers to a time when the rule is not enforced. This one's right. Expression II is also correct, because the college agrees to take the applicant and sends an *acceptance* letter. The only wrong one here is Expression III *(the car over <u>they're</u>),* which needs *there,* a place, not the contraction *they're* ("they are").

862. **III. (our school <u>principal</u>)**

For Expression I *(cause and <u>affect</u>)* you want *cause and effect,* because *effect* means "result." Expression II *(walking <u>passed</u> the bank)* is also wrong; *passed* is a verb, but here you need *past.* Expression III is right; the *principal* is the head of the school. *Tip:* Remember that the *princi<u>pal</u>* is your pal.

863. **I. and III. (I. historians studying the <u>past</u>; III. special <u>effects</u>)**

The *past* ("events prior to the present time") is what historians study, so Expression I is correct. Expression II *(<u>principals</u> of fair play)* isn't correct because here you need *principles,* or "rules." (*Tip:* Notice that both *principle* and *rule* end in *le.*) Expression III is fine, as it refers to exploding buildings, ghosts, aliens, and whatever else Hollywood experts create under the title of special effects.

864. **I. (time <u>passed</u> slowly)**

Time moves along, so the verb *passed* is appropriate for Expression I. Expression II *(illness that <u>effected</u> her)* needs *affected* ("influenced"), so it's incorrect. So is Expression III *(when <u>principles</u> scold students),* where *principals* ("school officials") scold, not *principles* ("rules or standards").

865. **II. (<u>principal</u> reason to sign the treaty)**

Expression I *(<u>past</u> over when promotions were announced)* should say *passed,* as a verb of movement fits the meaning here. (The boss looked at everyone and *passed* over an employee.) Expression II is correct, because here you need an adjective (a description). As an adjective, *principal* means "most important." Expression III *(the <u>affect</u> of the drought on crops)* is wrong; the correct version is *effect* ("result") of the drought.

866. **II. (the <u>effect</u> of Barbara's actions)**

Expression I *(the parade moved <u>passed</u>)* already has a verb *(moved),* so *moved passed* *(passed* is also a verb) doesn't make sense. The word you want is *past* ("in front of, by"). Expression I is wrong. Expression II is correct, as *effect* ("result") works nicely here. Expression III *(the dome of the <u>capital</u> building)* improperly substitutes the city *(capital)* for the building *(capitol).*

867. **I. and III. (I. heat <u>affects</u> the players; III. <u>principles</u> of sportsmanship)**

The heat "influences" *(affects)* the players, so Expression I is right. Expression II *(<u>capitol</u> to invest)* should be *capital,* because you're talking about money. Expression III refers to "rules or standards," so *principles* is correct.

868. **I. (<u>principal</u> talking to the first graders)**

Expression I is correct because the school head, *principal,* is referred to here. Expression II *(spending interest income, not <u>capitol</u>),* though, should say *capital* ("money"), not *capitol* ("government building"). Expression III *(has an <u>affect</u> on Max's mood)* is also wrong because you want the noun *effect* ("result"), not the verb *affect* ("to influence").

869. **II. and III. (II. visiting the freshly painted and renovated <u>capitol</u>; III. factors that <u>affect</u> you)**

Expression I *(meeting the <u>principle</u> signers of the treaty)* is wrong because the meeting is of the *principal* ("most important") *signers,* not the "rules" *(principles).* Expression II works because a *capitol* is a building where government meets. (No one's painting and renovating a city!) Expression III is also right; the phrase refers to *factors that affect* ("influence") you.

870. **II. and III. (II. the <u>principles</u> of investing; III. side <u>effects</u> of this medicine)**

Paris is a city, so Expression I *(Paris, the <u>capitol</u> of France)* should say *capital* ("the seat of government"), not *capitol,* which is a building. In Expression II *principles* properly refers to "rules or standards." The unintended "results" *(effects)* mentioned in Expression III are also right.

871. II. (<u>capital</u> letters)

Who has an educational conference? *Principals* ("school officials") do. Expression I (*principles' educational conference*) incorrectly substitutes *principles* ("rules"). Important letters are *capital letters,* so Expression II is fine. Expression III (*passed tense verb*) should be *past tense verb* — a verb that refers to events before the present moment.

872. I. and II. (I. to <u>effect</u> change; II. upon <u>further</u> consideration)

Surprised? *Effect* is usually a noun meaning "result," but it can, on rare occasions, be a verb meaning "to bring about." Expression I is correct. So is Expression II, because you want a word meaning "additional," and *further* is perfect. Expression III (*not the principle reason*) is wrong, though; you need *principal* ("most important") here. *Principle* is a noun meaning "rule or standard."

873. I. (ran <u>farther</u> than a marathoner)

Farther is the word you want for distance, so Expression I is right. Expression II (*compliments to the chef on a great meal*) should be *compliments* ("praise"), not *complements* ("what completes or makes better"). Expression III (*historic novels, including those with little readership or influence*) improperly substitutes *historic* ("of major importance") for *historical* ("referring to history").

874. II. and III. (II. <u>historical</u> documents; III. <u>complimentary</u> tickets)

You buy *stationery* ("office supplies"), not *stationary* ("fixed, unmoving"), so Expression I (*stationary for class, including an extra package of paper*) is wrong. Expression II works because documents created in the past are *historical* — "a record of history." Expression III is a winner because the tickets are "free," or *complimentary.*

875. I. and II. (I. <u>stationary</u> bicycle at the health club; II. no <u>further</u> trouble)

Expression I is right; a *stationary bicycle* doesn't move. Expression II is also a winner because *further* means "additional." However, Expression III (*all in the passed*) fails; *passed* is a verb meaning "gone by." The word you want here is *past.*

876. II. (<u>stationery</u> store having a back-to-school sale)

Expression I (*curtains in complimentary colors*) is wrong; it should say *complementary colors* — colors that go well with other items in the room and improve the overall look. Expression II is perfect, because a *stationery store* sells school and office supplies. Expression III (*the principals of good writing*) fails because *principals* are school officials or important participants in a situation. *Principles* ("rules") is what you want here. Expression III is incorrect.

877. All of the expressions

The *shoes* blend perfectly with whatever you're wearing; that is, they *complement your outfit.* A treaty is important, especially when it ends a war, so *historic* is also properly placed. *Principal* is correct, too, as the dancers are important, those who take the *lead roles.*

878. **None of the expressions**

You're buying *history textbooks,* not books that are remnants of the past. You travel *farther* in distance, and the paper you write on is *stationery.* All these expressions are wrong.

879. **III. (needing <u>further</u> study)**

Paper goods, including wedding invitations, are sold in *stationery* stores, so Expression I *(shopping for wedding invitations at a <u>stationary</u> store)* is faulty. Expression II *(<u>complementary</u> gift when you spend more than $500 on merchandise)* also fails because *complimentary* ("free") is the word you want here. Only Expression III makes the grade, because *further* means "additional."

880. **I. (<u>compliments</u> for the hero)**

Expression I is correct; a *compliment* is a bit of praise, something a hero should receive. Expression II *(<u>further</u> south along this road)* isn't, because *farther* is the word you want for distance. Expression III *(<u>historical</u> first human step on the moon)* is also problematic, because the first human step on the moon was extremely important in history — in other words, *historic.*

881. **III. (what the <u>historical</u> records show)**

Expression I *(<u>farther</u> reading)* should be *further* ("additional") *reading.* Expression II *(<u>complements</u> on her fine performance)* requires a word meaning "praise," such as *compliments.* Both I and II are wrong. Expression III is fine because *historical* refers to anything that comes from the past, such as *records.*

882. **As, because, unusual (As I said, I agreed to direct this play because it's very unusual.)**

The word *as* introduces subject-verb statements such as *I said. Since* is a time word, not a synonym for *because. Unique* means "one of a kind," an absolute concept. Therefore, the play can be *very unusual* but not *very unique.*

883. **whether, no change, no change (Elena wonders whether George likes the subject, because he seldom mentions it.)**

When *or not* is implied, the word you need is *whether,* not *if.* Here *Elena wonders whether or not George likes the subject.* The verb *likes* is proper, as is *because.*

884. **Because, unusual, no change (Because birds can fly, they see the world from an unusual point of view, one that humans achieve only if they're in an airplane.)**

Since is a time word, but the meaning you want here is *because. Unique* is an absolute — a one-of-a-kind. The sentence mentions that humans can attain a bird's point of view from airplane windows, so *unusual* (or *rare* or a similar word) is appropriate, not *unique. If* is fine in this sentence because it introduces a condition.

885. No change, whether, no change (Since yesterday, Alex has phoned me five times, asking me whether I'll sell him the unusual vase — quite rare — I found during my trip to Mexico.)

You need a time word in this sentence, and *since* fits nicely. Because the sentence presents two alternatives (selling or not), *whether* works better than *if. Quite rare* tells you that the vase is *unusual,* but not *unique* (the only one of its kind).

886. Because, no change, no change (Because the concert is sold out, Kira asked whether it would be broadcast, as she'd love to see the event.)

The sentence needs *because* to introduce a reason, not the time word *since. Whether or not it would be broadcast* is the implied meaning. *As* properly introduces a subject-verb statement *(she'd love).*

887. Delete *like* and the comma after *like,* no change, no change (Joe is trustworthy, so if he says he's been ill since Monday, he's telling the truth.)

Most grammarians dislike this use of *like* — even in speech. *If* introduces a condition in this sentence, a perfect job for that word. *Since* is a time word, also perfect for expressing the time period *since Monday.*

888. No change, no change, as (Whether you like the role or not, I expect you to do as we agreed and go on stage.)

When you see *or not,* you know that *whether* is a good choice. The verb *like* fits well in this sentence, but the second *like* doesn't. Because you're introducing a subject-verb statement *(we agreed),* use *as,* not *like.*

889. No changes

Everything works in this sentence: *try to* means "attempt to," *a number of* means "some," and *because* introduces a reason.

890. No change, no change, rather (Because the number of lions in the zoo is rather hard to estimate, Jana will have to guess.)

Because introduces a reason, so it's proper in this sentence. *The number of* refers to a specific number (even when you don't know how many!), so that expression works also. *Kind of* means "type of." Substitute *rather* (or *somewhat* or a similar expression).

891. No change, a number of, because (This kind of plant and a number of others need little water, because they are native to the desert.)

Kind of means "type of," so the first underlined expression is correct. *A number of* means "some," the intended meaning of the second underlined expression, so you have to make a change there. *Since* is a time word; use *because* to introduce a reason.

892. No change, no change, rather (Since Miranda emigrated from South Africa last year, she's been rather busy establishing her business.)

The time word *since* makes sense in the context of this sentence, as does the verb *emigrated,* because Miranda left South Africa. *Sort of* is not a substitute for *rather* — a better choice. (You may think of other correct alternatives, such as *somewhat, a bit,* or a similar phrase.)

893.

No change, as, no change (If he plays as I know he can, that pianist will be welcomed as an immigrant in dozens of countries.)

> *If* is correct because it introduces a condition. Change *like* to *as* because you have a subject-verb statement *(I know)* following. *Immigrant* is correct because the countries will welcome the pianist *into* their societies.

894.

No changes

> *Since* is a time word, totally justified by the context of this sentence. Louis left France, so *emigrated* is also correct. If *architectural students* are checking out your house, chances are you're in a *unique* (one of a-kind) structure. Everything in the original sentence is correct.

895.

try to, rather, no change (Jacqueline will try to calm down, but she's rather upset because she has to pay overdue fees for her library books.)

> Jacqueline won't do two things *(try* and *calm down);* she'll *try to calm down. Sort of,* which means "type of," isn't appropriate here; substitute *rather* (or *somewhat* or a similar expression). *Because* introduces a reason, so it's correct.

896.

No changes

> Because she was going into the city, *immigrating* is correct. Ellen is the subject of two verbs, each of which expresses a different action *(tried,* as in *tasted,* and *liked). Tried and* is therefore a good fit for this sentence. Finally, *sort of* in this sentence means "type of" — also a good use of language. Everything is correct!

897.

Try to, as if, no change (Try to look as if you were born here; don't let the tourists know you're a recent immigrant to this country.)

> One action is the point here, so the proper expression is *try to. Like* shouldn't introduce a subject-verb expression *(you were born),* so *as if* is better. *Immigrant* works because the person being ordered around in this sentence came *to* this country.

898.

No changes

> *Like* is proper here because it doesn't introduce a subject-verb expression. *Try and* is also okay, as you're talking about two actions (trying and failing). *A number of* means "some," a meaning that fits the context here. All okay in this sentence!

899.

No changes

> You should begin this sentence with *if,* not *whether,* because you're talking about a possibility. *Disinterested* means "fair" — the meaning you want here. *Try to* means "attempt to" — also a suitable expression for this sentence.

900.

No change, too, no change (Robbie implied that the phone bill was too high as he remarked, "I could fly there and talk in person for less!")

> *To imply* is "to hint," as Robbie's remark does. *Two* is a number, and the sentence calls for *too,* which means "overly." *As* properly introduces the subject-verb statement *(he remarked).*

901.

uninterested, no change, rather (Yawning to show that she was uninterested, Jasmine made a number of attempts to be excused from the meeting, which was rather boring.)

Disinterested means "fair," and in this sentence you need *uninterested*. *A number of* means "some," a good fit here. *Sort of,* which means "type of," isn't properly placed here; substitute *rather* (or *somewhat* or a similar expression).

902.

No change, emigrate, no change (Deciding whether to emigrate from the country where he was born, Andreas considered the number of visas issued each year and calculated his chances of receiving one.)

Two alternatives (to leave or not to leave) appear here, so *whether* works well in this sentence. *Emigrate* is "to leave one's country," so *immigrate* is misused in this sentence. *The number of* refers to a specific (though unspecified) number of visas, so that expression is correct in this context.

903.

No change, infers, a number of (In this sort of mystery novel, the detective often infers the identity of the murderer after gathering a number of clues.)

Sort of is appropriate in this sentence because the intended meaning is "type of." The detective, however, *infers the identity of the murderer. To imply* is "to hint." *To infer* is "to deduce," what you do when you figure out a mystery. *A number of* means "some" — the meaning you want in this sentence.

904.

No changes

Uninterested means "not interested," the meaning this sentence requires. *A number of* is a substitute for "some," which makes sense in this context. Finally, *try to* is just what you want in the last portion of the sentence, because only one action (an attempt to secure dinner) is expressed. All's well in this sentence.

905.

rather, uninteresting, two (Mark was rather happy when the uninteresting professor left the university two weeks before Mark was scheduled to be her student, because he liked to be entertained as much as enlightened by his teachers.)

Kind of means "type of," not the meaning you want here. Substitute *rather,* an expression that limits Mark's happiness. (You can also choose *somewhat.*) *Disinterested* is "fair," but the sentence calls for *uninteresting.* (You can also substitute any synonym for *boring.*) Finally, you need a number *(two),* not *too,* which means "overly."

906.

try to, no change, no change (The program will try to assist new immigrants in their adjustment to a new country.)

Only one action *(assist)* is in this sentence, so *try to* is the expression you want. *Immigrants* are people who have come into the country, so it's the correct term in the context of this sentence. The possessive *their* is also correct.

907.

I. and II. (I. already finished, and it's only 9 o'clock; II. thinking about you every day)

Already means "so soon" or "by this time." It's used correctly in Expression I. Expression II is right, too, as *every day* refers to today, tomorrow, the day after that — in other words, every single day. *Altogether* as one word means "completely," so it's misused in Expression III *(the choir, altogether in the rehearsal hall, waiting to perform)*. There you need *all together,* that is, the entire group in one spot.

---

908. **I. and II. (I. to meet again <u>someday</u>; II. <u>every</u> <u>body</u> in the morgue)**

An adverb referring to an unspecified time, *someday,* fits nicely in Expression I. *Every body* is the right term for Expression II, because you're talking about *bodies.* (If you want to write about an entire group of people, use the single word, *everybody.*) Expression III *(seven snacks, <u>already</u> for the children's lunchboxes)* is wrong; it works better with *all ready* — the entire group of snacks prepared, no further work required.

---

909. **II. (not hungry because she's eaten <u>already</u>)**

Expression I *(visits his uncle <u>some times</u>)* is faulty because the intended meaning is "occasionally," so *sometimes* is the proper word. Expression II correctly explains that *she's eaten* before this time, a definition of *already.* Expression III *(the entire jury, <u>altogether</u> in the courtroom)* is wrong; when a group is assembled in one spot, they're *all together.* The single word, *altogether,* means "completely" — not the meaning you need for this statement.

---

910. **I. and II. (I. <u>altogether</u> corrupt, not a shred of honesty left; II. <u>everyday</u> dishes, not the ones for special guests)**

Expression I works well with *altogether,* which means "completely." Expression II is another winner, as *everyday* means "ordinary." Expression III *(spending <u>sometime</u> on exam prep)* falls short because *sometime* as one word means "at an unspecified time." Here you want *some time,* a period of time — say, an hour — for exam prep.

---

911. **III. (<u>everybody</u> on the staff, with no exceptions)**

The intended meaning of Expression I *(<u>some times</u> sings professionally)* is "occasionally," so the adverb needed here is *sometimes.* Expression II *(to be a star <u>some day</u>)* is incorrect, too, because *some day* as two words refers to a particular day (Tuesday, for example) that isn't named. As a single word, *someday* means "at an unspecified time." Expression III is fine, as *everybody* refers to the whole group.

---

912. **II. and III. (II. <u>everyday</u> chores, but nothing extra; III. buying <u>some place</u> on 16th Street)**

Expression I *(the family, <u>altogether</u>)* refers to the family gathered as a group, so *all together* is appropriate, not the single word *altogether,* which means "completely." Expression II properly uses *everyday* to mean "common or ordinary." Expression III is correct as well, as *some place* means "a place."

---

913. **I. (a fitness plan for <u>every</u> <u>body</u> with a few extra pounds on it)**

In the context of Expression I, *every body* makes sense, because you're talking about physical *bodies.* Expression II *(to meet <u>someday</u> next week, but not Monday)* is wrong because the context *(but not Monday)* emphasizes a day. Therefore, *some day* is a better choice. Expression III *(books Maxine read <u>all</u> <u>ready</u> but would like to read again)* needs *already,* because the context requires "by this time" or "before this point in time."

914. **I. and II. (I. <u>someplace</u> to relax, such as a spa; II. a document that is <u>altogether</u> meaning-less, as if it were written by a two-year-old)**

Expression I is fine, because the sentence requires an adverb *(someplace)* to describe *relax.* Expression II properly inserts *altogether* ("completely") to explain exactly how *meaningless* the document is. Expression III *(calling <u>any time</u>)* mistakenly uses a noun *(time)* and a description *(any)* where you need an adverb, *anytime.*

915. **I. (<u>all ready</u> for the trip — bags packed and passport renewed)**

Expression I is a winner because *all ready* means "completely prepared," which describes the situation here. Expression II *(<u>every day</u> negotiations, nothing historic)* fails because you're not talking about a day; instead you need a word meaning "ordinary," and *everyday* fits perfectly. Expression III *(if the boss has <u>anytime</u> this week)* wrongly places the adverb *anytime* where you need a noun *(time)* and a description *(any).* The intended meaning is "a period of time."

916. **All of the expressions**

The fitness fanatic in Expression I *(lifting weights <u>every day</u>)* doesn't take a break from lifting weights day after day. Therefore, *every day* works here. Expressions II and III *(hoping to run for office <u>sometime</u>* and *planning to meet Helen <u>someday</u>)* correctly rely on the adverbs *sometime* and *someday* to refer to an unspecified time in the future.

917. **II. (permission to log on to the computer <u>sometimes</u>)**

Expression I *(dressed-up seniors, <u>already</u> for the prom)* fails because the seniors are pre-pared, or *all ready,* for their big celebration. Expression II works, because *sometimes* means "occasionally." Expression III *(going home in one car, <u>altogether</u>)* errs by substi-tuting *altogether* ("completely") for *all together* ("gathered in the same place").

918. **I. (getting revenge <u>someday</u>)**

Expression I correctly points to an unspecified time in the future with the adverb *some-day. Altogether* ("completely") makes more sense in Expression II *(a plan that is <u>all together</u> ambitious and inspiring)* than *all together,* which means "in unison." Expression III *(devoting <u>anytime</u> to volunteer work)* is also wrong, as it requires *any time* to refer to a period of time.

919. **I. and II. (I. finding <u>some place</u> in the orchestra, perhaps in the string section; II. <u>everyday</u> challenges for elderly residents)**

The noun-description combo, *some place,* is perfect here, because you're talking about a spot in the orchestra. Therefore, Expression I is correct. Expression II also works, because *everyday* means "ordinary," the sort of challenges any elderly person might encounter. Expression III *(going out because I <u>all ready</u> did my homework)* is wrong, as *already* ("by this time") is the word you want.

920. **III. (call <u>anytime</u>, day or night)**

The group huddled under the awning is *all together,* or "gathered," so Expression I *(sheltering from the storm, <u>altogether</u> under the awning)* is wrong. (*Altogether* means "completely.") Expression II *(asking for <u>sometime</u> off from work)* wrongly puts an adverb, *sometime,* where you need a noun and a description *(some time)*. *Anytime,* in Expression III, is a winner; in this context the adverb means "at all times."

921. **I. (my <u>sometime</u> friend, now my enemy)**

Expression I relies on a rare, older meaning of *sometime,* "once." This expression talks about someone who was once a friend but now isn't. Expression II *(<u>Everyday</u> of the week)* is wrong because you're talking about *days,* which is a noun. Therefore you need a noun-description combo, *every day.* Expression III *(<u>all together</u> majestic and inspiring)* is wrong because the context requires a word meaning "completely" *(altogether).*

922. **I. and III. (I. vampires, not <u>altogether</u> dead; III. nine months old and walking <u>already</u>)**

Vampires in films and novels aren't completely, or *altogether,* dead. Therefore, Expression I is correct. Expression II *(film making its debut <u>someday</u> next month)* is wrong because it requires a noun and a description *(some day),* not the adverb, *someday.* The debut will be on a particular day. Expression III is a winner, because *already* may mean "so soon."

923. **I. and II. (I. may burst out laughing at <u>any time</u>; II. has <u>sometimes</u> acted on Broadway)**

Expression I is right because you need a noun *(time)* to act as the object of the preposition *at.* Expression II is also fine because *sometimes* means "occasionally." Expression III *(danced, <u>altogether</u>, in the chorus line)* is wrong; *altogether* means "completely," but here you need *all together* ("in unison").

924. **a lot, would've, had (Greg has a lot of friends who would've taken care of him if they had known he was ill.)**

Written as two words, the expression *a lot* is acceptable in informal writing. (If you're aiming for the most formal level of expression, use *many.*) *Would of* is never acceptable. Substitute the contraction *would've.* The long form, *would have,* is also correct. *Had of* isn't Standard English. Go for *had* all by itself.

925. **No change, could, each other (If it's all right with Mike, Tracy and he could help each other with their physics homework.)**

All right is always two words in Standard English. *Might could* isn't correct; use one or the other, but not both together. *Each other* should never be written as one word.

926. **might've, anywhere, that ("I might've known!" shouted the detective, who added that she had never believed the murder weapon could be anywhere near that crime scene.)**

Might've is the contraction of *might have;* either one can replace *might of,* which is never correct. *Anywheres* and *that there* aren't Standard English expressions. Use *anywhere* and *that.*

927. **This, himself, no change (This notebook he bought himself, but Isabel purchased that one for him.)**

This here and *hisself* aren't Standard English; use *this* and *himself*. *That,* as used in this sentence, is correct.

928. **themselves, had, no change (The rowers reassured themselves that if they had won, they would've treated the losing team more politely.)**

Theyselves and *had of* aren't correct in Standard English; use *themselves* and *had*. *Would've* is a contraction of *would have*. Both are proper English expressions.

929. **should've, this, no change (Betsy should've watered the plants yesterday; now this garden has a lot of dead plants.)**

Should of and *this here* aren't Standard English expressions. Substitute the contraction *should've* (or the long form, *should have*) and *this*. *A lot* is correct in informal writing, as long as you write it as two words. As a single word it's always incorrect. (If you're aiming for the most formal level of expression, use *many* in this sentence instead of *a lot of*.)

930. **nowhere, could've, no change (Sam is nowhere to be found; he could've told me his location when we spoke with each other.)**

Nowheres isn't Standard English; substitute *nowhere*. *Could've* is a contraction of *could have*. Both expressions are correct, but *could of* is never acceptable in proper English. *Each other* should always be written as two words.

931. **himself, no change, no change (After falling, the skater checked himself for a minute and then said he was all right, though he could've been lying.)**

Hisself is not correct in Standard English. Substitute *himself*. *All right* is proper English; the single word, *alright,* isn't. *Could've* is a contraction of *could have*. Both expressions are fine, but *could of* isn't Standard English.

932. **No change, that, anywhere (A lot of work went into that art exhibit, the best examples of Picasso's work anywhere.)**

The two-word expression, *a lot,* is acceptable in informal English. (The most formal level of expression would require *much* instead of *a lot of*.) *That there* and *anywheres* aren't proper. Substitute *that* and *anywhere*.

933. **This, a lot, etc. (This janitor was assigned a lot of mopping, painting, etc.)**

This here and *and etc.* aren't correct in Standard English. The proper expressions are *this* and *etc.* alone. *A lot* is informal but acceptable, as long as it's written as two words. (If you're aiming for the most formal level of expression, use *much* in this sentence and substitute *and so forth* or a similar phrase for the abbreviation *etc.*)

934. themselves, no change, should've (The shoppers themselves packed their purchases (groceries, clothing, dishes, etc.), but the clerk should've taken care of that chore.)

Theirselves isn't correct in Standard English. The right word is *themselves. Etc.* is fine in informal writing. (If you're aiming for the most formal level of expression, use *and so forth* or *and other items.*) *Should of* is never correct. What you want is *should've,* a contraction of *should have.* Both expressions are right for this sentence.

935. each other, themselves, no change (James and Matt comforted each other, reminding themselves that they would've won the spelling bee had it not been canceled.)

Each other is never correct as one word. *Theirselves* isn't Standard English; substitute *themselves.* The contraction *would've* (short for *would have*) is correct. Never write *would of,* an incorrect expression.

936. anywhere, no change, that (Shelly was frantic because she couldn't find her pet bird anywhere, but the parrot was all right, hiding in that closet.)

Anywheres isn't Standard English; drop the letter *s,* and you're fine. *All right* is appropriately written as two words. *That there* is nonstandard; use *that* by itself.

937. nowhere, should've, etc. (With nowhere to go, Aaron and Betsy should've stayed home, but instead they drove around nearby suburbs, including Babylon, Massapequa, Bayshore, etc.)

Nowheres is never correct. The proper word is *nowhere. Should of* doesn't exist in Standard English either. You want the contraction *should've* or the long form *should have. And etc.* is overkill; end with the abbreviation *etc.* or, more formally, with *and so forth* or *and other towns.*

938. might've, this, no change (Winnie might've chosen this blue sweater if she had known it was available.)

Might of isn't Standard English. Go for the contraction *might've* or the long form, *might have. This here* is also nonstandard. Drop the *here* and you're fine. The last underlined word, *had,* is just what you need here.

939. No changes (The boys upset themselves when they spoke with each other about the math test, which should've been easier than it was, in their opinion.)

Themselves, each other, and *should've* are all correct in Standard English.

940. could not have been, themselves, etc. (Max and his friends, who could not have been more bored, entertained themselves by naming the Presidents — Washington, Lincoln, Kennedy, etc.)

Could of isn't Standard English. You can't make a contraction out of a negative, so substitute *could not have been. Theirselves* is also nonstandard; try *themselves.* One *etc.* is enough! Or, if you're being strictly formal, drop the abbreviation altogether and plug in *and others* or a similar expression.

941. **had, that, would've (If I had written that anonymous letter, the grammar would've been correct!)**

Had of and *that there* both contain extra words. Drop *of* and *there* and you're fine. *Would of* isn't Standard English. Go for the contraction, *would've,* or the long form, *would have.*

942. **everywhere, no change, might've (They sold similar cars everywhere, but in this dealership the owner might've given you a better price.)**

Everywhere never includes the letter *s. This* is correctly placed in this sentence. *Might of* is nonstandard. Try the contraction *might've* or the long form, *might have.*

943. **ought, that, anywhere (Yang ought to apply for that scholarship, because then he can achieve admission anywhere.)**

Everything underlined in this question has something extra — and wrong. *Had ought* should be *ought, that there* should be *that,* and *anywhere* (without the letter *s*) is Standard English.

944. **hadn't, everywhere, might've (If Mr. Mellon hadn't tried to satisfy his curiosity by looking everywhere for clues, his neighbors might've avoided calling the police.)**

Hadn't of is never correct. Drop the *of* and you're fine. *Everywheres* is also nonstandard. Delete the letter *s* for the correct version, *everywhere. Might of* is wrong. Try the contraction *might've* or its long form, *might have.*

945. **No changes (Ms. Johnson, who ought to know where the photos could've been stored, asked Annie and Sascha to help each other figure out where their work was.)**

Ought properly stands alone; it should never be paired with *had. Could've* is the correct contraction of *could have. Each other* should always be written as two words.

946. **would've, had, no change (Wendy would've given Jim a ride, if she had seen him waiting for the train all by himself.)**

The contraction of *would have* is *would've.* Either expression is correct, but *would of* is nonstandard. So is *had of;* drop *of* and you're fine. *Himself* is correct in Standard English.

947. **ought, himself, no change (Johnny ought to be more careful with himself, because he could have pulled a muscle by exercising too much.)**

Never use *had* with *ought. Hisself* is nonstandard; the correct word is *himself. Could have* (or its contraction, *could've*) is correct.

948. **herself, would've, could've (Eloise herself told me that she would've spoken more candidly if she could've.)**

Herself is always written as one word. The contractions *would've* and *could've* are proper English, as are their long forms, *would have* and *could have.*

949. ought not, could not have, etc. (Darius ought not to complain about his score on the test because he could not have done better on algebra, geometry, etc.)

Had never accompanies *ought* or *ought not* in Standard English. *Could not of* is never correct. The proper expression is *could not have* or the contraction *couldn't have*. *And etc.* doubles up where a simple *etc.* is what you need. (To be more formal, substitute *and so forth* or a similar expression.)

950. All right, no change, each other ("All right, sit down anywhere," declared Miss Echeva, "and help each other with your grammar homework.")

Alright is nonstandard; the correct spelling is *all right* (two words). *Anywhere* is Standard English for "any place" and is correct here. *Each other* should always be written as two words.

951. No change, ought, no change (Finding himself in a difficult situation, the spy ought to give up on his mission, and everything will turn out all right.)

Himself is the proper pronoun for this situation. *Had* should never be paired with *ought*. *All right* should always be written as two words, not as *alright*.

952. Do, because, no change (Do not mix business with pleasure, because you're not on duty now.)

Don't (short for *do not*) is negative and shouldn't precede *not*. Otherwise your sentence says, "Do not not . . . ." *Being that* is not Standard English. Change it to *because, as,* or a similar word. (Don't substitute *since*. Although many people equate *since* and *because*, *since* is actually a time word.) *You're* is positive, so *you're not* presents no problems.

953. anything, no change, school (May didn't know anything about spelling, and her handwriting was different from ours because she never attended school.)

The contraction *didn't* (short for *did not*) is already negative, so *nothing* creates a double negative. Change it to *anything*. *Different from* is correct. *Never* is negative, so *no school* also creates a double negative. Drop *no* and the problem is solved.

954. Because, can, no change (Because it's summer, you can expect no freezing rain or different weather.)

Being that isn't Standard English; you can substitute *because* or *as* or *considering that*. (Don't use *since*, which is a time word.) *Can't* is negative, but the sentence already mentions *no freezing*, so change *can't* to *can*. *Different,* in this sentence, is fine all by itself.

955. knew, anything, no change (Greta knew nothing, wouldn't do anything, and refused any help.)

Didn't is negative, and so is *nothing*. To eliminate the double negative, change *didn't know* to *knew*. The next verb, *wouldn't do,* is also negative and shouldn't pair with the negative word *nothing*. Change *nothing* to *anything,* and you're fine. *Refused* means "said no to," but *any* isn't negative, so no double negative pops up here.

956. **can get, no change, no change (Mick can get no satisfaction when he complains to Customer Service that he hasn't received any new guitars, although he has paid for three.)**

Can't is a negative (short for *cannot*), so *no* creates a double negative. Insert *can get* in place of *can't get* and the double negative disappears. *Hasn't* (short for *has not*) is negative, but here it's properly followed by *any*. No change is needed. Nor do you have to change *has paid,* which is simply a positive statement.

957. **any lies, regardless, anything (Zach won't tell any lies, regardless of who's asking for information, so do not explain anything to him.)**

Won't (short for *will not*) is negative, but so is *no*. Change *no lies* to *lies* to eliminate the double negative. *Irregardless* isn't correct in Standard English; substitute *regardless.* *Do not* is negative, and *nothing* creates a double negative. Change *nothing* to *anything* to correct the sentence.

958. **No changes (The dog should give you no trouble, being a gentle animal, unless you do not feed him.)**

Should give is positive, so it doesn't conflict with *no trouble. Being* is a fine word when it doesn't pair up with *that* to form *being that,* a nonstandard expression. The next verb is negative, but it's not a double. All is correct in this sentence.

959. **No changes (No, Ellie did not tell her aunt that Karl had completed nothing.)**

The first *no* is separated from the sentence by a comma, so it functions as an introduction to the sentence and doesn't create a double negative. The other two verbs are correct.

960. **can't help thinking, no change, different from (Jacques can't help thinking that, regardless of salary, his work is no different from his boss's.)**

Can't help but think is a double negative; change it to *can't help thinking. Regardless* is correct, but *different than* is nonstandard. Substitute *different from.*

961. **Regardless, that, no change (Regardless of what he says, the reason I changed jobs is that I didn't feel respected.)**

Irregardless isn't Standard English; substitute *regardless. The reason is . . . because* is also nonstandard. Go for *the reason is . . . that. Didn't* is negative, but it's not a double negative — no problems there!

962. **Because, should have, ever (Because Katie is dieting, she should have no candy, ever.)**

Being that isn't correct in Standard English. Substitute *because* or *as* or a similar word. (Don't use *since,* which is a time word.) *Shouldn't* is negative, so it can't pair with *no candy.* Change it to *should have. Never* also creates a double negative (actually, the original is a triple negative!). Substituting *ever* solves the problem.

963. anything, regardless, couldn't help charging (Steve claimed that he had not done anything; regardless, the district attorney couldn't help charging him with burglary.)

The expression *had not done* is negative, so *nothing* creates a double negative. Change *nothing* to *anything* and the problem is solved. *Irregardless* is nonstandard; substitute *regardless*. *Couldn't* is a negative word, and so is *but*. Together they make another double negative. Use *couldn't help charging* instead.

964. No change, no change, had (Walter's approach to the problem was different from Hannah's, but he had expected no criticism from her.)

Different from is Standard English, as is the use of *but* as a conjunction. No changes for these two! However, *hadn't* (short for *had not*) is negative, and so is *no criticism*. To eliminate the double negative, use *had* instead of *hadn't*.

965. any, no change, no change (Don't you know any better, regardless of the fact that you haven't been taught manners in a formal way?)

Don't (short for *do not*) is negative, so it makes a poor pair with *no better*. Substitute *any better* for *no better* and the sentence is, well, better! *Regardless* and *haven't* are correct here.

966. that, could, no change (The reason Nick moved is that he could hardly stand his supervisor's denial of any guilt.)

The reason is . . . that is correct, not *the reason is . . . because*. *Couldn't hardly* is a double negative, which you correct by changing *couldn't* to *could*. *Any* is fine in the context of this sentence.

967. No changes (No engineer but Martin has ever stepped in that room, and you can hardly blame him for bragging about his courage.)

Everything works in this sentence. The first *no* establishes a group, and the preposition *but* properly removes *Martin* from that group. The adverb *ever*, which means "at any time," properly describes the verb *has stepped*. *Can hardly* is a proper English expression.

968. couldn't help weaving, that, no change (Charlotte couldn't help weaving a beautiful web; the reason was that she was not an ordinary spider.)

Couldn't help but weave is a double negative; change it to *couldn't help weaving*. *The reason is . . . that* is correct, not *the reason is . . . because*. The single *not* in the last portion of the sentence is fine.

969. No changes (Judy could scarcely believe her eyes; the reason is that a flying saucer hadn't ever landed on her lawn before!)

Everything is fine in this sentence. *Could scarcely* and *hadn't ever* aren't double negatives, and *the reason is that* is the correct expression.

970. **No change, no change, ever (Do you know neither Latin nor Greek, or haven't you ever studied an ancient language?)**

Neither/nor is a paired conjunction, so these words don't count as a double negative. *Haven't* (a contraction of *have not*) is negative, so *never* creates a double negative. Substitute *ever* and the error vanishes.

971. **had only, could hardly, no change (King Leo had only five knights, and winning the war was something he could hardly imagine, except under different and unlikely circumstances.)**

Hadn't but is a double negative; go for *had only* or *had but* instead. *Couldn't hardly* is also a double negative that should be changed to *could hardly*. (Another way to correct this expression is to delete *hardly*.) In the context of this sentence, *different* is fine as written.

972. **many, no change, no change (Imelda has many shoes, far more than Jessie, but less time to shop.)**

You can count *shoes,* so *many* is the word you want here. (*Much* is for things you measure, such as *much salt.*) *More* both counts and measures; in this sentence, it's a counting word. *Less* is a measuring word, so *less time* makes sense.

973. **No changes (Much time has passed since Ellery noticed that many trees had some buds on their branches.)**

You measure time, so *much* is correct here. *Trees* are counted, so *many* is the proper word. *Some* works for both counting and measuring. Everything's right in this sentence.

974. **fewer, no change, many (Put fewer books on that shelf, which appears less sturdy than the one over there, which holds many thick volumes.)**

You count books, so *fewer* is better than *less,* which is a measuring word. *Less* pairs nicely with *sturdy,* a quality you measure. *Many,* a counting word, should attach to *volumes,* which may be counted.

975. **No change, no change, fewer (The soup needs a little pepper to spice it up; be sure to prepare less than you did last time, as we expect fewer guests.)**

A little and *less* are measuring words, so they're properly applied to *pepper* and *soup* in this sentence. For *guests,* which you can count, you need *fewer.*

976. **among, no change, much (Let's keep the secret among the three of us, because if more people know, our error will attract much attention.)**

Between is appropriate when you have two elements, but here you have *the three of us,* so *among* is the correct preposition. *More* is a great, all-purpose word, proper for both counting (the situation here) and measuring. Because you measure, not count, *attention,* you need *much,* not *many.*

977. **number, more, no change (Considering the number of hours I spent adding more vocabulary words to my flash cards, I should have scored much higher on the test.)**

Generally you measure time, but here time is broken into *hours,* which you count. Therefore, *number* is better than *amount. Much* doesn't work with *vocabulary words,* because you count them. *More* or *many* is a better choice. Did you stumble over the last underlined word? True, you count points to figure out a score, but here you're dealing with the abstract concept *higher,* so *much* is better. **Tip:** Never attach *more* to a comparative term such as *higher.*

978. **No change, no change, between (When Jack is among friends, he is less nervous than when the conversation is between him and only one other person.)**

Among is the preposition for groups of three or more; *between* is the preposition for a pair. In this sentence, the first underlined word applies to *friends,* and the third applies to *him and only one other person.* Therefore, you want *among friends* and *between him and only one other person.* The middle part of this question correctly attaches *less* to *nervous. Less* and *least* create negative comparisons — *less* for a comparison between two elements and *least* for three or more.

979. **No change, less, no change (This dial shows the amount of electricity consumed, which is less than last year but much more than the goal we set.)**

Electricity is measured, so *amount* is properly placed here. *Less,* an adjective, is correctly used after the linking verb *is. Lesser* is a noun, as in *the lesser of two evils,* and doesn't fit this context. The third underlined expression is tricky. *More* adapts to both measured and counted elements, so *more electricity* (the implied meaning) is correct. *Much* is an adverb, intensifying the abstract quality *more.* It, too, is correct in this sentence.

980. **Among, no change, no change (Among your options are law, banking, and education. The first two guarantee many salary increases, but the last may give you more success.)**

Three options appear, so *among,* a preposition for a group of three or more, is proper. *Many* is correct because it applies to *increases,* not to *salary. More* is one of those wonderful words that work for both counting and measuring.

981. **No change, no change, less (Dr. Henry pays much attention to his students, though he gives many more homework assignments and less extra credit work than other teachers.)**

You can't count *attention,* so *much* (a measuring word) is fine here. You can count *assignments,* so *many more* works well. *Fewer* is incorrect, though, because *work* isn't something you count. *Less* is the word that should attach to *extra credit work.*

982. **much less, no change, no change (Charlie and Rose have much less money between them than they'd like, but it is as much as they need.)**

In theory you count *money,* so *many fewer* seems correct. However, the singular word *money* is more abstract than, say, *dollars,* so it merits the measuring words *much less. Between* is correct because you're talking about two people. *Much* is a pronoun here, referring to the *money.*

983. **No change, fewer, no change (Many have complained that the rugs have fewer natural fibers and soil more easily than they used to.)**

The pronoun *many* represents *people,* so this counting word is correct. You can count fibers, so *fewer* is proper and *less* isn't. *More* creates a comparison with the word it's attached to *(easily)* and is also correct. The two-word comparative forms of adjectives and adverbs always rely on *more* and *less.*

984. **No change, no change, much (The card read, "Much love to my many fans who give me so much applause.")**

Love can't be counted, so *much* is the proper word. You can count *fans,* so *many* also works. *Applause,* on the other hand, is something you measure, so *much* is the word you need.

985. **Many more, no change, no change (Many more quilts are much better than fewer on a cold night like this!)**

The counting words *many more* and *fewer* should attach to *quilts,* which can be counted. *Better* is an abstract quality — nothing you can count! — so *much* works well with it.

986. **No change, many, no change (Sayed had much to be thankful for, such as many friends, few enemies, and a loving family.)**

Much is generally a measuring word, but *friends, enemies,* and *family* appear to be things you count. However, *much* in this sentence applies to the idea of *thankfulness,* even though that word doesn't appear in the sentence. The second underlined word should be *many,* as it's attached to *friends* — definitely something you count. You can also count *enemies,* so *few* works fine with that noun.

987. **I. (raise the flag)**

To raise is "to lift," and when you *raise the flag,* you lift it on the flagpole. Expression I is correct. Expression II *(lay down for a nap now)* is wrong because *to lay* is "to place, to put down." Here you want *lie,* which means "to rest or recline." Expression III *(setting on the chair)* fails because *sitting* is what you're doing when you're plopped on a chair. *To set* is "to place."

988. **II. (the sun, which rose at 5 a.m.)**

To set is "to place," the meaning you need in Expression I *(sit the fragile antique desk in the corner). Sit,* in this context, is wrong. Expression II is correct because the sun *rose* ("lifted itself"). Expression III *(has laid in bed for ten hours)* should be *has lain,* because that's the present perfect form of the verb *to lie,* which means "to rest or recline."

989. **II. and III. (II. who had sat in the shade on a blanket; III. laid railroad tracks near the station)**

The audience members lift themselves to a standing position, so *rising* ("lifting oneself") is the proper verb for Expression I *(the audience, raising for a standing ovation),* not *raising. Had sat,* in Expression II, is correct. The past perfect form of *to sit* is *had sat.* Expression III is fine as well, because someone placed railroad tracks, and *laid* is the past-tense form of *to lay.*

990. **III. (raised the shelf two inches higher)**

To set is "to place," so in Expression I *(because yesterday he sat the birdcage near a window)* you need that verb, not *to sit.* The proper form here is *he set the birdcage. Has lain,* in Expression II *(has lain the picnic basket on the ground),* is also wrong, because you need the present perfect form of *to lay* ("to place"), which is *has laid.* Expression III is a winner: *to raise* is "to lift," and here someone *raised* ("lifted") *the shelf.*

991. **II. and III. (II. rise for the singing of the national anthem; III. lay down for a nap about an hour ago)**

An informal expression often used in the South, *to set a spell* isn't correct in formal English. Use it in conversation if you want, but in formal writing, you need *sitting for a while* or a similar phrase. Therefore, Expression I *(setting a spell, to relax)* is wrong. *Rise* is correct in Expression II, because people lift themselves to their feet for the anthem, and *to rise* is "to lift oneself." Expression III employs *lay,* the past-tense form of *to lie* ("to rest or recline").

992. **I. and II. (I. peasants rose in rebellion; II. laid flowers in front of the shrine)**

The peasants "lifted themselves up" to oppose the rulers, so *rose,* the past tense of *to rise,* is correct in Expression I. Expression II is right because *laid* is the past tense of *to lay,* which means "to place." Expression III *(has set still for the photographer)* is wrong; *has sat* is the present perfect form of *to sit,* and you *sit still* when your picture is being taken.

993. **II. and III. (II. raises an important point at the meeting; III. the diamond, set in a gold ring)**

You know you need past tense in Expression I *(lay the suitcase on the bench and left it there)* because one of the verbs, *left,* is in that tense. The past tense of *to lay* ("to put or place") is *laid,* not *lay,* which is the past tense of *to lie* ("to rest or recline"). Therefore, Expression I is incorrect. Expression II properly includes the verb *raises,* because when you *raise a point,* you bring it up. (Of course, in this context the movement isn't physical.) Expression III is right because the diamond was placed, or *set,* in a gold ring.

994. **II. (sitting in the principal's office, waiting for an appointment)**

You place carpet on a floor, so the verb form you need in Expression I *(lying carpet on the floor)* is *laying* ("putting or placing"), not *lying.* Expression II is fine; you're in a chair, waiting, so you're *sitting.* Expression III *(Raise and shine! It's time to get out of bed!)* refers to getting up in the morning, so you want *rise,* not *raise.*

995. **I. (robbers lying in wait for a victim)**

The robbers are resting, as they wait for a victim. They are, as Expression I says, *lying.* Expression II *(has laid on the sofa, pretending to sleep)* should read *has lain,* as that's the present perfect form of *to lie* ("to rest or recline"). Expression III *(sitted on the window ledge)* has the right verb (to sit) but the wrong form. The past tense of *to sit* is *sat.*

996. **III. (his rising hope, as he listened to those encouraging words)**

You place, or *set decorations in the carton*, so Expression I *(will sit the decorations in the carton, ready for storage)* doesn't work. *Was lain* in Expression II *(was lain to rest in the town cemetery)* is incorrect. After death, the body is *laid to rest,* or "placed" in the cemetery. Expression III properly uses *rising,* as hope increases, or lifts, by itself, even if *encouraging words* are a motivating factor.

997. **I. and III. (I. set aside funds for college tuition; III. laying eggs)**

Expression I refers to placing money in a special account in order to pay for college tuition. Therefore, *set,* or "place," is correct. Expression II *(stirring yeast into the mixture and waiting for the bread to raise)* is wrong because the bread *rises,* or "lifts," by itself, once the yeast is present. Expression III is correct. The hen doesn't appear in this phrase, but she's "placing" her eggs in the nest, or *laying* them.

998. **II. (sat on a jury)**

If you're *not moving a muscle,* as Expression I *(laying still, not moving a muscle)* says, you're *lying* ("resting"), not *laying* ("placing"). Expression II is a little strange, but it's correct. You must sit down in the jury box during a trial, so *sat* (the past tense of *to sit*), is the right verb. You lift your own expectations to a higher level, according to Expression III *(rising your expectations and doing better work as a result),* so *raising* is proper here.

999. **I. and II. (I. raise money for the homeless; II. had set goals for himself)**

When a charity asks for money, it's trying *to raise,* or "lift" the amount available. Expression I is correct. So is Expression II, which talks about a man who *had set,* or "had put in place," *goals for himself.* Expression III *(plants laying dormant for the winter)* is wrong; it should read *lying dormant,* as the plants are "resting" for the winter.

1,000. **I. and II. (I. a position on the issue that laid her open to defeat in the next election; II. raising a fuss)**

Expression I refers to a politician who placed herself in danger of losing an election. Because "place" is the meaning here, *laid,* the past tense form of *to lay,* is correct. Expression II is right also, as *raising a fuss* is the same as "lifting" the level of controversy or disagreement. Expression III *(sat down on paper a record of all that had happened)* fails because you "place," or *set down,* words on a page.

1,001. **I. (set the story in the Victorian era)**

Expression I works nicely because the author "places" the story in a particular time and location, in this case, Victorian England. Therefore, *set* is the verb you want. Expression II *(will rise the stakes)* doesn't work because the stakes must be "lifted," or *raised,* by someone; they don't lift themselves. Expression III *(yesterday lay claim to)* refers to the past *(yesterday),* so you need the past tense of *to lay,* which is *laid.* Why *to lay?* Because you placed a claim on something — land, championships, whatever.

Index

About the Author

Geraldine Woods credits her four-decade career as an English teacher and grammarian to ultra-strict nuns armed with sentence diagrams and 5-inch-thick English texts who terrorized her in elementary school, which, when she attended, was called grammar school. She is the author of nearly 50 books, including *English Grammar For Dummies, English Grammar Workbook For Dummies, Grammar Essentials For Dummies, Wiley AP English Language and Composition, Wiley AP English Literature and Composition, Research Papers For Dummies,* and *College Admission Essays For Dummies,* all published by Wiley. She is also the author of *Punctuation, Simplified and Applied,* published by Webster's New World. With Peter Bonfanti and Kristin Josephson, she wrote *SAT For Dummies* and *PSAT/NMSQT For Dummies* (Wiley). She loves her family, New York City, Jane Austen, and the Yankees.

Dedication

This book is dedicated to my colleagues — the administrative professionals who answer more than 1,001 questions every day with courtesy and competence: Mary Boyle, Delores Busby, Laura Cassino, Barbara Connolly, Diana Gonzalez, Sherri Jefferson, Olive Keegan, Mindy Lisman, Doreen McDonald, Lorna Mercaldi, Noreen Murphy, and Frances Raffa.

Author's Acknowledgments

I appreciate the efforts of Elizabeth Rea and Christy Pingleton, Wiley editors who worked with diligence and intelligence to improve this book. I also thank Allyson Lynch and Candace Greer, the technical editors, whose attention to detail and relevant commentary were extremely helpful. I also owe a debt of gratitude to Lindsay Lefevere of Wiley and Lisa Queen of Queen Literary.

Publisher's Acknowledgments

Executive Editor: Lindsay Sandman Lefevere

Project Editor: Elizabeth Rea

Copy Editor: Christine Pingleton

Technical Editors: Candace Greer, Allyson Lynch

Project Coordinator: Phillip Midkiff

Project Manager: Laura Moss-Hollister

Cover Image: ©iStockphoto.com/jehandmade

Apple & Mac

iPad For Dummies,
5th Edition
978-1-118-49823-1

iPhone 5 For Dummies,
5th Edition
978-1-118-35201-4

MacBook For Dummies,
4th Edition
978-1-118-20920-2

OS X Mountain Lion
For Dummies
978-1-118-39418-2

Blogging & Social Media

Facebook For Dummies,
4th Edition
978-1-118-09562-1

Mom Blogging
For Dummies
978-1-118-03843-7

Pinterest For Dummies
978-1-118-32800-2

WordPress For Dummies,
5th Edition
978-1-118-38318-6

Business

Commodities For Dummies,
2nd Edition
978-1-118-01687-9

Investing For Dummies,
6th Edition
978-0-470-90545-6

Personal Finance
For Dummies, 7th Edition
978-1-118-11785-9

QuickBooks 2013
For Dummies
978-1-118-35641-8

Small Business Marketing
Kit For Dummies,
3rd Edition
978-1-118-31183-7

Careers

Job Interviews
For Dummies, 4th Edition
978-1-118-11290-8

Job Searching with
Social Media
For Dummies
978-0-470-93072-4

Personal Branding
For Dummies
978-1-118-11792-7

Resumes For Dummies,
6th Edition
978-0-470-87361-8

Success as a Mediator
For Dummies
978-1-118-07862-4

Diet & Nutrition

Belly Fat Diet For Dummies
978-1-118-34585-6

Eating Clean For Dummies
978-1-118-00013-7

Nutrition For Dummies,
5th Edition
978-0-470-93231-5

Digital Photography

Digital Photography
For Dummies,
7th Edition
978-1-118-09203-3

Digital SLR Cameras &
Photography For Dummies,
4th Edition
978-1-118-14489-3

Photoshop Elements 11
For Dummies
978-1-110-40821-6

Gardening

Herb Gardening
For Dummies, 2nd Edition
978-0-470-61778-6

Vegetable Gardening
For Dummies, 2nd Edition
978-0-470-49870-5

Health

Anti-Inflammation Diet
For Dummies
978-1-118-02381-5

Diabetes For Dummies,
3rd Edition
978-0-470-27086-8

Living Paleo For Dummies
978-1-118-29405-5

Hobbies

Beekeeping
For Dummies
978-0-470-43065-1

eBay For Dummies,
7th Edition
978-1-118-09806-6

Raising Chickens
For Dummies
978-0-470-46544-8

Wine For Dummies,
5th Edition
978-1-118-28872-6

Writing Young Adult Fiction
For Dummies
978-0-470-94954-2

Language &
Foreign Language

500 Spanish Verbs
For Dummies
978-1-118-02382-2

English Grammar
For Dummies, 2nd Edition
978-0-470-54664-2

French All-in One
For Dummies
978-1-118-22815-9

German Essentials
For Dummies
978-1-118-18422-6

Italian For Dummies,
2nd Edition
978-1-118-00465-4

e Available in print and e-book formats.

Math & Science

Algebra I For Dummies,
2nd Edition
978-0-470-55964-2

Anatomy and Physiology
For Dummies,
2nd Edition
978-0-470-92326-9

Astronomy For Dummies,
3rd Edition
978-1-118-37697-3

Biology For Dummies,
2nd Edition
978-0-470-59875-7

Chemistry For Dummies,
2nd Edition
978-1-1180-0730-3

Pre-Algebra Essentials
For Dummies
978-0-470-61838-7

Microsoft Office

Excel 2013 For Dummies
978-1-118-51012-4

Office 2013 All-in-One
For Dummies
978-1-118-51636-2

PowerPoint 2013
For Dummies
978-1-118-50253-2

Word 2013 For Dummies
978-1-118-49123-2

Music

Blues Harmonica
For Dummies
978-1-118-25269-7

Guitar For Dummies,
3rd Edition
978-1-118-11554-1

iPod & iTunes
For Dummies,
10th Edition
978-1-118-50864-0

Programming

Android Application
Development For Dummies,
2nd Edition
978-1-118-38710-8

iOS 6 Application
Development For Dummies
978-1-118-50880-0

Java For Dummies,
5th Edition
978-0-470-37173-2

Religion & Inspiration

The Bible For Dummies
978-0-7645-5296-0

Buddhism For Dummies,
2nd Edition
978-1-118-02379-2

Catholicism For Dummies,
2nd Edition
978-1-118-07778-8

Self-Help & Relationships

Bipolar Disorder
For Dummies,
2nd Edition
978-1-118-33882-7

Meditation For Dummies,
3rd Edition
978-1-118-29144-3

Seniors

Computers For Seniors
For Dummies,
3rd Edition
978-1-118-11553-4

iPad For Seniors
For Dummies,
5th Edition
978-1-118-49708-1

Social Security
For Dummies
978-1-118-20573-0

Smartphones & Tablets

Android Phones
For Dummies
978-1-118-16952-0

Kindle Fire HD
For Dummies
978-1-118-42223-6

NOOK HD For Dummies,
Portable Edition
978-1-118-39498-4

Surface For Dummies
978-1-118-49634-3

Test Prep

ACT For Dummies,
5th Edition
978-1-118-01259-8

ASVAB For Dummies,
3rd Edition
978-0-470-63760-9

GRE For Dummies,
7th Edition
978-0-470-88921-3

Officer Candidate Tests,
For Dummies
978-0-470-59876-4

Physician's Assistant Exam
For Dummies
978-1-118-11556-5

Series 7 Exam
For Dummies
978-0-470-09932-2

Windows 8

Windows 8 For Dummies
978-1-118-13461-0

Windows 8 For Dummies,
Book + DVD Bundle
978-1-118-27167-4

Windows 8 All-in-One
For Dummies
978-1-118-11920-4

e **Available in print and e-book formats.**

Take Dummies with you everywhere you go!

Whether you're excited about e-books, want more from the web, must have your mobile apps, or swept up in social media, Dummies makes everything easier .

Visit Us

Like Us

Follow Us

Watch Us

Join Us

Pin Us

Circle Us

Shop Us

Dummies products make life easier!

- DIY
- Consumer Electronics
- Crafts

- Software
- Cookware
- Hobbies

- Videos
- Music
- Games
- and More!

For more information, go to **Dummies.com®** and search the store by category.

FOR
DUMMIES®
A Wiley Brand